PHOENIX
EATS + DRINKS

CHRISTINA BARRUETA

PHOTOGRAPHY BY
JOANIE SIMON

PHOENIX
EATS + DRINKS

RECIPES FROM THE
CITY'S FAVORITE
RESTAURANTS AND BARS

Figure.1
Vancouver / Toronto / Berkeley

Copyright © 2025 by Christina Barrueta
Recipes copyright © 2025 by individual restaurants
Recipes are chef-tested.

25 26 27 28 29   5 4 3 2 1

All rights reserved, including those for text and data mining,
artificial intelligence training, and similar technologies.
No part of this book may be reproduced, stored in a retrieval
system or transmitted, in any form or by any means, without the
publisher's prior written consent or a license from Access Copyright.

Cataloguing data is available from
Library and Archives Canada

ISBN 978-1-77327-268-9 (hbk.)

Design by Naomi MacDougall | DSGN Dept.
Photography by Joanie Simon
Styling by Brendan McCaskey

Editing by Tanya Trafford
Copy editing by Pam Robertson
Proofreading by Breanne MacDonald
Indexing by Iva Cheung

Printed and bound in China by Shenzhen Reliance Printing Co., Ltd.
Figure 1 Publishing Inc.
Vancouver BC Canada
www.figure1publishing.com

Figure 1 Publishing is located in the traditional, unceded territory of
the xʷməθkʷəy̓əm (Musqueam), Sḵwx̱wú7mesh (Squamish),
and səlilwətaɫ (Tsleil-Waututh) peoples.

For my husband, Ernesto, who drives me all over the city so I can sip, taste, and savor every corner of our culinary world. I know it means I don't cook for you as much these days (sorry about that!), but you never complain. Your love and understanding fuel this adventure, and I couldn't do it without you.

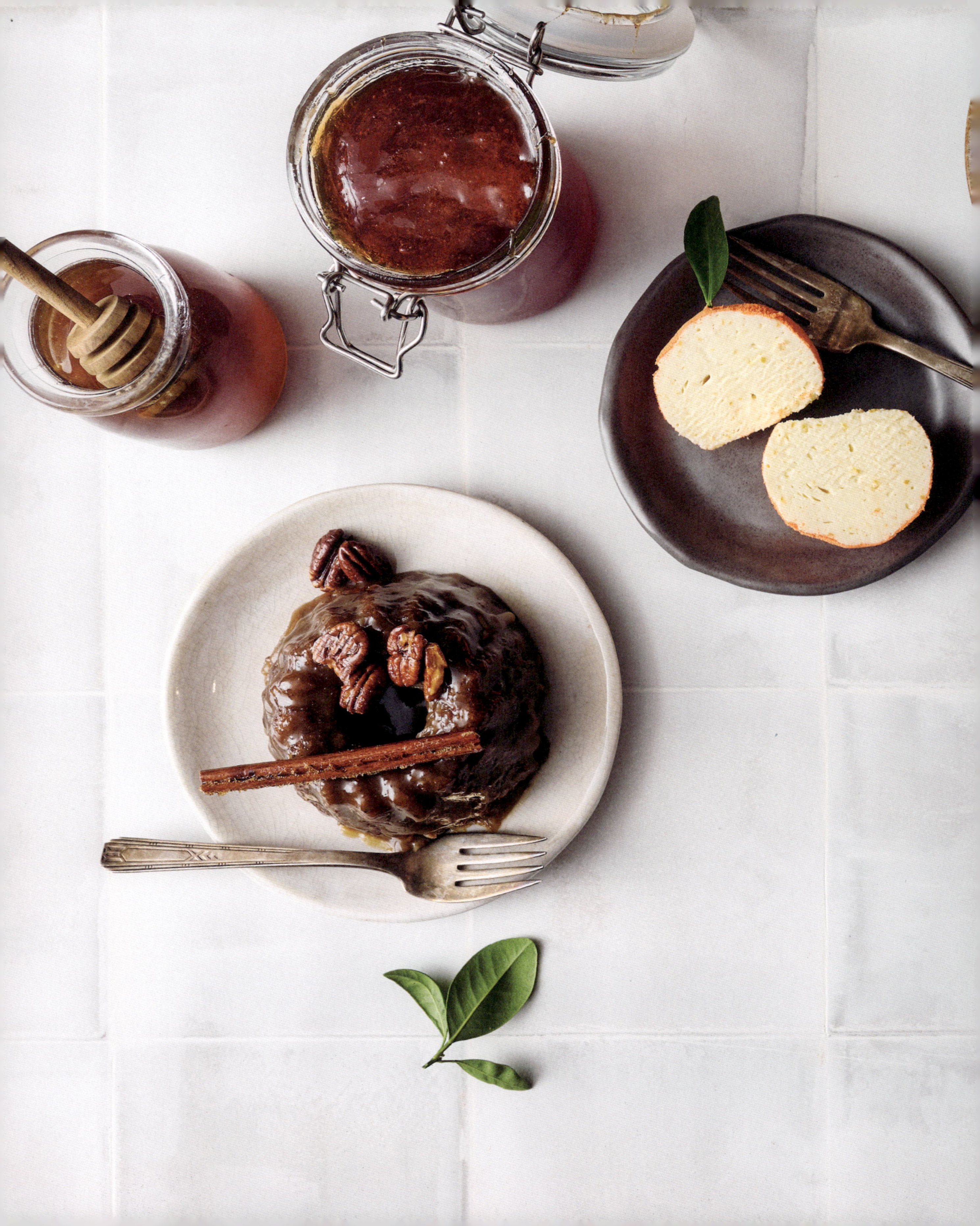

Contents

9 Introduction
12 The Restaurants
14 The Recipes
267 Acknowledgements
268 Index
276 About the Author

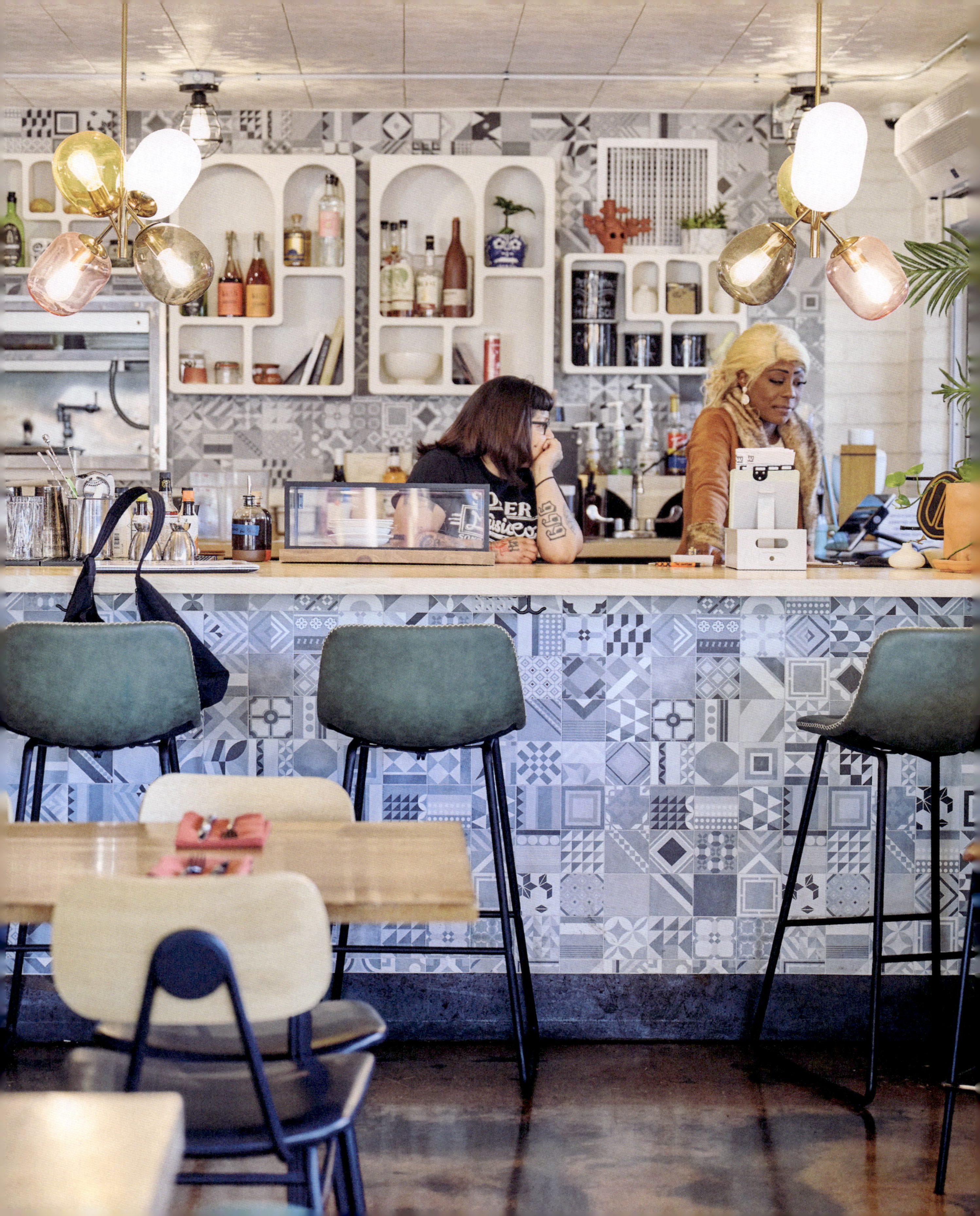

Introduction

When I invited readers to join me on a journey through the Valley of the Sun with my first cookbook, *Phoenix Cooks*, I didn't expect the overwhelming response. Eager pre-orders saw it climb to #1 in New Release categories like Southwestern U.S. Cooking, Gourmet Cooking, and Food & Wine on Amazon. And there it was, sitting pretty at #3 for Amazon's Southwest Cookbook Gift Ideas, right behind heavyweights like Joanna Gaines's *Magnolia Table* and Ree Drummond's *The Pioneer Woman*.

PHOENIX magazine named it the "Most Anticipated Cookbook" in their 2020 Best of the Valley issue and I found myself under the bright lights of news shows like *Good Morning Arizona* and gracing the pages of magazines from *Phoenix Home & Garden* to *Modern Luxury Scottsdale*. An unforgettable highlight was learning that copies had made it to tables in New York's James Beard House when our Phoenix tourism board partnered with Arizona chefs for a special dinner.

And then there were the fun, unexpected sightings: A copy of *Phoenix Cooks* in the lobby of a Sedona resort; stacked alongside *Franklin Barbecue* and Sean Brock's *South* at a local butcher shop; and even perched on a bookshelf in my room at the Westin Tempe. As it landed on lists like *City Lifestyle*'s "Gifts for a Foodie" and *Visit Arizona*'s "The 10 Most 'Arizona' Gifts You Can Buy," I was thrilled to see that supporters viewed it as more than a cookbook. They saw it as I'd hoped they would—as an ode to the city and a snapshot in time, capturing Phoenix coming into its own as a gastronomic destination.

Now, five years later, I'm extending you another invitation. In this second helping, I'm revisiting familiar faces with fresh concepts and introducing a new group of chefs making their mark on our city. I'm also expanding beyond the plate and turning your attention to the glass. Across the Valley, liquid alchemists have been shaking, stirring, and pouring their way into the national spotlight and it's time to share their stories too.

Since our first adventure, Phoenix's culinary and beverage scene hasn't just grown—it has exploded. Acclaimed restaurateurs and celebrity chefs from around the country, like *Top Chef* alumnus Angelo Sosa (page 224), have found their way to (and fallen in love with) our corner of the country. Our homegrown talent continues to make the pages of national magazines, compete on popular cooking shows, and collect accolades like cacti collect rain.

In the last year alone, James Beard Foundation award-winning chef Christopher Gross of Christopher's at Wrigley Mansion (page 48) added another jewel to his crown with the 2024 DiRōNA Award of Excellence, and young talent

Lawrence Smith of Chilte (page 40) captured both a 2024 *Food & Wine* Best New Chef distinction and a 2025 James Beard Foundation semifinalist nod as Emerging Chef. Not to be outdone, Valentine (page 230) proved lightning can strike twice in the same kitchen, with Donald Hawk and Crystal Kass both nabbing James Beard Foundation nominations: Hawk for Best Chef: Southwest and Kass for her pastry prowess as Outstanding Pastry Chef or Baker.

On the cocktail front, Little Rituals (page 140) received their second James Beard Foundation award nomination for Outstanding Bar, Century Grand (page 36) landed a coveted spot on *Forbes* magazine's "North America's 50 Best Bars" list, Bitter & Twisted (page 32) earned two prestigious Pinnacle Guide pins, BARCOA Agaveria (page 22) made *USA Today*'s "Bars of the Year" lineup, and rising star Jax Donahue at Wren & Wolf (page 250) was announced as a James Beard Award semifinalist for Outstanding Professional in Cocktail Service.

As you flip through these pages, I hope you'll feel the same excitement I felt while compiling the recipes. Some dishes might challenge you, while others will wrap you in the comfort of familiar flavors. All of them, however, share the creativity and spirit that define Phoenix's food and drink scene. There are dishes that speak to our multicultural heritage, cocktails that capture the essence of the desert, and techniques that showcase the ingenuity of our culinary artists.

From a restaurant at a historic mansion helmed by a James Beard Foundation Award–winning chef (page 48) to a cocktail lounge celebrating all things agave (page 22), it's diversity that defines our vibrant city. Whether you're a longtime resident or a curious visitor, a seasoned home cook or an aspiring mixologist, this book is an invitation to experience the flavors of Phoenix in your own kitchen and home bar. It's a celebration of how far we've come—and a glimpse into the exciting future that lies ahead.

So, fire up your stoves and fill up your cocktail shakers, and join me on another delicious journey through the Valley of the Sun.

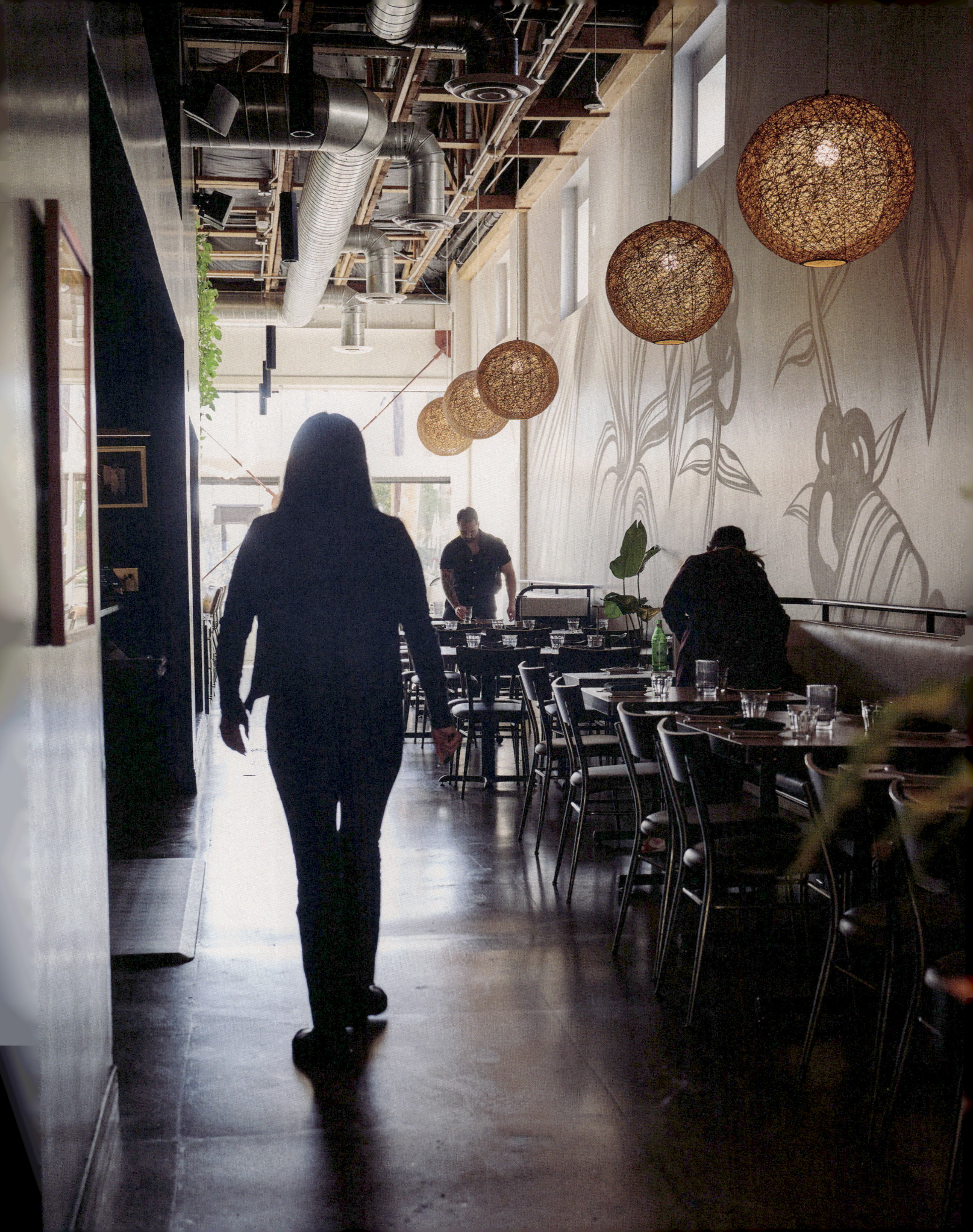

The Restaurants

16 **AFTERMATH BAR & KITCHEN**
Austin Finley, Charles Barber Jr.

22 **BARCOA AGAVERIA**
David Tyda, Ryan Oberholtzer, Nick Fiorini, Jourdain Blanchette

26 **BARLEY & SMOKE**
Michael Mahalick

32 **BITTER & TWISTED COCKTAIL PARLOUR**
Ross Simon

36 **CENTURY GRAND**
Jack Allen, Alex Montoya, Mat Snapp

40 **CHILTE**
Lawrence "LT" Smith

48 **CHRISTOPHER'S AT WRIGLEY MANSION**
Christopher Gross

58 **ELEMENTS**
Gregory James

68 **ELLIOTT'S STEAKHOUSE**
Michael Testa, Nick Gibbs, Michael Regan, Brent Tratten

74 **EMBER**
Jolie Skwiercz, Willard Thompson

80 **EVO**
Saul Velazquez

86 **FABIO ON FIRE PIZZERIA ITALIANA**
Fabio Ceschetti

90 **FIRE AT WILL**
Dom Ruggiero

96 **FIRST & LAST**
Robb Hammond, Delena Humble-Fischer

100 **FRASHER'S STEAKHOUSE AND LOUNGE**
George Frasher

106 **HONEY + VINE**
Adam Rzeczkowski

112 **THE HOUSE BRASSERIE**
Drew Hatfield, Dustin Wheeler, Joe Ieraci

118 **THE ITALIAN DAUGHTER**
Vittorio Colafranceschi

122 **JOE'S FARM GRILL**
Tim Peelen

128 **THE JOY BUS DINER**
Jennifer Caraway

134 **J.T. PRIME KITCHEN & COCKTAILS**
Alex Trujillo

140 **LITTLE RITUALS**
Aaron DeFeo

144 **MELINDA'S ALLEY**
PJ Vader Baron

150 **THE MEXICANO**
Rigo Martinez

156 **THE MICK BRASSERIE**
Brent Menke, Michael Winneker

162 **MIRACLE MILE DELI**
Josh Garcia

166 **NELSON'S MEAT + FISH**
Christopher Nelson

172 **OSTERIA MIA**
Mario Rana

176 **PA'LA**
Jason Alford

180 **PARADISE VALLEY BURGER CO.**
Bret Shapiro

186 **THE PHOENICIAN TAVERN**
Ashley Traynor

190 **PHOENIX CITY GRILLE**
Cory Asure, Uriel Telix

196 **PIZZERIA VIRTÙ**
Gio Osso

204 **POPPY'S OFFICE**
Adam Downey, Matt Keeler

208 **RENATA'S HEARTH**
Daniel Weber

214 **ROUGH RIDER**
Kyla Hein, Ian Herschberg

218 **T. COOK'S**
Mireya Ryan

224 **TÍA CARMEN/KEMBARA**
Dejan Djukic, Angelo Sosa

230 **VALENTINE**
Crystal Kass, Donald Hawk

236 **VECINA**
James Fox

242 **WEFT** & **WARP**
ART BAR + **KITCHEN**
Sam DeMarco, Ethan Blanset

250 **WREN** & **WOLF**
Jackson "Jax" Donahue,
Ivan Gonzalez

254 **ZINC BISTRO**
Aaron Gonzalez, Matt Carter

260 **ZUZU**
Russell LaCasce

The Recipes

Cocktails

- 142 Breakfast of Champions
- 252 Chil-te-bell
- 38 Dead Man's Pocket Watch
- 73 Elliott's Steakhouse Freezer Martini
- 23 Elote Moda
- 24 Espiritu de Café
- 146 First Street Last Word
- 188 Fresno Blueberry Margarita
- 116 Grapefruit-Ginger Rye Sour
- 148 Heart of Gold Old-Fashioned
- 187 Lavender Fairway
- 37 Mandrake
- 205 100 Grand
- 141 Pleasure Island
- 206 Silver Fox
- 34 Split Decision
- 217 The Sea Queen Punch
- 33 Tropic Like It's Hot
- 99 Verde de la Vida

Appetizers

- 98 Albacore Tuna Tartare Toast
- 135 Bacon-Wrapped Dates with Chipotle Aioli
- 160 Escargot on Brioche with Brie and Bordelaise Sauce
- 114 Foie Gras on Brioche with Pichuberry Chutney and Mushroom Caramel
- 216 Fried Cauliflower with Pickled Onions and Malt Aioli
- 108 Honey Whipped Feta with Roasted Olives
- 94 Iberico Ham Croquettes with Harissa Aioli and Manchego Cheese
- 228 Kembara's Lamb Spring Rolls with Cilantro Yogurt
- 42 Prawns with Peanut Mole
- 210 Sea Bass and Blue Crab Ceviche with Passion Fruit Leche de Tigre
- 158 Shrimp Tartine with Creole Butter Sauce
- 167 Smoked Salmon Dip
- 110 Wagyu Meatballs with Pomodoro Sauce and Whipped Ricotta

Salads, Sides, and Lighter Fare

- 262 Blistered Romanesco with Whipped Fromage
- 132 Causa Rellena de Pollo with Salsa a la Huancaína
- 20 Charred Brussels Sprouts with Pickled Sultanas, Goat Cheese, Bacon Lardons, and Mustard Vinaigrette
- 256 Endive Salad with Foie Gras, Mimolette Cheese, and Hazelnut Mustard Vinaigrette
- 240 Faroe Island Salmon Tacos with Yuzu Kosho Aioli
- 124 Grilled Wedge Salad
- 178 Japanese Sweet Potatoes with Aleppo Chili Crisp
- 168 Octopus Salad
- 238 Papas Verde with Green Chorizo
- 101 Peppercorn Steak Soup
- 226 Tía Carmen's Southwest Tri-Tip Kebabs

Mains

28	Bao Buns with Hoisin-Glazed Pork Belly and Pickled Fresno Chiles
136	Beef Short Rib Ravioli with Gorgonzola Cream Sauce
198	Bistecca alla Fiorentina
251	Braised Pork Shank Chili Verde
119	Casarecce Trapanese (Pasta with Sicilian Pesto of Trapani)
184	Cinco Diablo Burgers
88	Cioppino
54	Crepe of Atlantic Skate with Scallop Mousse and Lobster Sauce
50	Duck Three Ways
87	Eggplant Parmigiana Panini
222	Elote Rigatoni
70	Filet au Foivre
258	Fruits de Mer with Uni Beurre Blanc, Caviar, and Smoked Salmon Roe
126	Goat Cheese–Stuffed Lamb Burgers
18	Grilled Pork Chop with Jeow Som and Summer Peach Salad
163	Hungarian Stuffed Cabbage
31	Jamaican Jerk–Rubbed Salmon with Crispy Rice and Mango Salsa
130	Jennifer's Famous Birria de Chivo
174	Lupara
173	Pappardelle with Rabbit Ragu
212	Pollo Pibil with Guasacaca and Pickled Red Onions
244	Porcini Lasagna
154	Quesabirria Tacos
192	Ribeye Steaks with Tepary Bean Chili and Pico de Gallo
120	Risotto alla Nerano
232	Sarsaparilla-Glazed Lamb Ribs with Chayote Salad
177	Seared Polenta with Tomatoes and Sausage
247	Shawarma Spiced Lamb Shank with Garlic Sauce, Herb Salad, and Saffron Couscous
60	Sonoran Eggs Benedict with Polenta, Braised Short Ribs, Rosemary Hollandaise, and English Muffin Chips
152	Sonoran Molcajete
92	Stacked Enchiladas
264	Sticky Icky Iberico Spareribs with Funky Daikon Salad
82	Striped Bass with Gremolata, White Bean Ragu, and Corn Nage
164	The Mile Burger
220	Vegan Spaghetti Bolognese with Vegan Ricotta
200	Virtù Timballo
75	Yellowtail Crudo with Cucumber Pico de Gallo, Avocado Mousse, and Ponzu

Desserts

234	Burnt Desert Blossom Honey Flan
194	Buttermilk Pie with Caramel Sauce and Fresh Berries
76	Desert Blossom Sticky Toffee Date Cake with Prickly Pear Jam, Blood Orange Semifreddo, and Praline Pecans
46	Elote Cheesecake
181	Fried Ice Cream Shake
104	Gooey Butter Cake
64	Monkey Bread with Apples, Candied Pecans, Cajeta, and Five-Spice Royal Icing
84	Vanilla Pots de Crème

AFTERMATH BAR & KITCHEN

Austin Finley, Charles Barber Jr.

For Charles Barber Jr., Zinc Bistro (page 254) was a launching pad for a career that continues to flourish. After more than fifteen years behind its famous zinc bar, he cofounded Hush Public House to rave reviews. But Barber wasn't done. In 2021, he ventured out on his own to open Aftermath, followed by two Born & Bred locations in 2023 and 2024.

Barber's food philosophy, steered by culinary director Austin Finley, is a delicious balancing act of refined but unpretentious. "The menu is eclectic New American," he says. "Not being tied to one specific style gives us the freedom to explore." About 30% of the menu is seasonal, but beloved staples remain, like the award-winning Aftermath Burger, the four-cheese leek-studded Aftermac, and roasted brussels sprouts with mustard vinaigrette (page 20). These signature creations rub elbows with more globe-trotting dishes, like oysters dressed in a Calabrian chile ponzu and fried rice flecked with crabmeat and house-fermented kimchi, not to mention sophisticated nightly specials like foie gras and duck lasagna.

The vibe inside is just as inviting as the menu. White brick walls, comfy black booths, and local art give the space a laid-back, industrial-chic feel. "It's elevated but approachable, just like our food," Barber notes.

Looking ahead, Barber is focused on building something timeless. Reflecting on Zinc Bistro's enduring success, he shares that he'd "love to be like Zinc, which has been around for twenty-three years, with thousands of loyal customers. Sure, we could go super outrageous like some restaurants are doing now, but will that show longevity? Our goal is to strike a balance—be eclectic, push boundaries, but still be approachable for everyone."

▶ Grilled Pork Chop with Jeow Som and Summer Peach Salad

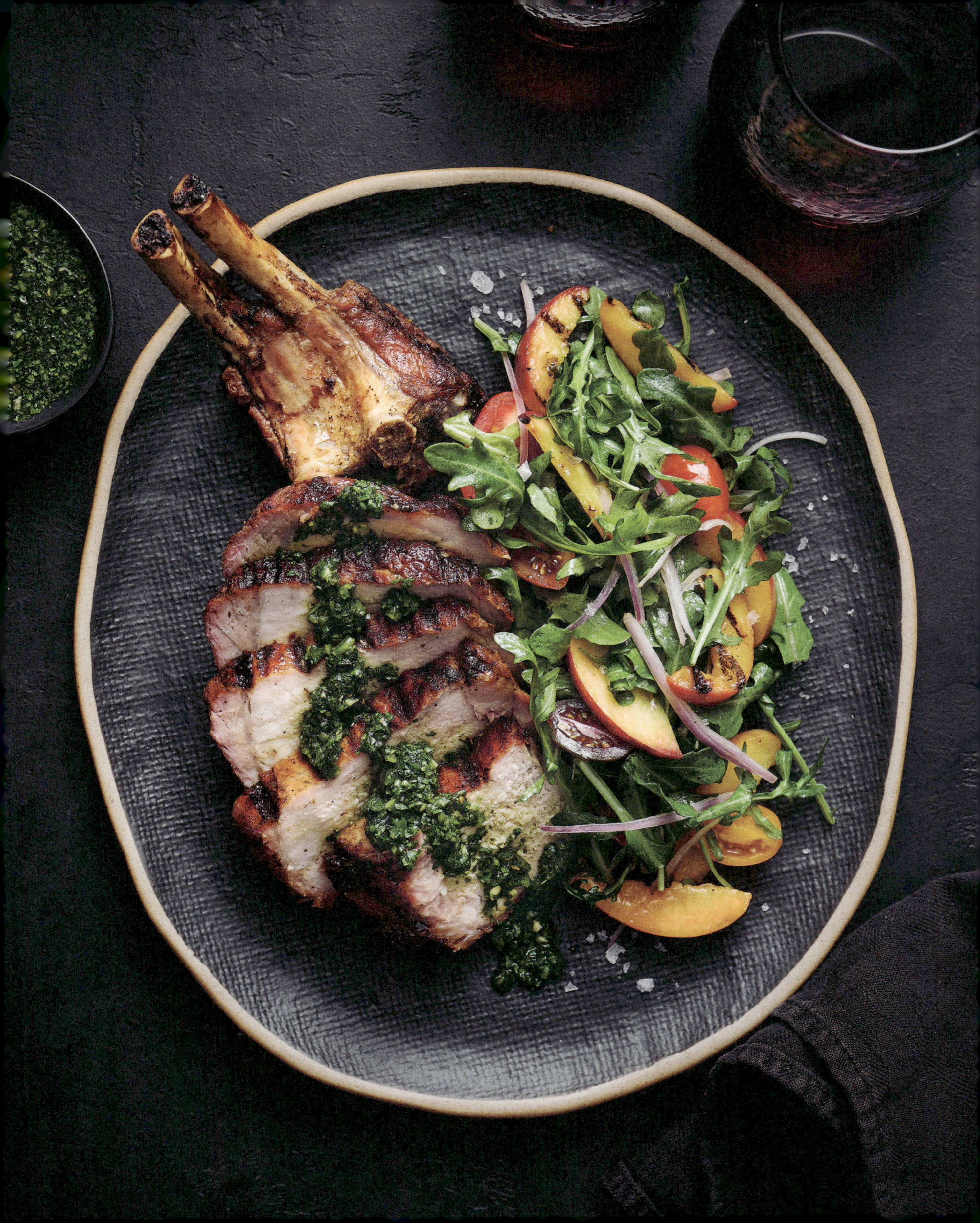

JEOW SOM

6 cloves garlic
8 green Thai chiles
½ tsp kosher salt
¼ tsp MSG (optional)
½ cup fish sauce, plus more to taste
2 Tbsp granulated sugar, plus more to taste
2 limes, juiced, plus more to taste
½ cup minced cilantro

SUMMER PEACH SALAD

1 peach, pitted and halved
1–2 tsp canola–olive oil blend
2 cups baby arugula
½ cup halved cherry tomatoes
¼ cup thinly sliced shallots
1 tsp lemon juice
1 Tbsp extra-virgin olive oil
Flaky sea salt and cracked black pepper, to taste

ASSEMBLY

1 (16-oz) bone-in pork chop, preferably Berkshire or other heritage breed
Kosher salt and cracked black pepper, to taste
2–3 cups Summer Peach Salad (see here)
½ cup Jeow Som (see here)

Grilled Pork Chop with Jeow Som and Summer Peach Salad

SERVES 2 While a juicy sixteen-ounce pork chop is the centerpiece, this east-meets-southwest dish also showcases Arizona's peak-season peaches, in a colorful salad, and jeow som, a vibrant sauce popular in Laotian and Cambodian culture. Grind the garlic and chiles for jeow som in a mortar and pestle for the best flavor, although you can mince the ingredients or use a food processor if you prefer.

Jeow Som Place garlic, chiles, salt, and MSG (if using) in a mortar. Using a pestle, crush ingredients until a rough paste forms. Add fish sauce, sugar, and lime juice, and mix until well combined. (If the ingredients exceed the capacity of your mortar, transfer the paste to a separate container before stirring in the remaining ingredients.)

Taste and adjust seasoning by adding more fish sauce for saltiness, sugar for sweetness, or lime juice for tartness. Stir in cilantro.

Refrigerate jeow som until ready to serve, for up to 1 day.

Summer Peach Salad Preheat grill to high.

Brush cut surfaces of peach halves lightly with canola–olive oil blend and grill cut side down until grill marked but not too soft, 2–3 minutes. Remove from grill and allow to cool completely, then slice into ¼-inch slices.

In a bowl, combine peaches, arugula, tomatoes, and shallots. Just before serving, dress with lemon juice and olive oil. Season with salt and pepper to taste.

Assembly Approximately 1 hour before cooking, remove pork from the refrigerator and allow to come to room temperature. Generously season all sides with salt and pepper, being liberal with salt due to the thickness of the cut.

Preheat grill to high.

Place pork chop on the hottest part of the grill. Grill for 2–3 minutes on each side, or until there are good grill marks and caramelization. Move to the cooler part of grill to continue cooking indirectly. Turn occasionally to ensure even cooking, until a meat thermometer shows an internal temperature of 150°F–155°F for medium to medium-well.

Allow to rest for half the time it took to cook to allow juices to redistribute and make the pork more tender and flavorful.

To serve, slice pork chop from the bone, then slice boneless loin into ½-inch-thick slices. Arrange slices in a fanned-out pattern on one side of a serving platter with the bone standing up on its side at the fan's base for presentation.

Plate peach salad next to the pork chop and spoon jeow som over the pork.

PICKLED SULTANAS
½ cup sultanas (golden raisins)
¼ cup water
¼ cup white wine vinegar

MUSTARD VINAIGRETTE
½ cup Dijon mustard
½ cup white balsamic vinegar
¼ cup sherry vinegar
3 cloves garlic
Kosher salt and black pepper, to taste
1 cup canola–olive oil blend

BACON LARDONS
¼ lb slab bacon
1 Tbsp water

Charred Brussels Sprouts with Pickled Sultanas, Goat Cheese, Bacon Lardons, and Mustard Vinaigrette

SERVES 2–4 Brussels sprouts have gone from loathed to loved and at Aftermath, they're a crowd-pleaser. This dish brings out the best in them, combining tangy, creamy, and smoky elements for a perfect balance of flavors. Finished with a zippy mustard vinaigrette, it's no wonder this is one of the restaurant's bestsellers.

Pickled Sultanas Place sultanas in a heatproof bowl.

In a saucepan over high heat, bring water and vinegar to a boil. Pour over sultanas and allow to rehydrate at room temperature until plump, about 30 minutes.

Store in the refrigerator for up to 1 week.

Mustard Vinaigrette Place all ingredients, except oil, in a blender. Blend on medium speed until garlic is fully puréed. Gradually add oil in a slow stream until vinaigrette is emulsified.

Store in the refrigerator for up to 1 week. Extra vinaigrette can be used as a salad dressing, marinade, or glaze for roasted vegetables.

Bacon Lardons Cut bacon into ½-inch slices, then into ½-inch-thick rectangles (lardons).

Place bacon in a cold sauté pan with water. Cook over medium heat until fat begins to render. Stir occasionally until bacon starts to fry in rendered fat. Once fat becomes foamy, bacon should be crispy.

Remove bacon lardons with a slotted spoon and set on a paper towel–lined plate to drain. Reserve bacon fat for other uses.

ASSEMBLY

3 cups brussels sprouts

2–3 Tbsp canola–olive oil blend

Kosher salt and black pepper, to taste

½ cup Bacon Lardons (see here)

¼ cup Mustard Vinaigrette, plus more to taste (see here)

¼ cup crumbled goat cheese

¼ cup Pickled Sultanas (see here)

1 Tbsp thinly sliced chives

Assembly Turn on broiler.

Trim brussels sprouts by cutting off tough stem end and peeling away yellow or damaged outer leaves. Cut sprouts in half lengthwise.

In a large bowl, toss sprouts with enough oil to lightly coat. Season generously with salt and pepper.

Spread sprouts out on a sheet pan in an even layer. Place under broiler until they begin to take on color and char slightly. Lower temperature to 450°F and roast until tender but not mushy, 5–10 minutes.

Transfer sprouts to a bowl and toss with bacon lardons and mustard vinaigrette. Season to taste with salt and pepper.

To serve, arrange brussels sprouts and lardons in a serving dish. Sprinkle with goat cheese and pickled sultanas, drizzle with more vinaigrette, and garnish with chives.

BARCOA AGAVERIA

David Tyda, Ryan Oberholtzer, Nick Fiorini, Jourdain Blanchette

When David Tyda and his partners Ryan Oberholtzer, Nick Fiorini, and Jourdain Blanchette opened BARCOA Agaveria in 2021, they were inspired by Mexico's rich culture. "There's such diversity, and each spirit tells a story," Tyda says. "It sounds cliché, but we constantly remind our staff to honor the person who made the spirit so that it translates to the guest's experience." It's an ethos woven through every aspect, from drinks to decor.

The colorful street-level Cantina serving classics from margaritas to mezcalitas is "meant to be warm and welcoming," says Tyda. "Everything you see is from Mexico." He loves when guests tell him that the wooden bar reminds them of their *abuela*'s cabinets—"it's like that hearth that holds the family heirlooms… and mezcal and tequila."

Downstairs, the vibe shifts. "It's darker and sexier, more like modern Guadalajara," says Tyda, but with a similar attention to detail. He gestures to pillows hand-stitched with agaves and tables crafted from Mexican Parota wood. On the wall, cow skulls with intricate beadwork catch the eye. "They're an ancient art form from the Huichol, an indigenous tribe between Nayarit and Jalisco," he explains.

And then there are the four hundred rabbits. Underneath the staircase is an art installation featuring hand-painted alebrijes, paying homage to Mayahuel, the goddess of agave spirits. According to legend, she birthed four hundred rabbits and tasked them with guarding pulque, a fermented agave drink. "But they drank it all," Tyda laughs, "so each rabbit represents a different state of drunkenness" brought to life.

"We're more than just a bar," Tyda says, "and I think that resonates with people. Before we opened, I could picture the energy here, and it has exceeded my expectations."

PILONCILLO SYRUP

1 (8-oz) cone of piloncillo (see Note)
½ cup (4 oz) water

ASSEMBLY

1 strip of dried corn husk, for garnish (optional)
1 oz Mezcal Vago Elote
1 oz Abasolo Ancestral Corn El Whisky de Mexico
1 tsp Nixta Licor de Elote
¼ oz Piloncillo Syrup (see here)
2 dashes Angostura aromatic bitters
2 dashes Angostura orange bitters
1 orange peel, cut into a 1-inch-wide strip with minimal white pith, for garnish

Elote Moda

SERVES 1 This reimagined old-fashioned pays homage to Mexico's ten-thousand-year history with corn. Sweetened with piloncillo's molasses notes, it features a unique corn liqueur, a whisky made from ancestral cacahuazintle corn, and a smoky mezcal distilled with roasted corn. It's a historical blend that marries one of the earliest printed cocktail recipes with Mexico's agricultural heritage.

Piloncillo Syrup In a saucepan over medium heat, stir together piloncillo and water, until sugar is dissolved. Remove from heat and allow to cool. Transfer syrup to a glass jar and store in the refrigerator for up to 6 months.

This recipe can be scaled up, maintaining a 2:1 ratio of piloncillo to water.

Assembly If desired for presentation, tie the dried corn husk around a rocks glass.

Combine all liquid ingredients in a mixing glass. Add ice and stir until well chilled, 12–15 seconds. Strain into the prepared rocks glass over a large ice cube.

To express the orange peel, hold it over the glass with the outer side facing down and give it a gentle squeeze to release the oils onto the surface of the drink. Drop the expressed peel into the glass alongside the ice cube.

NOTE Piloncillo, a raw Mexican sugar, is commonly packaged as cone-shaped blocks. Look for piloncillo at Mexican markets, including Los Altos Ranch Market and Food City, as well as from online retailers. Grate or finely chop before use for easier measuring.

COFFEE-INFUSED LICOR 43
1 (750-mL) bottle of Licor 43
1 cup ground coffee

SPICY COCOA POWDER
¼ tsp cayenne
1½ Tbsp cocoa powder
½ tsp ground cinnamon

VEGAN CHOCOLATE CREAM
½ oz Bols Crème de Cacao White
1¾ oz Silk dairy-free heavy cream

ASSEMBLY
1 oz Azuñia Reposado Tequila
1 oz Coffee-Infused Licor 43 (see here)
½ oz Narano Bitter Orange Liqueur
½ oz Kalani Coconut Liqueur
Vegan Chocolate Cream, for garnish (see here)
Spicy Cocoa Powder, for garnish (see here)

Espiritu de Café

SERVES 1 At BARCOA, the upstairs Cantina serves a classic carajillo with Licor 43 and espresso, a drink that some say traces its roots to Spain where workers would mix coffee with liquor for a quick boost. But if you venture downstairs you'll find a forty-eight-hour infusion with a float of vegan chocolate cream that turns the traditional cocktail into an inspired espresso martini.

Coffee-Infused Licor 43 Combine Licor 43 and coffee in a glass mason jar or other container. Allow to infuse for 48 hours.

Strain through a coffee filter into a pitcher and pour into a glass bottle or the original Licor 43 bottle. Discard grounds. The infusion can be stored indefinitely in a cool, dark space, although flavor may change over time.

Spicy Cocoa Powder In a bowl, whisk together cayenne, cocoa powder, and cinnamon until evenly combined.

Vegan Chocolate Cream Pour ingredients into a small squeeze bottle and shake vigorously until blended. Use immediately or refrigerate until needed, shaking well before use.

Assembly Pour all ingredients, except vegan cream and cocoa powder, into a mixing glass.

Add ice and stir until well chilled, 12–15 seconds. Strain into a coupe glass.

Stand a bar spoon in the center of the drink, with the bowl end touching the bottom of the glass. Holding the squeeze bottle at a 45-degree downward angle, position the tip of the bottle halfway up the handle of the spoon. Carefully squeeze chocolate cream so that it runs down the spoon handle and spreads gently and evenly on the surface in a ¼-inch layer. Garnish with a dusting of spicy cocoa powder.

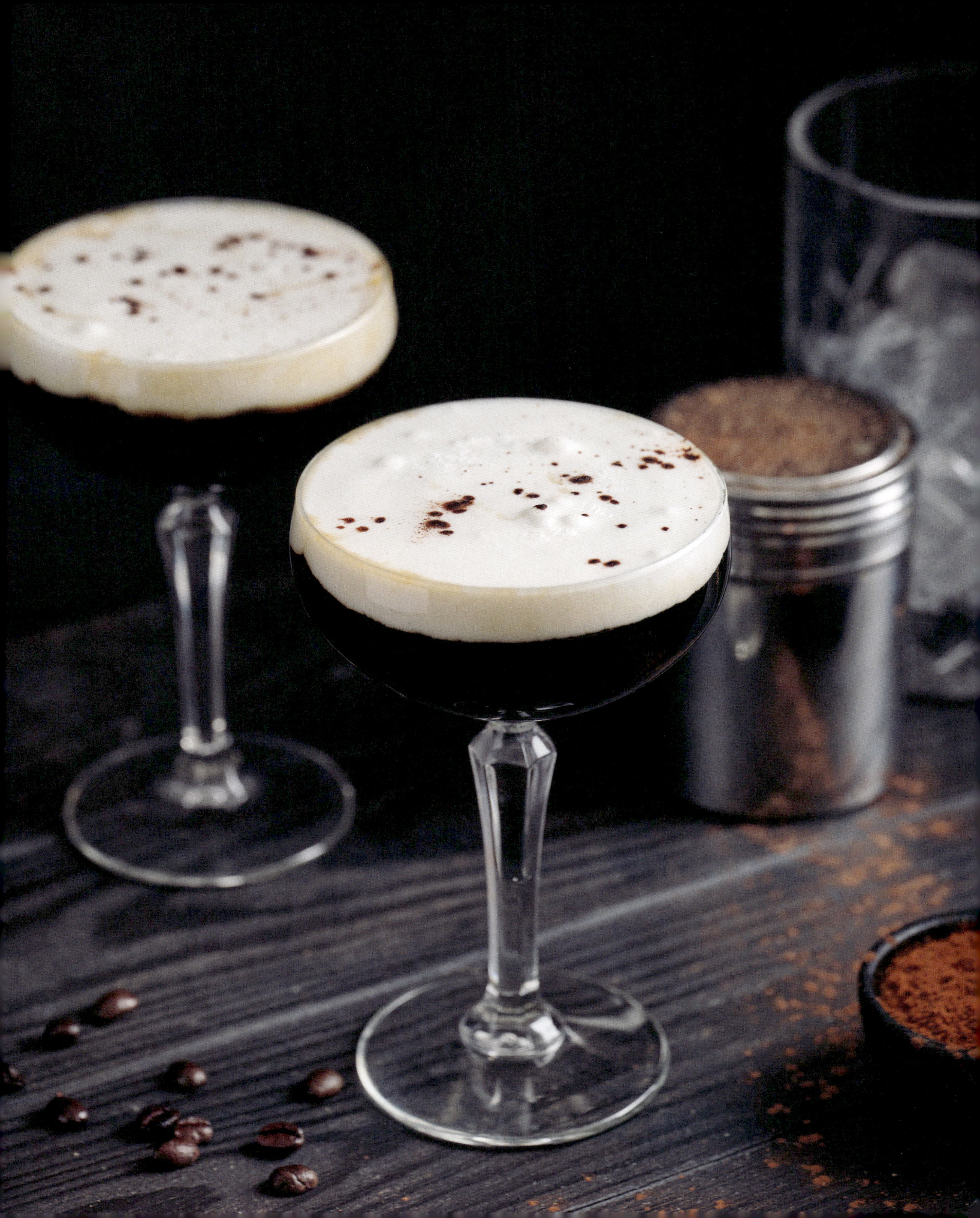

BARLEY & SMOKE

Michael Mahalick

At Barley & Smoke, executive chef Michael Mahalick and co-owners Matthew and Kristina Frosch have created the intimate vibe of a secret supper club. Accessed through a discreet entrance in their casual pub, Peoria Artisan Brewery, the thirty-seat lounge opened in 2024 and introduced northwest Peoria to a new era of fine dining and craft cocktails.

"The space was available when we first opened the brewery and we thought it would be great for a lounge-type spot," Mahalick recalls, "but it didn't work out at the time. Then one day, Matt said, 'Hey, that spot's available again. Want to open a speakeasy?' And I was like, hell yeah."

The talented chef, whose impressive résumé includes stints at the Boulders, Blue Hound Kitchen & Cocktails, and DeSoto Central Market, has created a space that is both sophisticated and comfortable. "It's like you're stepping into the kitchen at my house for that intimate look into what we do," he says, praising the blue and gold accents and ambient lighting that frame his open Hestan-equipped kitchen.

The menu reflects Mahalick's bold creativity with global influences. Oysters with marrow jam and gin and tonic mignonette? Yes, please. Puffy bao buns stuffed with smoked pork belly glazed in a homemade hoisin sauce (page 28)? They're a signature. For Mahalick, the timing was perfect: "Peoria's food culture was evolving with more upscale restaurants, so it was a good time for us to do something fancier."

His ultimate goal? "I want people to leave satisfied and say, 'Man, I'm coming back here.' But not 'I'm coming back here for my birthday next year,'" he says. "I want them to say, 'I'm coming back next week.'"

▶ Bao Buns with Hoisin-Glazed Pork Belly and Pickled Fresno Chiles

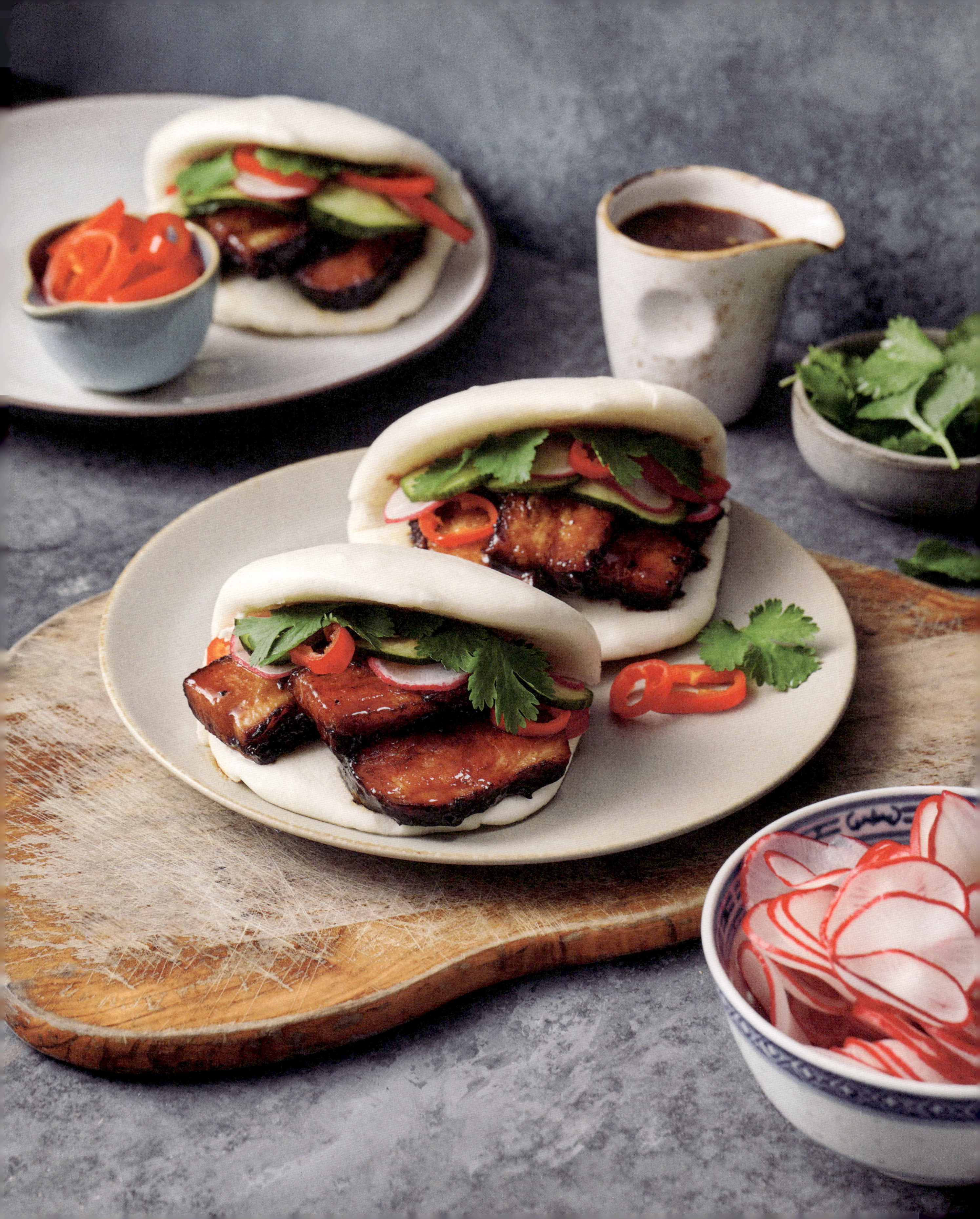

PICKLED FRESNO CHILES

2 Fresno chiles, sliced
1 cup water
1½ cups unseasoned rice wine vinegar
½ cup granulated sugar
1 Tbsp pickling spice

HOISIN GLAZE

½ cup soy sauce
4 Tbsp smooth peanut butter
2 Tbsp dark brown sugar
4 tsp unseasoned rice wine vinegar
4 tsp sesame oil
2 tsp sambal, or to taste (see Note)
2 cloves garlic, minced
1 small shallot, minced
¼ tsp ground black pepper
Pinch of five-spice powder

DRY RUB

½ cup black pepper
¼ cup kosher salt
2 Tbsp granulated garlic
2 Tbsp dark brown sugar

SMOKED PORK BELLY

1 lb skinless pork belly
3 Tbsp Dry Rub (see here)

Bao Buns with Hoisin-Glazed Pork Belly and Pickled Fresno Chiles

SERVES 2 At the restaurant, Michael Mahalick smokes his pork belly over mesquite and pecan wood. No smoker? No problem. Here he has included a braising method that delivers equally mouthwatering results. Bao buns, also known as Chinese steamed buns, are soft white buns with a characteristic fluffy texture. Look for frozen bao buns at Asian markets like Lee Lee International Supermarket and H Mart.

Pickled Fresno Chiles Place chiles in a heatproof container.

In a saucepan over high heat, combine water, vinegar, sugar, and pickling spice. Bring to a boil, stirring until sugar is dissolved.

Pour hot pickling liquid over the chiles and allow to cool to room temperature. Keep chiles submerged with a plate if necessary.

Pickled chiles will keep in the refrigerator for up to 1 month.

Hoisin Glaze Combine all ingredients in a bowl and whisk until smooth.

Dry Rub In a bowl, mix pepper, salt, garlic, and brown sugar until evenly combined.

Dry rub can be stored in an airtight container in a cool, dark place for up to 6 months. Leftover rub can be used to season steaks, brisket, ribs, chicken, and roasted vegetables.

Smoked Pork Belly Preheat smoker to 225°F. (Plan on smoking the pork belly the night, or day, before you will be serving.)

Place pork belly on a sheet pan and generously coat all sides with the dry rub, letting any excess fall on the pan. Allow to season for 1 hour at room temperature.

Smoke pork belly until internal temperature reaches 200°F, about 7 hours.

Allow to cool at room temperature for 1 hour, then refrigerate until completely chilled.

BRAISED PORK BELLY

1 lb skinless pork belly
1 quart chicken stock
1 yellow onion, cut in quarters
1 stalk celery, cut in thirds
3 cloves garlic, smashed
2 bay leaves
2 Tbsp liquid smoke
3 Tbsp Dry Rub (see here)

ASSEMBLY

¾ lb Smoked or Braised Pork Belly (see here)
4 bao buns
2 Tbsp canola oil
Hoisin Glaze (see here)
½ English cucumber, thinly sliced, for garnish
2 radishes, thinly sliced, for garnish
Pickled Fresno Chiles, for garnish (see here)
Cilantro, for garnish

Braised Pork Belly Preheat oven to 400°F. Place pork belly in a 12- × 14-inch baking dish. Add remaining ingredients, except dry rub, ensuring pork belly is partially submerged in the braising liquid with a portion visible above the surface. Sprinkle dry rub over exposed surface of the pork belly.

Cover dish with plastic wrap, and then aluminum foil. Braise in oven for 4 hours, or until fork tender.

Allow to cool at room temperature for 1 hour, then refrigerate until completely chilled.

Assembly Slice smoked (or braised) pork belly into ½-inch × 2-inch slices.

Add water to a medium-sized pot with a steamer basket, ensuring water does not touch bottom of basket. Place over medium-high heat, cover, and bring to a boil.

Once water is boiling, place bao buns in the steamer basket, leaving space between them to allow for expansion. Cover pot and steam buns for 5 minutes. Keep warm by reducing heat to low, removing lid, and covering pot with a damp cloth.

While buns are steaming, add oil to a cast-iron skillet over medium-high heat. Sear pork belly until dark golden brown, 3–4 minutes per side. Add hoisin glaze, stir to coat, and simmer for 1 minute.

Remove bao buns from steamer. Gently open bao buns and divide pork belly between the 4 buns. To serve, drizzle with hoisin glaze and garnish with cucumber and radish slices, pickled Fresno chiles, and cilantro.

NOTE Sambals are flavorful chili pastes popular in Indonesian, Malaysian, and Singaporean cuisine. Look for sambals—such as sambal oelek, made from ground red chilies, salt, and vinegar—in the Asian foods aisle of grocery stores, at Asian markets, and online retailers.

Barley & Smoke

MANGO SALSA

1 cup peeled and diced mango
1 Tbsp dark brown sugar
1 tsp kosher salt
¼ tsp jerk seasoning
¾ tsp finely chopped cilantro
¾ tsp finely chopped flat-leaf parsley
Pinch of chipotle powder
1 lime, juiced

ASSEMBLY

4 cups water
1 Tbsp salt
2 cups jasmine rice
2 bay leaves
4 (6-oz) skinless salmon fillets
3 Tbsp jerk seasoning
5 Tbsp canola oil, divided
Kosher salt and black pepper, to taste
Mango Salsa (see here)
4 Tbsp sliced scallions, for garnish

Jamaican Jerk–Rubbed Salmon with Crispy Rice and Mango Salsa

SERVES 4 Michael Mahalick drew inspiration from the Caribbean's bold flavors for this dish that combines the smoky kick of jerk seasoning with salmon and spicy-sweet mango salsa. "The flavors go so well together and the crispy rice gives it texture," he notes. Use your preferred jerk seasoning or Mahalick's personal favorite: Spiceology Jamaican Jerk Rub.

Mango Salsa Place all ingredients in a bowl, stir to combine, and let sit for 30 minutes at room temperature for flavors to meld.

Assembly In a medium pot, bring water and the 1 tablespoon of salt to a boil over high heat. Add rice and bay leaves. Reduce heat to low, cover, and simmer for 10 minutes, until water is absorbed and rice is tender. If it's not, cover and cook for an additional 2–3 minutes. Spread rice out on a baking sheet to cool.

Preheat oven to 350°F.

Pat salmon fillets dry and season with jerk rub on both sides.

Heat 2 tablespoons of oil in a heavy-bottomed ovenproof pan or cast-iron skillet over medium-high heat.

Once oil is hot and you see a wisp of smoke, sear salmon fillets for 1–2 minutes on each side.

Transfer pan to oven and bake until salmon reaches 125°F for medium, or your desired temperature.

While salmon is baking, heat the remaining 3 tablespoons of oil in a heavy-bottomed sauté pan over medium-high heat. Once oil is hot and you see a wisp of smoke, add cooked rice, flattening it with a spatula so it covers the bottom of the pan. Sprinkle with a pinch of salt and pepper.

Cook rice for 4–5 minutes until it starts to brown and become crispy.

Using a wide spatula, flip rice cake. Cook for an additional 4–5 minutes, or until crispy.

Break up crispy rice and divide among individual plates, placing rice in the middle of each one. Top with a salmon fillet and ½ cup of mango salsa. Garnish with 1 tablespoon of sliced scallions per plate.

BITTER & TWISTED COCKTAIL PARLOUR

Ross Simon

In a city making waves for its award-winning cocktail scene, Bitter & Twisted Cocktail Parlour stands as tall as the historic Luhrs Building it resides in. Owner Ross Simon's journey began far from the desert, in the misty hills of Scotland, and led him to the bustling streets of London, including time spent at the legendary LAB bar.

Fast forward to 2014, and Simon's vision came to life in downtown Phoenix in an Art Deco building built in 1924 that once served as Arizona's Prohibition headquarters. Exposed brick walls speak of its history, while high-backed tufted booths invite you to sink in and stay awhile. But it's the cocktail list that steals the show with a "Book o' Cocktails" that has earned multiple nominations for World's Best Cocktail Menu at the Spirited Awards. Updated annually, it's a vividly illustrated tome of creative concoctions and classic inspirations, with themes that have ranged from fairy tales to 8-bit video games. Each page is a collaborative labor of love from Simon's talented brigade, showcasing both their greatest hits and their newest innovations.

While the accolades keep rolling in—including two coveted pins from the prestigious Pinnacle Guide—Simon stays focused on what matters most: the talent behind the bar. "Bitter & Twisted's spirit is defined by our passionate team," he notes. "For over a decade, genuine hospitality has been key with our people blending expertise and cocktail artistry to craft exceptional drinks and memorable experiences. The magic unfolds in the warm welcome, shared knowledge, and the cocktails we serve."

CINNAMON-GRAPEFRUIT SYRUP

2 cinnamon sticks
2 cups Monin cane syrup
⅔ tsp grapefruit oil (see Note)
⅛ tsp citric acid (see Note)

TROPICAL PURÉE

¼ cup La Fruitière passion fruit purée, or other high-quality brand of frozen purée
¼ cup La Fruitière pink guava purée
½ cup La Fruitière pineapple purée

ASSEMBLY

Chamoy, for garnish (see Note)
Tajín Clásico, for garnish (see Note)
1½ oz mezcal
1½ oz Tropical Purée (see here)
1 oz club soda
2 oz mango juice
½ oz lemon juice
½ oz Cinnamon-Grapefruit Syrup (see here)
Half orange slice, for garnish
Fresh mint, for garnish

Tropic Like It's Hot

SERVES 1 Inspired by the popular '80s U.K. juice drink Um Bongo, this cocktail is a playful tribute to Ross Simon's childhood. "As a kid growing up in Scotland, tasting fruits like guava was next level," he recalls of the drink, and the memory inspired him to make this adult version. "Mezcal adds a lovely smokiness but you can swap it out for your favorite spirit." For serving, Simon recommends a Pearl Diver tiki glass. "I love the acrylic ones for poolside," he adds.

Cinnamon-Grapefruit Syrup Toast cinnamon sticks in a dry skillet over medium heat until fragrant, 2–3 minutes.

In a small pot, heat cane syrup over low heat. Add toasted cinnamon sticks, grapefruit oil, and citric acid. Stir continuously until smooth and citric acid is dissolved.

Remove from heat and allow to cool. Transfer to an airtight container, such as a bottle, and refrigerate.

Leftover syrup will keep refrigerated for up to 2 months and can be used as a sweetener for cocktails and mocktails.

Tropical Purée Mix purées until combined. Tropical purée can be stored in the refrigerator for up to 10 days.

Assembly Prepare a Pearl Diver glass (or highball glass) by dipping the rim into chamoy and tilting and rotating so it is evenly coated; repeat with Tajín.

Combine all ingredients, except garnishes, in a cocktail shaker.

Whip-shake by adding 1½ cups crushed ice to the shaker and shaking vigorously for 7–10 seconds.

Pour contents, including ice, into prepared glass and top with fresh crushed ice. Garnish with orange slice and mint.

NOTE Citric acid is a natural acid found in citrus, while grapefruit oil is extracted from grapefruit peel. Both provide citrus notes that enhance the flavor profile of cocktails. Look for them in the baking or canning sections of grocery stores, specialty grocers, or online.

Chamoy is a syrupy Mexican condiment made from pickled fruit, chiles, and lime, while Tajín is a tangy-spicy seasoning made from chiles, lime, and salt. Both can be found at grocery stores and Mexican markets.

BANANA SAVEIRO MADEIRA

¼ oz Saveiro Vento do Oeste Madeira

4 tsp (20 g) organic banana extract

ASSEMBLY

1½ oz Tullamore D.E.W. Irish Whiskey

½ oz Monkey Shoulder Blended Malt Scotch Whisky

1 oz Banana Saveiro Madeira (see here)

¼ oz vanilla syrup

1 dash Scrappy's Cardamom Bitters

1 tsp vanilla sugar, or granulated sugar, for garnish

1 (½-inch-thick) slice banana, for garnish

1 section of banana leaf cut into a circle a little larger than banana slice, for garnish

2 flakes sea salt, for garnish

Split Decision

SERVES 1 This sophisticated cocktail combines Tullamore D.E.W. and Monkey Shoulder whiskies with banana Madeira and cardamom bitters for a silky, tropical sipper. The caramelized notes of banana enhance Madeira's natural sweetness and richness, and the bruléed banana on a banana leaf adds a lush garnish. Banana leaves, available at markets like Lee Lee International Supermarket and Food City, can be found bundled fresh in the produce section or pre-cut and packaged in the frozen aisle.

Banana Saveiro Madeira Whisk together ingredients until combined. Refrigerate until use.

Assembly Pour all ingredients, except garnishes, into a mixing glass. Add ice and stir until chilled and diluted, 12–15 seconds.

Pour over a large 2- × 2-inch ice cube in a double rocks glass.

Sprinkle a small amount of sugar on one side of the banana slice. Using a kitchen torch, brûlée until caramelized and golden brown.

To serve, sit banana leaf on surface of ice cube, place banana slice on top, and garnish with sea salt.

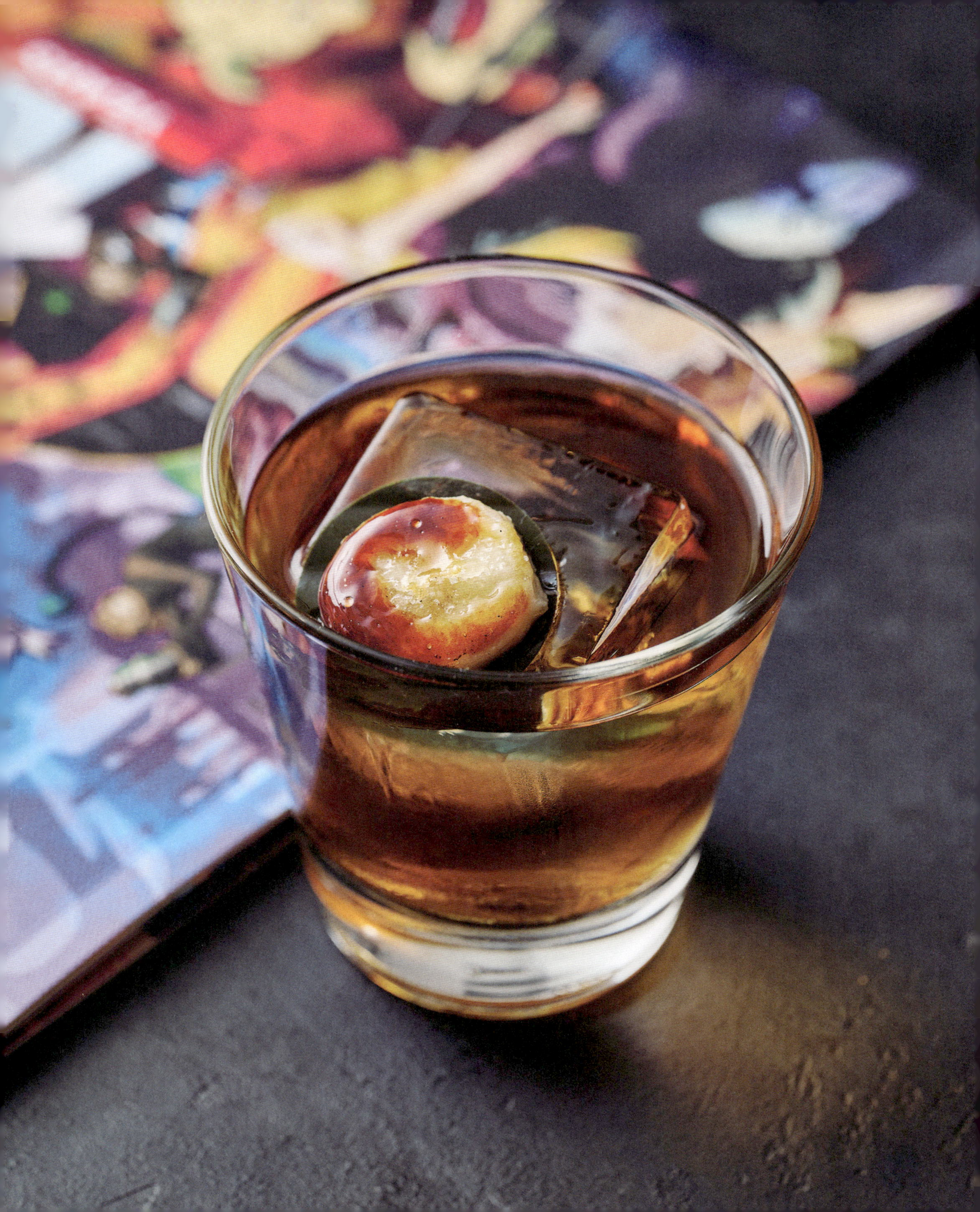

CENTURY GRAND

Jack Allen, Alex Montoya, Mat Snapp

"**While our guests** enjoy escapism, they're served world-class cocktails with world-class hospitality," says Mat Snapp, executive vice president of operations at Barter & Shake Cocktail Entertainment. At Century Grand, named one of North America's 50 Best Bars and Best U.S. Cocktail Bar by the Tales of the Cocktail Foundation, you're transported a century back in time through state-of-the-art sound, lighting, and video effects at three unique concepts led by bar chef Alex Montoya and director Jack Allen.

It's all aboard at Platform 18, where guests ride a lavish 1920s Presidential Pullman-inspired train car gliding past a New York landscape. The historical narrative unfolds around a fictitious steel magnate named Hollis Cottley Pennington and a clandestine meeting of "bootleggers, crime families, and the badass women who were in charge of New York's nightlife in the '20s, like Helen Morgan and Texas Guinan," says Snapp.

At M.E. Lee's House of Exotic Imports (formerly Grey Hen Rx) you'll discover a Chinatown curiosity shop tucked behind a Peking duck restaurant. Order the Very Special Walnut Shrimp cocktail, and it arrives in a Chinese to-go box with a vintage nickel to use in a nearby phone booth to unlock more hidden stories.

Completing the trifecta is UnderTow, offering a nautical escape in the belly of a spice trading vessel with dramatic lightning storms and changing porthole views. "Our inspiration is a return to the good life, a 'Return to Paradise,'" explains Snapp. "This menu combines all the best tiki classics, a few vintage UnderTow favorites, and the newest cocktails from the entire UnderTow team."

"Our storytelling is one of the magnetic qualities of Century Grand," he continues, summarizing the bar's philosophy. "If we can invite guests into our space and have them forget where they are, even for a moment, then we've done our job."

BEET-INFUSED CAMPARI

½ lb red beets, unpeeled

1 (750-mL) bottle of Campari

RASPBERRY JACKED HENDRICK'S GIN

1 cup individually quick-frozen raspberries

1 (750-mL) bottle of Hendrick's Gin

CHAMPAGNE FOAM

¾ cup Champagne, or sparkling wine

2 Tbsp simple syrup (1:1 ratio of granulated sugar dissolved in water)

1 large egg white

ASSEMBLY

¾ oz fresh lemon juice

¼ oz simple syrup (1:1 ratio of granulated sugar dissolved in water)

¼ oz Beet-Infused Campari (see here)

¼ oz Combier Crème de Peche de Vigne liqueur

½ oz Giffard Crème de Pamplemousse Rose liqueur

1½ oz Raspberry Jacked Hendrick's Gin (see here)

2 oz Champagne Foam (see here)

2 fresh rose petals, for garnish

Mandrake

SERVES 1 "Often mistaken for a love potion," as the menu says, this scarlet libation cast a spell when it debuted at Grey Hen Rx. Beet-infused Campari lends earthy depth while raspberry-infused gin provides a botanical backbone with a berry twist.

Beet-Infused Campari Trim tops and roots from beets, then wash and chop into 1-inch pieces. Place beets in a large mason jar and add Campari. Infuse at room temperature for 45 minutes, agitating occasionally. Strain through a fine-mesh sieve and transfer to original Campari bottle.

Store in a cool, dark place or in the refrigerator. Infused Campari can be stored indefinitely, although flavor may change over time.

Raspberry Jacked Hendrick's Gin Place frozen raspberries in a large mason jar and add gin. Agitate jar to combine.

Infuse at room temperature for 24 hours, agitating occasionally.

Strain through a fine-mesh sieve or cheesecloth and transfer to original gin bottle.

Store in a cool, dark place or in the refrigerator. Infused gin can be stored indefinitely, although flavor may change over time.

Champagne Foam Measure ingredients into a container with a pour spout. Do not blend or mix.

Pour into an iSi container (a charged canister that foams and whips). Follow the manufacturer's instructions and charge. Shake vigorously to mix contents, then charge container once more.

Refrigerate iSi container for at least 30 minutes to allow foam to stabilize.

When ready to use, shake the iSi container again to re-aerate the mixture.

Charged foam can be stored in the iSi container in the refrigerator for up to 2 days. Shake container before use.

Assembly To a shaker, add all ingredients in order, except foam and rose petals.

Fill with ice and shake vigorously for approximately 10 seconds.

Double strain (pour through shaker strainer and then through a fine-mesh strainer) into a chilled coupe glass.

Using the iSi container, gently top with champagne foam and garnish with rose petals.

BASIL OIL

½ cup basil leaves
⅓ cup extra-virgin olive oil

ASSEMBLY

1 fresh basil leaf
2 drops soy sauce
1 dash chocolate bitters
1 dash Angostura bitters
1 dash St. George Absinthe Verte
½ tsp Verjus Blanc (see Note)
¼ oz Giffard Crème de Fraise des Bois strawberry liqueur
¼ oz Martini & Rossi Riserva Speciale Bitter
¼ oz Mattei Cap Corse Quinquina Blanc
2 oz WhistlePig Whiskey
3 drops Basil Oil, for garnish (see here)
1–2 skeleton leaves, for garnish
Mini cocktail clothespin, for garnish

Dead Man's Pocket Watch

SERVES 1 This sophisticated Platform 18 libation is anchored by robust WhistlePig Whiskey with craft additions adding fruity brightness and herbal complexity (and an unexpected umami pop via a touch of soy sauce). To garnish, look for mini cocktail clothespins and skeleton leaves at craft stores or online retailers.

Basil Oil Bring a pot of water to a boil over high heat. Prepare an ice bath by filling a bowl with half ice and half water.

Blanch basil in boiling water for 15 seconds. Using a small hand strainer or slotted spoon, immediately transfer basil to ice bath to stop the cooking process. Once cooled, remove basil and pat dry.

In a blender, blend oil with blanched basil until smooth.

Set up a gravity filter by placing a fine-mesh strainer lined with a coffee filter over a bowl. Pour basil oil into coffee filter. Allow to slowly filter through, then discard solids and transfer oil to a glass jar.

Assembly In a mixing glass, muddle basil leaf to release its oils.

Add all ingredients in the order of the recipe, except garnishes.

Add ice and stir until well chilled, approximately 10 seconds or 30 revolutions.

Strain into a chilled martini glass and clip 1–2 skeleton leaves to the glass with a mini cocktail clothespin. Garnish with basil oil.

NOTE Verjus, the tart juice of unripe grapes, comes in two varieties: verjus blanc (white) and verjus rouge (red). Its gentle acidity, milder than vinegar or lemon juice, makes it a popular choice for bartenders looking for a softer acid profile in cocktails. You can find it at gourmet specialty markets and online retailers.

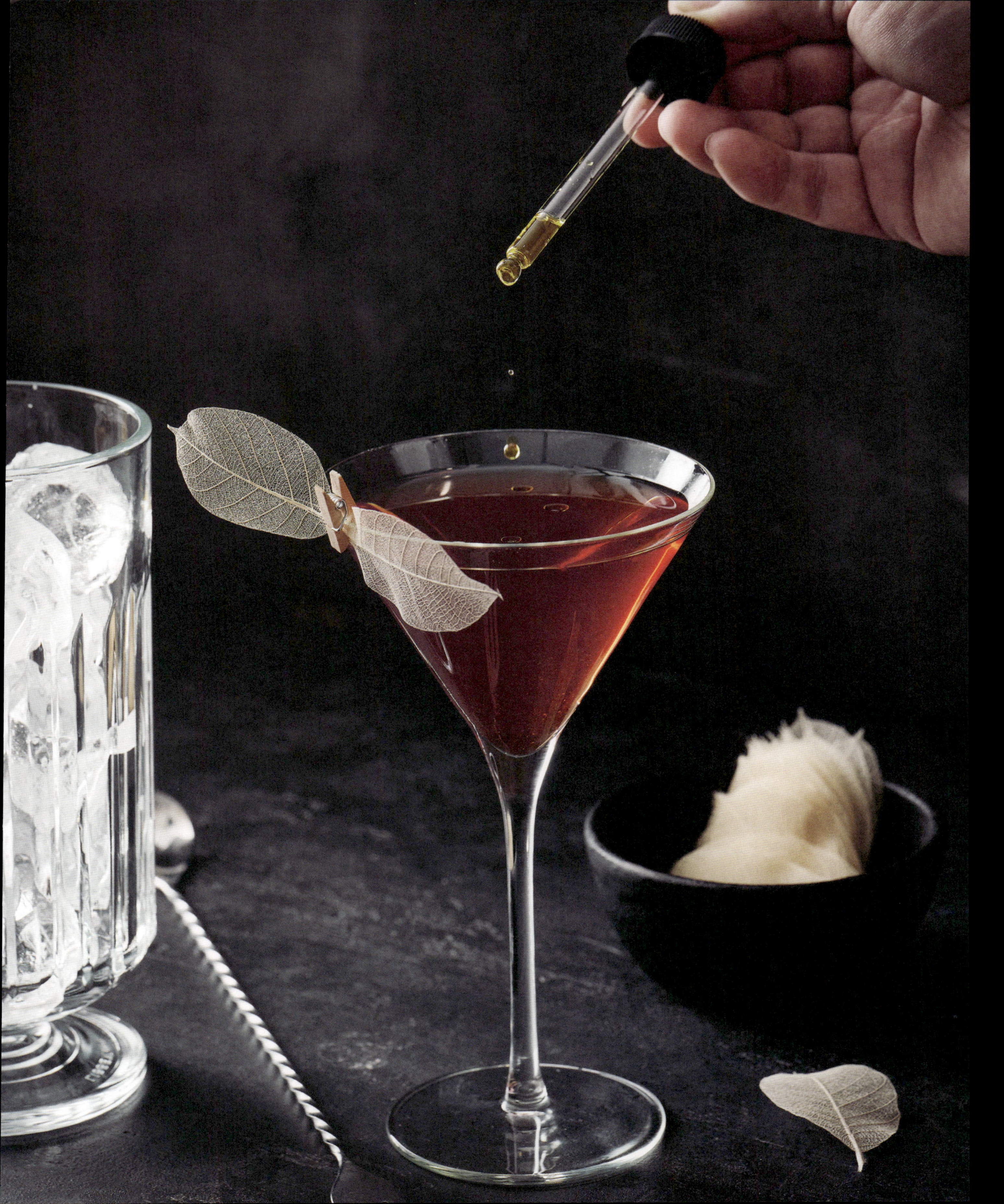

CHILTE

Lawrence "LT" Smith

"**What I love about** Chilte is that it's always evolving," says Lawrence "LT" Smith, the former NFL player who traded football for food. "I feel like every menu we put out is better than the last one." When Smith and his wife, Aseret Arroyo, launched Chilte in early 2023 in downtown Phoenix, it didn't take long for people to notice. Locals were buzzing, but so were the big names. *Forbes* and *Esquire* heaped praise, *Bon Appétit* named it one of the "24 Best New Restaurants of 2023," and *Food & Wine* honored Smith on their 2024 Best New Chefs list. Not bad for a rookie season.

After hanging up his cleats, Smith turned a hobby into a second career, sharpening his skills at the Arizona Culinary Institute and working his way through some of the city's best kitchens. When the pandemic hit, Smith and Arroyo transitioned to farmers' markets, hand-pressing tortillas for their birria and chorizo al pastor. With a loyal following, a food truck soon followed and by the time they found a permanent home in the historic Egyptian Motor Lodge, Phoenicians were ready for the full experience.

Chilte's menu reflects Smith's adventurous palate and willingness to blend tradition with unexpected surprises. Think mole with crunchy lamb neck flautas, aguachile spiked with chocolate, and squid ink tortillas folded around birria tacos and dunked in miso consomé.

"I want you to come in open minded and leave happy," says Smith, a 2025 James Beard Award semifinalist for Emerging Chef. "I love storytelling and evoking memories, and I hope you leave feeling like you were part of something really, really cool."

Chilte / 41

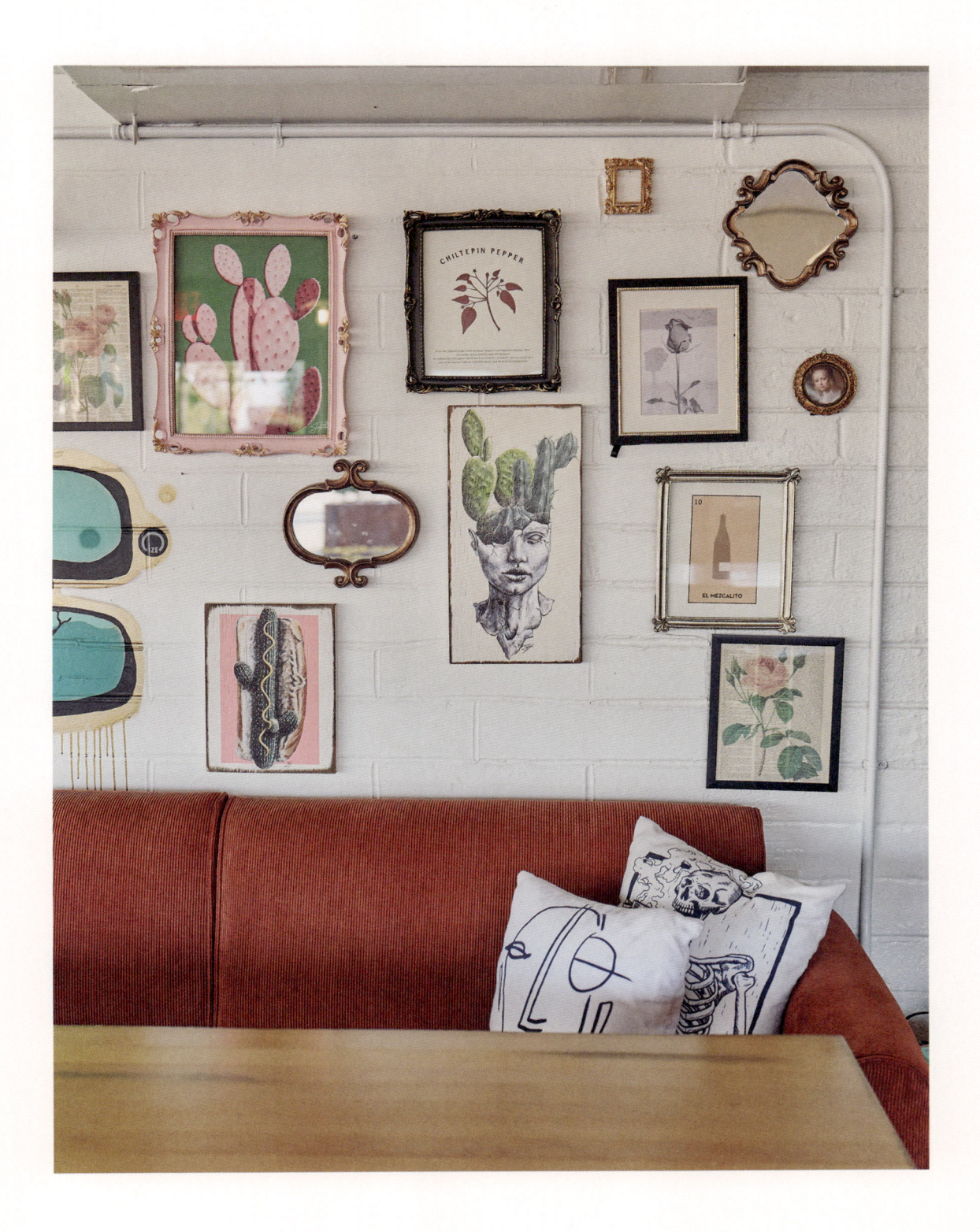

PEANUT MOLE

½ cup raw, unsalted peanuts

2 Tbsp unsalted butter

2 cloves garlic, crushed

2 canned chipotle peppers in adobo sauce + 1 Tbsp adobo sauce (see Note)

4 cups coconut milk

2 Tbsp orange juice

Kosher salt, to taste

SOY-HONEY GLAZE

1 Tbsp unsalted butter

½ cup soy sauce, or gluten-free tamari

2 Tbsp orange juice

2 Tbsp honey

Prawns with Peanut Mole

SERVES 4 A prime example of LT Smith's creative thought process, this appetizer draws inspiration from *camarones a la cucaracha*, a Mexican favorite of prawns coated in a spicy sauce, and merges it with Chinese honey walnut shrimp. "But rather than the traditional mayo-based sauce," Smith explains, "I imagined a rich peanut and chipotle mole with the candied walnuts adding a sweet relief from the spice."

Peanut Mole Heat an unoiled skillet over medium heat. Add peanuts and toast them, stirring frequently, for 3–5 minutes, until they are fragrant and light golden brown.

Melt butter in a pot over medium heat. Add toasted peanuts, garlic, chipotle peppers, and adobo sauce and cook for 3–5 minutes, stirring occasionally, until garlic is fragrant and peanuts turn a darker golden brown.

Slowly pour in coconut milk and orange juice to avoid splattering and increase heat to high to bring to a boil. Reduce heat to a strong simmer and reduce by a quarter, stirring constantly to prevent scorching. Once reduced, remove from heat and allow to cool slightly to prevent steam pressure buildup when blending.

Pour mixture into a blender. Be careful when blending hot liquids: Remove cap on blender lid and cover with a folded dish towel to allow steam pressure to escape and catch any splashes. Starting on slow and gradually increasing speed, blend until smooth and velvety.

Strain through a medium-mesh strainer into a bowl and season with salt to taste.

Sauce can be stored in the refrigerator for up to 5 days. Reheat to a simmer before serving.

Soy-Honey Glaze In a small pot over low heat, melt butter with soy sauce (or tamari), orange juice, and honey. Stir until honey is fully dissolved. Remove from heat and set aside.

MIXED HERBS

½ cup cilantro leaves

3 sprigs mint, leaves only

¼ cup chopped chives, cut into 2-inch lengths

Extra-virgin olive oil, or avocado oil

Flaky sea salt

ASSEMBLY

12 head-on prawns, U12 or larger, body peeled and deveined

Soy-Honey Glaze (see here)

Kosher salt, to taste

1–2 cups Peanut Mole (see here)

½ cup candied walnuts (homemade or store-bought)

Mixed Herbs, for garnish (see here)

2 limes, cut into wedges, to serve

Mixed Herbs Combine herbs in a small bowl. Toss with a small drizzle of oil and a pinch of salt.

Assembly Preheat grill to medium-high.

Brush prawns with soy-honey glaze and season with a pinch of salt.

Grill for 1–2 minutes per side, or until opaque and lightly charred.

To serve, spread ¼ cup of peanut mole on the bottom of each plate, adding more to taste. Arrange 3 prawns on top of the sauce, sprinkle with walnuts, and garnish with a generous pinch of herbs. Serve with lime wedges.

NOTE Canned chipotle peppers in adobo sauce are dried, smoked jalapeños packed in a tomato-based sauce with garlic, vinegar, and spices. You'll find them in the international aisle or Mexican foods section of grocery stores, at Mexican markets, and online. Unused peppers and sauce will keep in the refrigerator for 2–3 weeks, or purée the peppers and sauce together and freeze for later use.

44 / Chilte

▶ Elote Cheesecake

SABLÉE CRUST

3 cups all-purpose flour, or gluten-free flour
½ tsp kosher salt
1 Tbsp buttermilk
2 large egg yolks
2 cups (4 sticks) butter, room temperature, plus extra for greasing
1 cup granulated sugar

CHARRED CORN

4 ears of corn, shucked
1–2 tsp olive oil

CHEESECAKE FILLING

2 cups Charred Corn (see here)
5 leaves fresh epazote (see Note)
1 Tbsp vanilla paste
1 Tbsp heavy cream
1 cup sour cream
2 tsp lime juice
3 lbs Philadelphia cream cheese, softened
2 cups granulated sugar
1 cup gluten-free flour
4 large eggs, room temperature
4 egg yolks, room temperature

Elote Cheesecake

SERVES 6 "Growing up, cheesecake was at every family gathering," says LT Smith. "Now, I make it with my own twist, inspired by Mexican street corn. I add roasted corn, epazote, and cincho cheese for the perfect balance of sweet and savory." At Chilte, Smith often garnishes this cheesecake with whipped cream and jamaica (hibiscus) coulis but encourages experimenting with fruit or caramel sauces, fresh fruit, or citrus to create your own version.

Sablée Crust Combine flour and salt in one bowl and buttermilk and egg yolks in another. Mix well and set both aside.

Cream butter and sugar in the bowl of a stand mixer fitted with the paddle attachment on medium-high speed until light and fluffy. Reduce speed to medium-low and mix in buttermilk and egg mixture. Reduce speed to low and gradually mix in flour and salt until incorporated.

Remove dough from bowl and shape into a disk. Wrap in plastic wrap and refrigerate for at least 1 hour. Allow to come to room temperature before using (dough should be firm but malleable).

When ready to bake, preheat oven to 350°F.

Grease a 6- to 8-inch springform pan and line the bottom with parchment paper. Press approximately 3 cups sablée dough into an even layer about ½ inch thick on the bottom of the pan. (If you like, you can add more sablée to create a side crust.) Dock with a fork, then freeze for 10 minutes.

Remove from the freezer and bake for 10–15 minutes, until crust is golden brown. Allow to cool in pan.

Charred Corn Turn on broiler.

Set corn on a baking sheet and brush lightly with oil.

Set in oven about 6 inches from broiler. Rotate until charred and slightly blackened in spots, 8–10 minutes.

Remove from oven and allow to cool. Cut kernels off the cobs and set aside.

ASSEMBLY

Cheesecake Filling (see here)

Prepared Sablée Crust (see here)

Cincho or cotija cheese, for garnish (see Note)

Your favorite cheesecake toppings, for garnish

NOTE Epazote is a distinctive herb used in Mexican cuisine known for its pungent flavor that blends notes of citrus, mint, and anise. Fresh epazote can be found at Mexican grocers like El Super, Food City, and Los Altos Ranch Market, and at local farmers' markets. If unavailable, omit.

Cincho cheese, or queso cincho, is a firm, aged Mexican cheese with a salty, tangy flavor that is easy to grate. Look for it at Mexican markets such as El Super or Los Altos Ranch Market. If unavailable, substitute with cotija. Although it has a milder flavor and crumblier texture, it is readily available at local grocers.

Cheesecake Filling Purée corn, epazote, vanilla, heavy cream, sour cream, and lime juice in a food processor.

Place corn purée, cream cheese, sugar, and flour in the bowl of a stand mixer fitted with the paddle attachment. Mix until smooth and combined.

Add whole eggs and yolks one at a time, ensuring each is fully incorporated before adding the next.

Assembly Preheat oven to 300°F.

Pour cheesecake filling into baked sablée crust, leaving 1 inch of space at top of pan.

Wrap bottom of springform pan with foil (to prevent water seepage from the water bath).

Place pan in a larger baking dish. Fill baking dish with hot water until it reaches halfway up the sides of the springform pan.

Bake cheesecake for 45 minutes and check for doneness. The edges should be firm, and the center should have a slight jiggle and be golden brown on top. If needed, bake for 5–10 minutes more. To avoid cracking, jiggle gently and don't open oven door too often when checking.

Allow cheesecake to cool to room temperature in pan. Refrigerate for at least 4 hours and up to 3 days. (Cheesecake can also be frozen; thaw overnight in the refrigerator before serving.)

To remove from the pan, run a warm butter knife around the edge before releasing the clasp. When cutting, dip a sharp knife in hot water and wipe clean between cuts. Garnish with your favorite cheesecake toppings and a grating of cincho (or cotija) cheese.

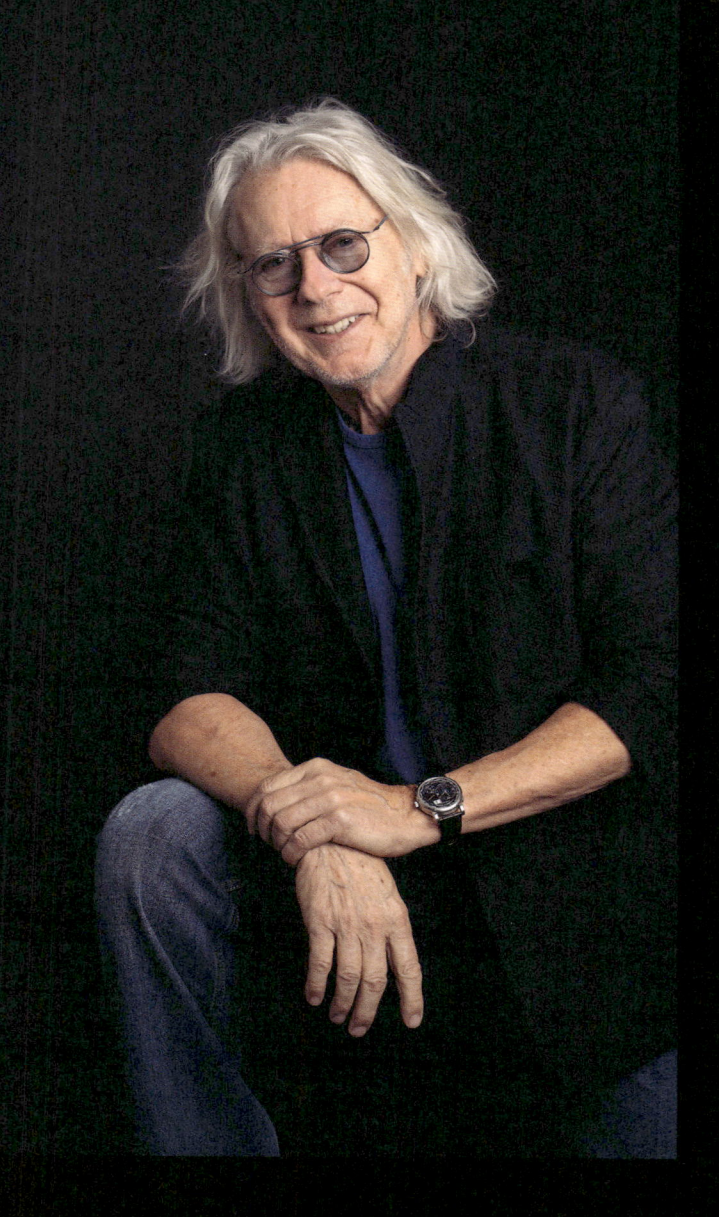

CHRISTOPHER'S AT WRIGLEY MANSION

Christopher Gross

When chewing gum baron William Wrigley Jr. gifted his wife, Ada, a hilltop mansion overlooking Phoenix in the 1930s, little did he know it would one day house a culinary destination that would draw people from all over the world. Enter Christopher's at Wrigley Mansion, where James Beard Award–winning chef Christopher Gross has created a dining destination that's equal parts theater, art gallery, and gastronomic wonderland.

"Christopher's is a modern, contemporary add-on to the mansion, a piece of art in keeping with the Venice Charter," explains Gross, referencing the architectural principle of combining historic buildings with modern additions for a contrast that honors context. "While it's obviously not a part of the original building, it blends in beautifully with its historic lines."

It's a stunning setting for his immersive approach to fine dining, where each element of the experience is as intentional as a brushstroke on a canvas. Brought to life by renowned architect Wendell Burnette, Gross's glass-walled perch combines his love for art and travel with global whimsy. A retractable ceiling echoes a Parisian restaurant, while the cutlery drawers at diners' tables pay homage to a Copenhagen favorite. Unique flourishes are part of the modern French tasting menu and include tableside apéritif carts and bronze cloches designed by Paolo Soleri. Even the hand-fired Blue Door Ceramics plates showcase Gross's artistry, bearing his own illustrated designs.

As Gross notes with characteristic grace: "The philosophy of the restaurant includes all those different elements. While guests come for my food, it's not just about me; it's about creating an entire dining experience."

Christopher's at Wrigley Mansion / 49

PORTIONING DUCK

2 (5- to 5½-lb) whole ducks

REDUCED DUCK STOCK

2 duck carcasses, cut up into smaller pieces, along with necks, wings, and trimmings (see here)
3–4 sprigs thyme
2 large cloves garlic, chopped
2 small shallots, sliced
½ tsp whole black peppercorns
2 fresh bay leaves, torn
2 cups chicken stock
2 cups veal stock, or 1 cup prepared veal demi-glace, such as D'Artagnan

Duck Three Ways

SERVES 4 Guaranteed to impress, this elegant dish features herb-basted duck breast, duck confit, and seared foie gras, all complemented by a savory duck sauce. Christopher Gross suggests serving with seasonal vegetables roasted or sautéed in the confit duck fat. Ingredients like duck fat, foie gras, and veal demi-glace can be sourced through your local butcher, or ordered online from specialty purveyors like Hudson Valley Farms and D'Artagnan Foods.

Portioning Duck Place ducks breast-side up on a cutting board and pat dry with paper towels. Using a sharp boning knife, remove necks, if attached, saving them for sauce.

Trim excess fat and skin but don't be too aggressive; you want to be sure all of the meat is covered by skin. To remove wings, cut through the joint where the wings meet the body. Set wings and trimmings aside, saving them for sauce.

To remove legs, trim excess skin and fat around the cavity to give a clearer view. Working with one leg at a time, grasp drumstick and pull leg outward from the body. Cut skin between leg and body to expose the joint and slice through the joint to detach the leg.

To remove breasts, feel for the breastbone that runs down the center of the duck. Working one side at a time, cut along the top of the breastbone to the bottom, slicing a few centimeters deep as close to the bone as possible. Use your fingers to separate the breast from the ribcage. (If needed, use boning knife to detach the breast, leaving the ribcage clean.) Slice through the skin to fully separate the breast. Once breast is free, remove tenderloin (refrigerate or freeze for another use).

You should have 4 breast halves and 4 legs. Cover and refrigerate, reserving bodies, wings, and trimmings for sauce.

Reduced Duck Stock Preheat oven to 400°F. Place duck carcasses, necks, wings, and trimmings on a roasting rack set over a baking sheet. Roast until dark brown, 15–20 minutes.

CONFIT DUCK LEGS

3–4 cloves garlic, chopped

1 Tbsp black peppercorns, coarsely ground

¾ cup kosher salt

4–6 sprigs thyme, leaves only, chopped

4 duck legs (see here)

2–3 cups duck fat, melted

ASSEMBLY

4 duck breast halves (see here)

Kosher salt, to taste

Cracked black pepper, to taste

Five-spice powder, to taste

2 sprigs of fresh herbs, such as thyme, rosemary, or sage, plus more for garnish

4 Confit Duck Legs (see here)

4 (2- to 3-oz) portions Hudson Valley Farms foie gras

1½ cups Reduced Duck Stock (see here)

2 Tbsp cold unsalted butter

Vegetables sautéed or roasted in duck fat, to serve

Shaved black truffles, for garnish (optional)

Maldon sea salt, for garnish

Transfer roasted duck parts to a large stockpot. Add remaining ingredients, along with more stock (or water) as needed to submerge duck. Bring to a boil over high heat, then reduce heat and simmer gently for 1 hour, skimming off and discarding any oil and foam. Strain through a fine-mesh sieve into a heatproof container, discarding bones and residue. Return stock to pot and simmer until reduced by half, 15–20 minutes.

Reduced stock can be stored in the refrigerator for up to 1 week.

Confit Duck Legs In a food processor, pulse garlic, peppercorns, salt, and thyme for 10–12 seconds to create a curing mix. Sprinkle generously on all sides of duck legs. Cover and refrigerate for at least 6 hours, or overnight.

When ready to prepare the confit, preheat oven to 200°F.

Rinse duck legs under cold water to remove residual curing mix. Drain on a paper towel–lined tray and pat completely dry. Place snugly in a deep roasting pan and add enough duck fat to completely submerge. Cover pan with foil and cook for 14–16 hours, or overnight.

Remove from oven and carefully pull away foil to release steam. The duck should be fork tender with little color. Allow to cool in pan for 20 minutes. Using a slotted spoon, transfer legs to a cooling rack over a sheet pan.

Strain and store duck fat in an airtight container in the refrigerator for up to 2 weeks. Duck fat can be used to sauté greens, roast potatoes and root vegetables, or flavor other dishes.

Assembly Turn on broiler.

With a sharp knife, score skin on duck breasts in a crosshatch pattern, cutting through skin but avoiding meat (to render fat and achieve a crispy skin). Generously season flesh side of each duck breast with salt and pepper and a pinch of five-spice powder.

Heat a heavy sauté pan over medium heat. Add duck breasts, skin-side down, being careful not to overcrowd the pan. (If needed, cook in batches.) As fat starts to render, add herbs. Sauté for 4–6 minutes, using a spoon to baste with herbs until all fat is rendered and skin is crispy and golden brown. Transfer breasts to a wire rack set over a baking sheet. Wipe sauté pan clean and

Christopher's at Wrigley Mansion

reserve. Meanwhile, place confit duck legs on a baking sheet and broil for 8–10 minutes, until skin is crispy but not burnt. Remove from oven and set aside. Lower oven temperature to 375°F.

Score foie gras in a crosshatch pattern and season generously with salt and pepper. In the same pan used for the duck breasts, sear foie gras over medium-high heat for 2–3 minutes per side, basting with its own fat. Transfer to the wire rack with the duck breasts.

Place rack and baking sheet in oven and bake foie gras and duck breasts for approximately 6–8 minutes for medium-rare. Remove and allow to rest on a cutting board for 3–4 minutes.

Meanwhile, in a saucepan over medium heat, reduce duck stock by half or until it reaches a consistency that will coat the back of a spoon (*nappe*), 10–15 minutes. Remove from heat and mount with butter (*monter au beurre*) by gradually whisking in small, cold pieces until butter is melted and sauce is smooth and glossy. Adjust seasoning if needed.

Place a duck leg on each serving plate, just to the side. Set a piece of foie gras on top. Pour duck sauce around duck leg and in center of plate. Slice duck breasts in half and place skin-side up next to the duck leg and foie gras.

Alternatively, for a more formal presentation, arrange foie gras, duck leg, and sliced duck breast in center of plate. Pour duck sauce around duck and foie gras.

Serve with sautéed or roasted vegetables, garnish with shaved truffles (if using), and finish with a sprinkle of Maldon salt.

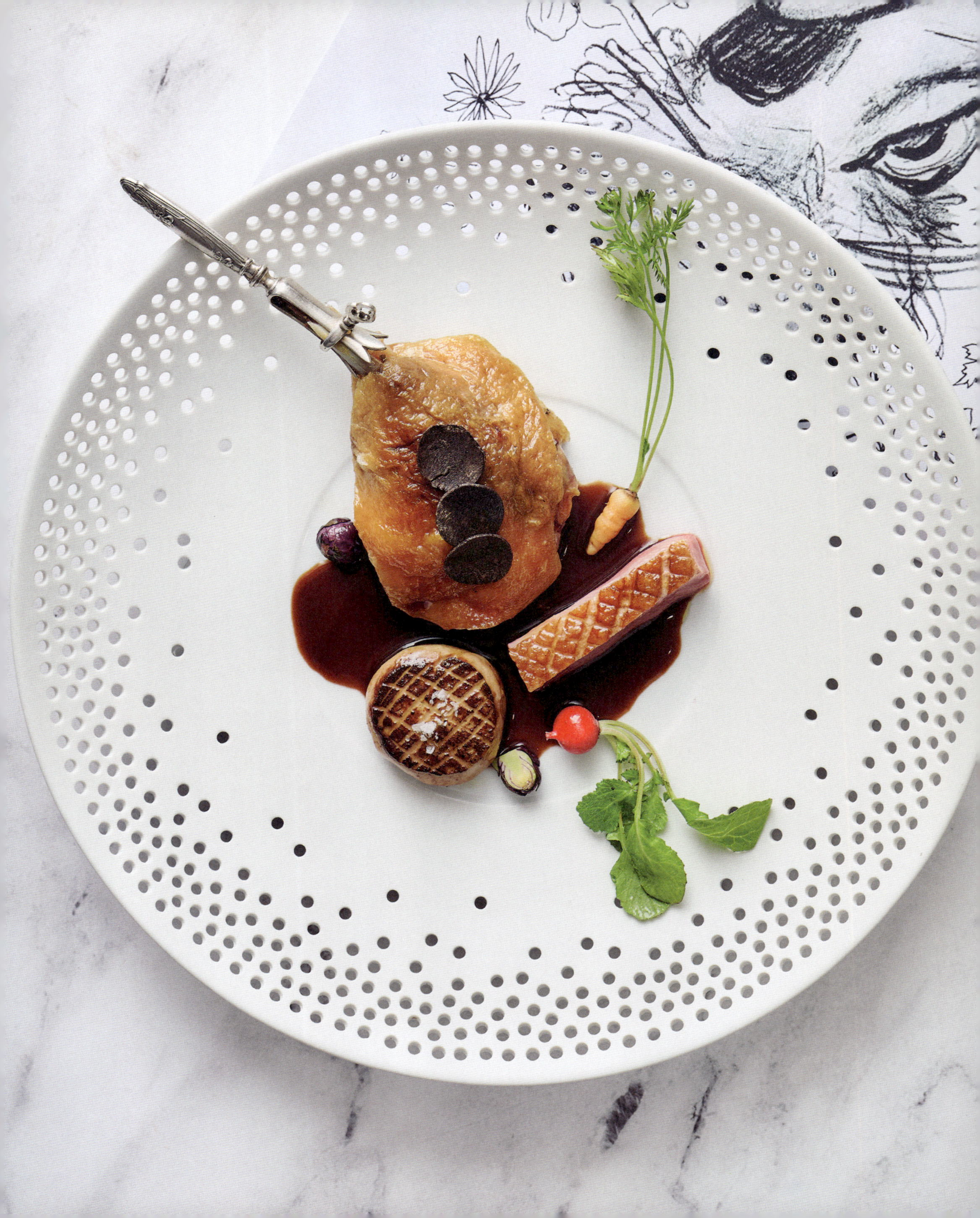

SCALLOP MOUSSE
3½ oz bay or sea scallops
1 tsp lobster roe (see Note)
1 large egg white
Kosher salt, to taste

SKATE ROLL
1 (5-lb) Atlantic skate wing, cleaned
1 cup Scallop Mousse (see here)

Crepe of Atlantic Skate with Scallop Mousse and Lobster Sauce

SERVES 4 This showstopper highlights skate, a ray fish prized for its flaky texture and subtle sweet flavor. Rolled and stuffed with scallop mousse, the skate is decorated by squid ink crepes that add a dramatic flair to its presentation. To save time, crepe batter can be made the day before serving and lobster stock can be purchased. Source skate, squid ink, lobster roe, and lobster stock from local fishmongers like Nelson's Meat + Fish (page 166) or online gourmet retailers such as L'Epicerie.

Scallop Mousse Place scallops and lobster roe in a small food processor and process for 30–40 seconds until mixture is smooth and pale green from the roe. Add egg white and process for another 20 seconds. Lightly season to taste with salt.

Transfer mousse to a piping bag and store in the refrigerator for up to 1 hour.

Skate Roll Pat skate wing dry with paper towels on a cutting board. With presentation side facing down (the side with fewer imperfections), trim into a rectangular shape.

Lay out a piece of plastic wrap double the size of the fish and place the skate in the center.

Pipe out a thin line of scallop mousse, ½–¾ inch in diameter, one-third of the way down. Use the plastic wrap to roll the skate wing tightly into a log shape and wrap completely. Refrigerate for 30–60 minutes.

Fill a pot with water and place a steamer insert inside, ensuring water level is below the bottom of the steamer. Heat over medium until it reaches a steady temperature of 140°F. Add plastic-wrapped skate roll, cover, and steam fish for 30 minutes. Monitor temperature, adjusting as needed. If it rises, briefly remove pot from heat to cool slightly before continuing. Scallop mousse visible at ends of roll should be bright orange-red, indicating it is cooked. If it's still green, steam a little longer.

Remove skate roll with tongs and transfer to an ice water bath (a large bowl filled with ice cubes and cold water) to chill completely.

LOBSTER SAUCE

2 Roma tomatoes, diced
½ cup minced yellow onion
1 clove garlic, minced
1 fresh bay leaf
⅓ cup tomato paste
½ cup brandy
2 cups lobster stock, or 1 lb lobster shells
½ cup heavy cream
½ cup cold unsalted butter
Kosher salt and black pepper, to taste

SQUID INK CREPES

½ cup all-purpose flour
Pinch of kosher salt
Pinch of black pepper
½ cup whole milk
2 tsp squid ink
1 Tbsp unsalted butter, for frying

Lobster Sauce Add tomatoes, onions, garlic, and bay leaf to a saucepan over medium heat. Cook for 2–3 minutes, until onions are translucent but not browned. Stir in tomato paste and cook for an additional minute. Add brandy and simmer until reduced by half, 3–5 minutes. Stir in stock (or lobster shells and 2 cups of water) and reduce by half again, 25–30 minutes. Pour in heavy cream. Simmer until the sauce reaches a consistency that will coat the back of a spoon (*nappe*), 15–20 minutes. Strain through a fine-mesh sieve into another small saucepan, discarding solids.

Over low heat, mount with butter (*monter au beurre*) by gradually whisking in cold unsalted butter 1 tablespoon at a time until smooth and glossy. Season with salt and pepper to taste and keep warm until ready to plate.

Squid Ink Crepes Combine flour, salt, and pepper and set aside. In a separate bowl, mix milk and squid ink. Blend dry and wet ingredients in a blender until smooth, 10–12 seconds. Chill batter in the refrigerator for at least 30 minutes, and up to 24 hours.

For each crepe, melt ½ teaspoon of butter in an 8-inch nonstick skillet or crepe pan over medium-high heat. Pour 3–4 tablespoons of batter into the pan, swirling to spread it thinly and evenly. The less batter used and the larger you can stretch the crepe, the thinner it will be.

Cook for 1–2 minutes until edges start to lift and bottom is lightly browned. Flip and cook for another 1–2 minutes, for a total of 2–4 minutes. Repeat with remaining batter, adding more butter to the pan as needed.

Stack finished crepes on a plate and keep warm under a clean dish towel.

ASSEMBLY

Skate Roll (see here)
Kosher salt and black pepper, to taste
1½ tsp unsalted butter
1 Tbsp canola oil
2 sprigs of fresh herbs, such as thyme, plus extra for garnish
1 cup Lobster Sauce (see here)
4 Squid Ink Crepes (see here)
Edible gold leaf, for garnish (optional)
Squid ink breadsticks, for garnish (optional)
Culinary plankton powder, for garnish (optional)

Assembly Once skate roll is cold and firm, remove plastic wrap and pat fish dry. Slice roulade into 4 even slices and sprinkle with salt and pepper.

Melt butter with oil in a large nonstick pan over medium-high heat. Add skate slices and herbs and sauté skate, basting frequently, until slices are golden brown, about 2 minutes per side. Transfer skate to a paper towel–lined plate to absorb any residual oil.

To serve, spoon ¼ cup of warm lobster sauce into the center of each plate. Place a skate slice on top, and blanket fish with a squid ink crepe, leaving one-quarter of the skate slice exposed. Garnish with fresh herbs and sprinkle crepe with edible gold leaf, if using. For a more formal presentation, garnish with squid ink breadsticks and plankton powder, if desired.

NOTE Lobster roe are the eggs of female lobsters and are sold both fresh and frozen. When raw, they appear dark green or black and have a soft jelly-like texture. The roe is also called lobster coral because upon cooking, it turns a bright orange-red color.

Christopher's at Wrigley Mansion / 57

ELEMENTS

Gregory James

Camelback Mountain rises like a sleeping giant in the Sonoran landscape, and along its northern slopes lies Sanctuary Camelback Mountain, where the Gurney's Resorts property unfolds across fifty-three acres. With its manicured gardens and beautiful vistas of nearby Praying Monk and Mummy Mountain, Sanctuary is one of Arizona's most luxurious destinations. Here executive chef Gregory James oversees every culinary experience, from Elements Restaurant and Jade Bar to celebratory banquets and private guest dinners. "Today I'm cooking for seven villa guests who wanted the freshest ingredients to guide us," he says. "I love creating bold flavors in unusual combinations, and my favorite way to cook is hyper-local, seasonal, and ingredient-driven."

It's a philosophy that has made Sanctuary's dining program, under his leadership, as memorable as the spectacular panoramas framed by Elements' floor to ceiling windows. Expressing his commitment to Arizona sourcing, James notes that "we need to support our farms. By promoting them and encouraging consumers and other businesses to buy from them, they'll continue to grow." This passion manifests in every carefully curated partnership, from the marbled perfection of Copper State Ranch's beef to the heritage grains grown by Hayden Flour Mills.

"I love the food community here," continues James, whose thirty years of experience span destinations in Arizona, Minnesota, California, and, most recently, the Inn at Perry Cabin in Maryland. (In 2022 he was crowned Restaurant Association of Maryland Chef of the Year.) Reflecting on his current role, he shares, "I just love being at Sanctuary. With almost twenty-five years of history, it's an iconic part of Arizona."

▶ Sonoran Eggs Benedict with Polenta, Braised Short Ribs, Rosemary Hollandaise, and English Muffin Chips

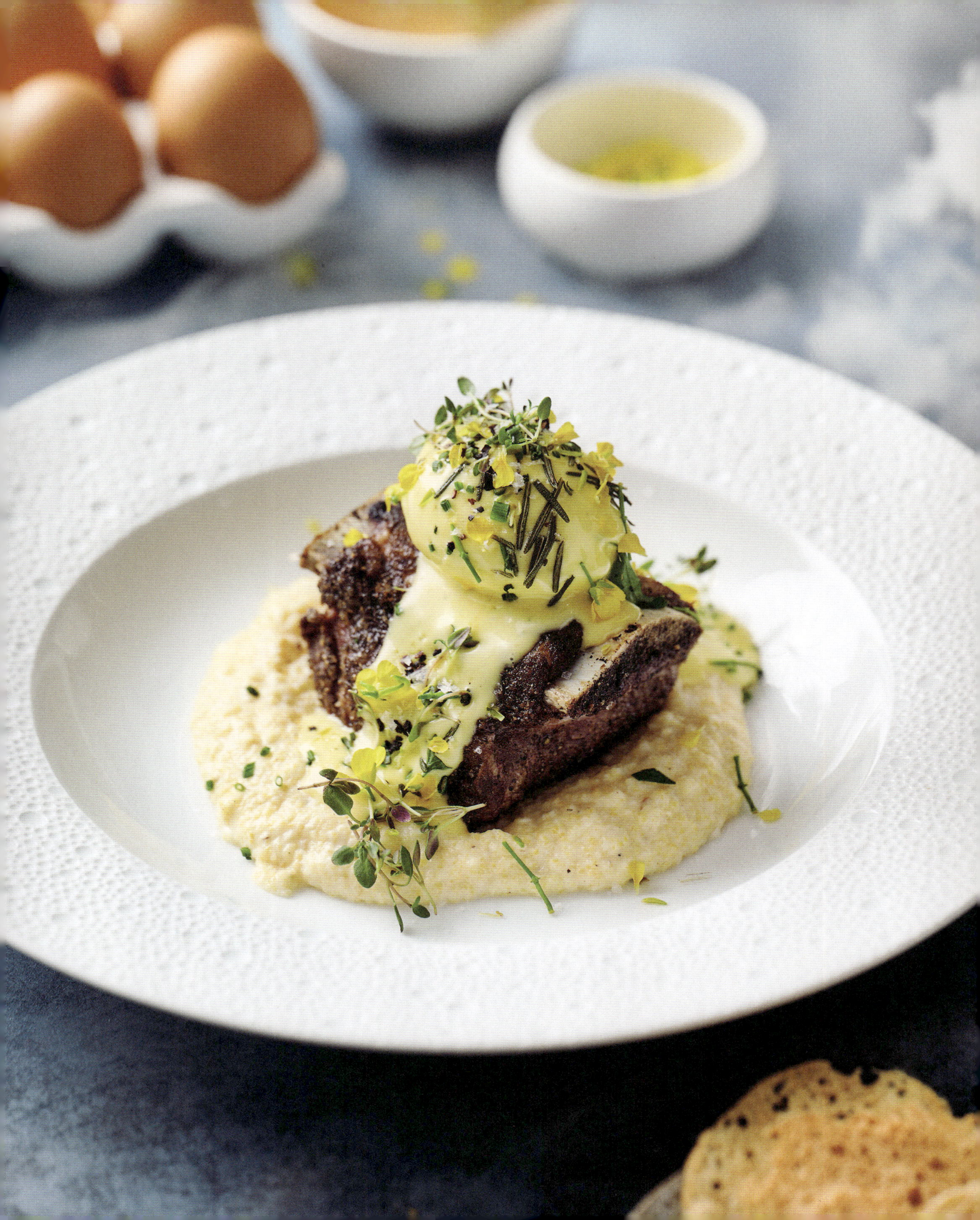

ENGLISH MUFFIN CHIPS

Cooking spray
2 Breadworks English muffins, frozen

COPPER STATE BEEF SHORT RIBS

3 lbs bone-in short ribs, at least 1½ inches thick
Kosher salt and freshly ground black pepper, to taste
2 Tbsp vegetable oil
2 large heads garlic, halved crosswise
1 medium onion, chopped
4 stalks celery, chopped
2 medium carrots, chopped
3 Tbsp tomato paste
2 cups dry red wine (about half a bottle)
2 cups beef broth
4 sprigs thyme

Sonoran Eggs Benedict with Polenta, Braised Short Ribs, Rosemary Hollandaise, and English Muffin Chips

SERVES 4 "It's all local," says Gregory James of this brunch favorite made with Hayden Flour Mills polenta, Copper State Beef short ribs, Two Wash Ranch eggs ("red pepper flakes in the chicken's diet gives the yolks a beautiful orange-red hue"), Breadworks English muffins, and Cutino hot sauce. The hollandaise? Scented with rosemary plucked from the property. "We shave the English muffins thin and bake until crispy," he adds. "Dip them in polenta, get that short rib and egg on them, and it's like a tostada."

English Muffin Chips Preheat oven to 300°F.

Line a baking sheet with parchment paper lightly coated with cooking spray.

Shave frozen English muffins as thinly as possible using a mandoline or serrated knife.

Place muffin slices on the prepared baking sheet. Top with another sheet of parchment paper and sandwich with a second baking sheet.

Bake for 25–30 minutes, or until chips are golden brown and crisp. Remove from oven and allow to cool.

Chips can be stored at room temperature in an airtight container for up to 1 week.

Copper State Beef Short Ribs Preheat oven to 275°F.

Pat ribs dry. Season on all sides with salt and pepper.

Heat oil in a large Dutch oven over medium-high heat. Once oil is hot and shimmering, add ribs (in batches to avoid overcrowding) and sear on all sides until dark and evenly browned, 6–8 minutes. Transfer seared ribs to a large plate.

Remove all but 2 tablespoons of the fat in the pan, keeping the browned bits. Reduce heat to medium and add garlic, cut-side down. Cook for 1–2 minutes and add onions, celery, and carrots. Sprinkle with salt and pepper and toss to coat. Sauté, stirring occasionally, until vegetables are softened but not browned, 5–10 minutes. Add tomato paste and stir to coat. Continue to cook, stirring occasionally, until tomato paste darkens slightly and starts to caramelize, 2–3 minutes.

POACHED EGGS
1 Tbsp kosher salt
2 Tbsp white vinegar
4 large fresh Two Wash Ranch eggs, cold

Add red wine and use a wooden spoon to stir and scrape up any browned or caramelized bits. Simmer 8–10 minutes, until slightly reduced. Stir in beef broth, and add thyme. Return short ribs to the pan, along with any juices that have accumulated. Nestle ribs into vegetables, bone-side up to ensure meat is submerged. If liquid does not completely cover meat, add more broth or water as needed. Bring contents to a simmer, then cover and transfer to oven.

Braise, undisturbed, for 3½ to 4 hours, or until ribs are fork tender and falling off the bone.

At this point, you can serve short ribs bone-in, as James prefers for presentation, or boneless. To remove bones, use tongs to transfer ribs to a plate, then carefully take out the bones. Return boneless ribs to the braising liquid to keep warm.

Braised short ribs can be prepared up to 4 days ahead and stored in the refrigerator in their braising liquid. To reheat, place ribs and braising liquid in a covered pot and warm over low heat, or warm in a 275°F oven.

Poached Eggs Fill a medium pot with water, leaving a 1-inch space from the top. Stir in salt and vinegar and bring to a simmer over medium heat. The water should have small bubbles forming, not a rolling boil.

Prepare an ice bath by filling a bowl with ice and enough water to cover.

Crack 1 egg into a small ramekin. Using the handle of a spatula or spoon, quickly stir water in one direction, creating a gentle whirlpool (this prevents the white from "feathering," or spreading out). Carefully lower egg into center of whirlpool.

Turn off heat immediately, cover pan, and set timer for 5 minutes. Don't stir or disturb egg in any way. Use a slotted spoon to transfer poached egg to ice bath and allow to cool. Repeat with remaining eggs.

Poached eggs can be refrigerated in cold water for up to 8 hours, then gently reheated in warm water before serving.

POLENTA

2 cups chicken broth
½ cup heavy cream
½ cup Hayden Flour Mills polenta (see Note)
2 Tbsp unsalted butter
1½ oz (¼ cup) finely grated Parmesan
½ tsp chili powder
½ tsp ground white pepper
1½ tsp kosher salt
4 dashes Cutino Sauce Co. hot sauce, or your favorite hot sauce

ROSEMARY HOLLANDAISE

3 large egg yolks
1 Tbsp dry white wine
1 tsp Worcestershire sauce
½ tsp Dijon mustard
¾ lb clarified butter or ghee, held warm at 130°F–140°F (see Note)
1 lemon, zested and juiced
1 Tbsp finely chopped rosemary
1 tsp kosher salt
½ tsp ground white pepper
Pinch of cayenne pepper

Polenta Over high heat in a heavy-bottomed saucepan, bring chicken broth to a boil. Stir in cream.

Gradually whisk in polenta until fully incorporated. Reduce heat to low and simmer for 20–25 minutes, stirring frequently to prevent sticking.

Whisk in butter and Parmesan until melted. Stir in chili powder, white pepper, and salt. Add hot sauce, then taste and adjust seasoning.

Keep warm until ready to serve.

Rosemary Hollandaise Prepare a double boiler by filling a medium saucepan with 1–2 inches of water and bringing it to a low simmer over medium-low heat.

In a stainless steel bowl that will fit snugly over the pan without touching the water, whisk together egg yolks, white wine, Worcestershire sauce, and mustard.

Place bowl over simmering water and whisk constantly for 3–5 minutes, or until mixture thickens and doubles in volume, forming ribbons when lifted.

Gradually pour in warm butter (or ghee) in a thin, steady stream while whisking vigorously. Be sure to keep the hollandaise warm, but not hot, to prevent breaking and separating.

Whisk in lemon juice and zest, rosemary, salt, white pepper, and cayenne. Taste and adjust seasoning.

Keep hollandaise warm in the double boiler with the heat turned off, stirring occasionally.

ASSEMBLY

4 Poached Eggs (see here)

3 cups Polenta (see here)

4 (4-oz) pieces of Copper State Beef Short Ribs (see here)

½ cup Rosemary Hollandaise (see here)

1 Tbsp chopped fresh herbs, such as rosemary and thyme

1 tsp Maldon sea salt

Edible flowers, for garnish (optional)

12 English Muffin Chips, to serve (see here)

Assembly Bring water to a boil in a heavy-bottomed saucepan over high heat, then reduce to a gentle simmer. Add poached eggs and gently warm for 1–2 minutes.

Spoon ¾ cup polenta into each serving bowl and top with a short rib. Place 1 poached egg on each short rib.

Top with hollandaise and sprinkle with fresh herbs and sea salt. Garnish with edible flowers, if using. Serve with English muffin chips for dipping.

NOTE Hayden Flour Mills polenta is a whole grain, non-GMO yellow corn polenta stone-ground by a family-owned business dedicated to sustainable farming practices and reviving heritage and ancient grains. Find it at specialty grocers like AJ's Fine Foods and Whole Foods, at the Hayden Flour Mills shop in Gilbert, or order directly from their website.

Clarified butter and ghee are butterfats with milk solids and water removed, reducing risk of hollandaise curdling or separating. Jarred ghee can be found at Middle Eastern or Indian markets and specialty grocers. To keep warm, place butter or ghee in a vacuum pack in a sous-vide water bath; preheat the oven to its lowest setting, turn it off, and place in a container inside; or hold in a double boiler with gently simmering water.

CAJETA

1 whole Mexican vanilla bean
4 cups goat milk, plus more if needed (see Note)
¾ cup sugar
½ tsp baking soda
⅛ tsp Diamond Crystal kosher salt

CANDIED PECANS

6 Tbsp dark brown sugar
1½ tsp ground cinnamon
½ tsp fine sea salt
½ tsp vanilla extract
1½ Tbsp water
2 tsp orange zest, optional
Pinch of cayenne pepper, optional
2 cups Arizona pecan halves

Monkey Bread with Apples, Candied Pecans, Cajeta, and Five-Spice Royal Icing

SERVES 4 "When I was twenty-one and an executive chef in Wisconsin, we always had monkey bread at Sunday brunch," Gregory James shares. "I've brought different iterations to everywhere I've worked." His Arizona version showcases local pecans, Anna apples from Schnepf Farms, a fourth-generation family farm in Queen Creek, and cajeta, a Mexican caramel. "You can make cajeta with cow's milk, but I love the tang of goat milk," says James.

Cajeta Using the tip of a sharp paring knife, split the vanilla bean pod lengthwise down the middle. Using the flat side of the blade, scrape out seeds and dark, sticky paste (reserve to flavor other desserts).

Place scraped pod in a pot over medium heat and add goat milk, sugar, baking soda, and salt. Warm, stirring occasionally with a heat-resistant spatula, until sugar dissolves and milk turns foamy and light, about 15 minutes.

Continue gently simmering, lowering heat if necessary, and stirring and scraping the sides of the pot frequently. As it thickens, stir more frequently to prevent scorching. After about 45 minutes, the cajeta should be a deep golden color and a spatula dragged across the bottom will leave a trail that remains open for 1–2 seconds before closing. Remove from heat and discard vanilla pod.

Pour cajeta into a measuring cup. If less than 1 cup, add more goat milk to reach that measure. Transfer to a heat-resistant, wide-mouthed glass jar.

Cajeta can be prepared ahead and stored in the refrigerator.

Candied Pecans Line a baking sheet with parchment paper or a silicone baking mat.

In a medium skillet over medium heat, combine brown sugar, cinnamon, salt, vanilla, water, and, if using, orange zest and cayenne pepper. Stir continuously until sugar dissolves smoothly into a bubbling sauce, about 1 minute.

FIVE-SPICE ROYAL ICING
1 egg white
1 cup confectioners' sugar
½ tsp vanilla extract
1 tsp five-spice powder

CARAMELIZED APPLES
4 medium Schnepf Farms Anna apples, or Pink Lady apples
2 Tbsp butter
1 tsp ground cinnamon
⅓ cup granulated sugar
5 Tbsp water, divided
4 tsp cornstarch

Add pecans and stir to coat. Continue to cook, stirring continuously, until pecans are candied and shiny, and smell nutty, 2–3 minutes. Watch carefully to avoid burning.

Working quickly and using a silicone spatula, transfer hot pecans to prepared baking sheet and spread out in one layer.

Allow pecans to cool, then break them apart. Candied pecans can be prepared ahead and stored in an airtight container for up to 2 weeks.

Five-Spice Royal Icing In a stainless steel bowl, beat egg white with a handheld or stand mixer on medium speed until frothy, 2–3 minutes. Reduce speed to low and gradually add in sugar, vanilla, and five-spice powder. Once fully incorporated, whip at medium-high speed until stiff, shiny peaks form, 5–7 minutes. The icing should be thick and hold its shape when you lift the beaters out of the bowl.

Icing can be prepared ahead and refrigerated in an airtight container for up to 7 days. Before using, bring to room temperature and whisk until smooth.

Caramelized Apples Peel and core apples and slice into thick slices.

In a saucepan over medium heat, melt butter and sprinkle in cinnamon. Stir in apples, sugar, and 3 tablespoons of water. Cover and cook, stirring occasionally, until apples are slightly softened, 4–6 minutes.

In a small dish, make a slurry by mixing cornstarch with the remaining 2 tablespoons of water until dissolved. Stir slurry into pot. Continue to cook, stirring occasionally, until apples are soft but not mushy, and filling is thickened. Simmer for another 2–3 minutes on low heat.

Remove from heat and set aside to cool. Caramelized apples can be prepared ahead and stored in the refrigerator for up to 3 days.

ASSEMBLY

¾ oz active dry yeast

¾ cup warm water (105°F–110°F)

½ cup (1 stick) unsalted butter, softened

½ cup granulated sugar

1 tsp kosher salt

1 oz milk powder (see Note)

2 large eggs

3 cups all-purpose flour

1 cup cake flour

1–2 Tbsp vegetable oil, for oiling bowl

Cooking spray

1 cup Cajeta (see here)

1 cup Candied Pecans, chopped (see here)

1 cup Caramelized Apples (see here)

Five-Spice Royal Icing (see here)

Confectioners' sugar, for garnish

NOTE While you can substitute cow's milk, goat milk gives traditional cajeta its distinctive flavor. Look for goat milk at specialty markets like Whole Foods, Trader Joe's, and Sprouts, and at most local grocers. A local favorite is Crow's Dairy goat milk.

Milk powder (or dried milk) is fresh milk with the water removed through evaporation. It adds richness to baked goods. Find it in the baking aisle of most grocery stores or online.

Assembly In a bowl, dissolve yeast in warm water. Let sit for 10 minutes, or until frothy.

In a stand mixer fitted with a dough hook on medium speed (or using a hand mixer), combine butter, granulated sugar, salt, and milk powder until well combined. Add eggs one at a time, scraping the sides of the bowl with a spatula after each addition. Gradually add both flours and mix until dough appears slightly shaggy but not thoroughly combined, 3–4 minutes. Let rest for 5 minutes, then add activated yeast and water.

Knead with the dough hook (or by hand) until smooth, 8–10 minutes. Test by stretching a piece of dough the size of a golf ball. If it stretches thin enough to let light through without tearing, it's ready. If it tears easily, continue kneading.

When it's ready, transfer dough to an oiled bowl and cover with plastic wrap. Leave in a warm place to proof until doubled in size, 1–2 hours.

Meanwhile, coat four 6-inch cast iron pans with cooking spray. In each pan, spread ¼ cup of cajeta evenly on the bottom and top with ¼ cup of chopped pecans, then ¼ cup of caramelized apples.

Once dough is doubled in size, punch down to deflate. Using scissors, divide into 30-gram (golf ball–sized) portions. Roll into balls by using your hands to tuck edges underneath, creating surface tension to tighten the dough into a smooth ball.

Place 8 balls in each pan, setting one in the center and the rest in a circle around it. Cover loosely with plastic wrap and allow to proof in a warm spot for 45 minutes to 1 hour, or until dough springs back slowly and leaves a small indent when poked (if indent fills immediately, it needs more time).

Meanwhile, preheat oven to 350°F.

When dough is proofed, bake monkey bread for 15–20 minutes, or until bread reaches 195°F internally on an instant-read thermometer. Remove from oven and let rest for 20 minutes.

To serve, run a knife around the edge of each pan. Place a serving plate on top, and invert monkey bread onto it. Drizzle generously with five-spice royal icing and dust with confectioners' sugar.

Elements / 67

ELLIOTT'S STEAKHOUSE

Michael Testa, Nick Gibbs, Michael Regan, Brent Tratten

In downtown Chandler's historic district, a 1912 theater has taken on a second act as Elliott's Steakhouse, a loving homage by owners Gavin Jacobs and Jackie Hall to Hall's late husband, Elliott. Their latest addition adds to a legacy that includes The Brickyard Downtown, The Hidden House, and Maple House. Soaring brick walls whisper of performances past, while a magnificent forty-seven-foot bar anchors the space beneath graceful arches. Above, the mezzanine dining room floats like a private box seat over the lively scene below.

In the kitchen, corporate chef Brent Tratten and executive chef Nick Gibbs bring a fresh take on steakhouse tradition. "It's classic fine dining with interesting twists," Tratten reveals, "like our play on steak au poivre (page 70) or our 16-ounce porcini-crusted ribeye. It's sliced into four pieces and we top each one with a truffle ricotta–filled agnolotti and truffle beurre blanc. It's just so good."

Guided by director of operations Michael Regan and beverage director Michael Testa, the cocktails at Elliott's Steakhouse command their own standing ovations. "We wanted the drinks to be of the same caliber," Regan explains. "Our specialty cocktails are inspired by culinary techniques, like the infused olive oil in the freezer martini (page 73). It pairs beautifully with seafood while being robust enough to complement heartier dishes."

It's a synchronicity that has contributed to the restaurant's resounding success. "It's awesome to have a bar program built on so much trust that I never have to think about it," recognizes Tratten. "The drinks are just as good as the food, and it's really special to have that whole package."

▸ Filet au Foivre and Elliott's Steakhouse Freezer Martini

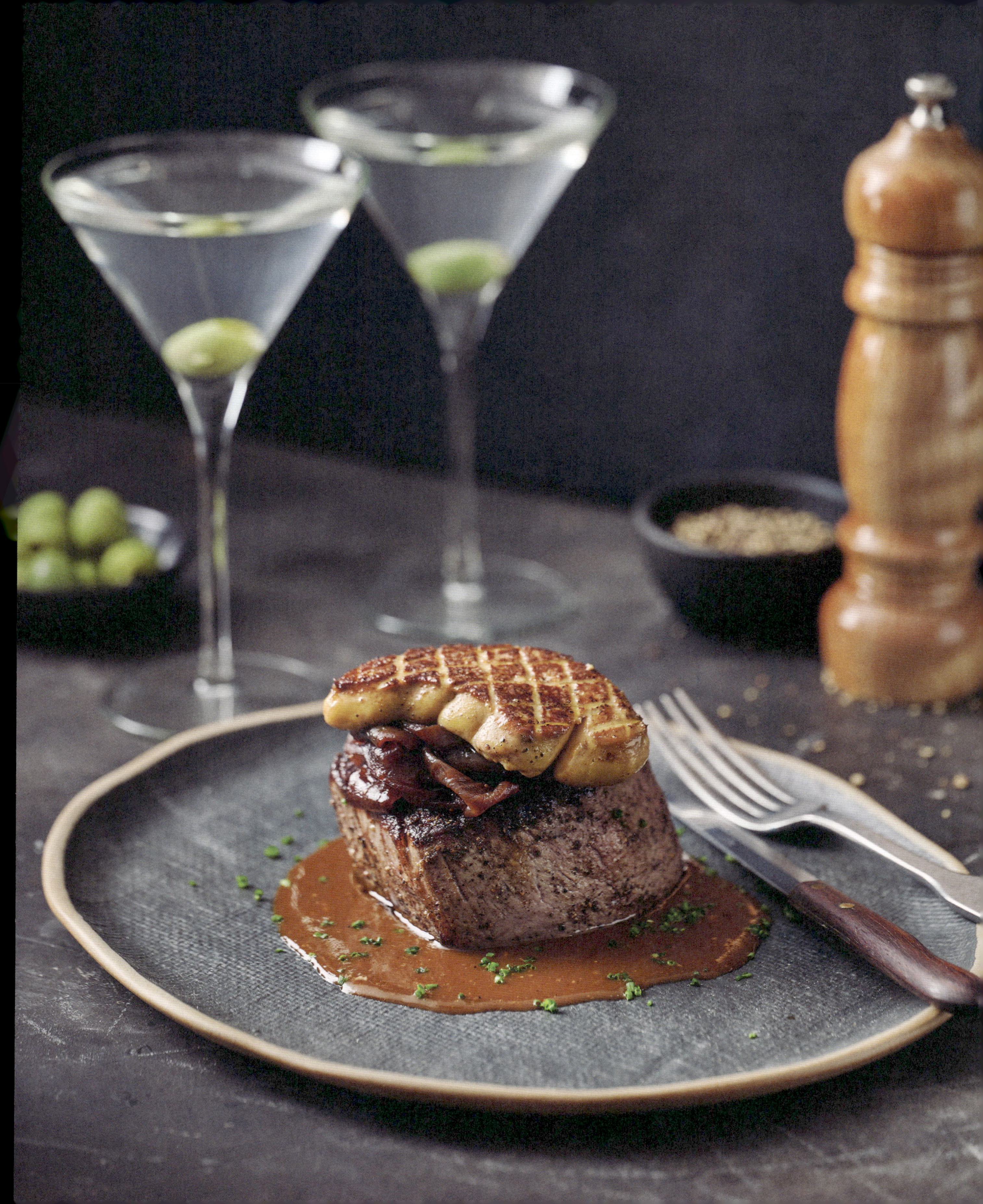

BALSAMIC ONIONS
3 cups thinly sliced white onions
2 cups balsamic vinegar
2 Tbsp granulated sugar
½ cup dry red wine, such as Burgundy

PEPPERCORN-BRANDY CREAM SAUCE
1 Tbsp diced shallots
1 strip bacon, chopped
4 cups red wine demi-glace
½ cup brandy
2 cups heavy cream
4 cloves garlic
2 Tbsp diced carrots
2 tsp ground black pepper
½ tsp pink peppercorns
1 Tbsp kosher salt

Filet au Foivre

SERVES 6 "We thought about putting a traditional steak au poivre on the menu," says Brent Tratten, "but I wanted to step it up with foie gras, and I love the sweet vinegary component of balsamic onions." Demi-glace and foie gras can be purchased at gourmet groceries and from online retailers like D'Artagnan Foods.

Balsamic Onions Bring all ingredients to a boil in a pot over medium-high heat. Reduce heat and simmer, stirring occasionally, until liquid is reduced by half and onions are soft, about 30 minutes.

Balsamic onions can be made up to 5 days ahead and stored in the refrigerator.

Peppercorn-Brandy Cream Sauce In a saucepot over medium heat, sauté shallots and bacon until shallots are soft, about 5 minutes. Add remaining ingredients and stir to combine. Simmer until reduced by a third, about 1 hour.

Blend with an immersion blender or blender until smooth. If using a blender, be careful when blending hot liquids: Remove cap on blender lid and cover with a folded dish towel to allow steam pressure to escape and catch any splashes. Purée the sauce in batches if needed, being careful not to fill the blender more than halfway. Starting on low speed and gradually increasing to high, blend until smooth.

Keep sauce warm.

ASSEMBLY

6 (6- to 8-oz) filets mignons

Kosher salt, to taste

¼ cup coarsely crushed black peppercorns

2 Tbsp oil with a high smoke point, such as canola, grapeseed, or avocado

6 (2-oz) portions of foie gras, chilled

Black pepper, to taste

Balsamic Onions (see here)

1½ cups Peppercorn-Brandy Cream Sauce (see here)

Minced chives, for garnish

Assembly Season filets with salt and then press crushed peppercorns on both sides to form a crust. Lightly oil 2 skillets and heat over medium-high heat.

Cook filets in one of the skillets, approximately 4 minutes per side for medium-rare. Time will vary depending on thickness of the steak; a probe thermometer will show a temperature of 115°F–120°F for medium-rare.

Meanwhile, using a sharp knife and shallow cuts, score the top of each piece of foie gras in a crosshatch pattern. Season with salt and pepper.

Sear foie gras in the second hot skillet, using a spoon to baste the foie gras in its own fat. Cook for approximately 2 minutes per side. When foie gras is ready, it will feel softened (when raw it feels firm). Be careful not to overcook as foie gras can render into fat if cooked too long. Remove, leaving residual fat in pan, and set aside.

Add balsamic onions to same pan and stir in fat until hot.

To serve, place a peppercorn-crusted filet on each plate and pour ¼ cup of peppercorn-brandy cream sauce onto it. Top with a heaping tablespoon of balsamic onions and a slice of seared foie gras.

Garnish with chives.

Elliott's Steakhouse

EVOO-INFUSED SIPSMITH GIN

1 bottle (750-mL) of Sipsmith Gin (see Note)

⅔ cup extra-virgin olive oil

FREEZER MARTINI

2¼ cups EVOO-Infused Sipsmith Gin (see here)

½ cup Casa Martelletti Vermouth di Torino Dry white vermouth

1¼ cups filtered water

ASSEMBLY

6 dashes Regans' Orange Bitters

1 bottle (32-oz) of Freezer Martini, fully chilled (see here)

6 Castelvetrano olives

6 lemon peels, cut into 1-inch-wide strips with minimal white pith, for garnish

Elliott's Steakhouse Freezer Martini

SERVES 6 A finessed twist on the classic, Michael Regan's recipe results in a perfectly chilled cocktail that pairs beautifully with steakhouse fare or stands alone as a sophisticated sipper. "A martini is the number one returned drink in a bar," says Regan. "Through trial and tribulation—drinking many martinis—I created our house freezer martini for the perfect dilution and temperature every time."

EVOO-Infused Sipsmith Gin Pour gin and oil into a gallon-sized zip-top bag. Place in a sous-vide bath at 135°F for 1 hour. Remove bag from water and allow to cool. (If you don't have a sous-vide circulator, pour ingredients into a large container like a mason jar and allow to infuse at room temperature for 6–8 hours, shaking once per hour.)

Pour contents into a freezer-safe container and freeze overnight, or until oil has risen to the top and solidified. Strain through a coffee filter into a pitcher and then pour into the gin bottle or another container. Discard solidified oil.

The infused gin can be stored indefinitely, although the flavor may change over time.

Freezer Martini Pour ingredients into a large freezer-safe resealable bottle and shake to combine.

Place in the freezer until fully chilled.

Assembly At least 2 hours before serving, place 6 martini glasses in the freezer.

For each cocktail, add 1 dash of bitters to glass, followed by ⅔ cup of chilled freezer martini.

Garnish each martini with an olive and expressed lemon peel. (To express, hold peel over the glass with outer side facing down and give it a gentle squeeze to release the oils onto the surface of the drink.) Discard peel.

NOTE The consistency of the freezer martini varies depending on your gin's alcohol content. Higher-proof gins will remain pourable, while others may freeze solid. If your freezer martini freezes, allow to rest briefly at room temperature until it can be poured.

EMBER

Jolie Skwiercz, Willard Thompson

Located on the ancestral lands of the Fort McDowell Yavapai Nation, We-Ko-Pa Casino Resort has a rich history tied to the Yavapai people, who are celebrated in the resort's concepts and design flourishes. In 2020, the property underwent an ambitious refresh, including a constellation of distinctive dining experiences: the Buffet and its global flavors; WKP Sports Bar, offering elevated pub fare; Ahnala, with American comfort dishes; and the crown jewel, Ember, a fine-dining steakhouse centered around the allure of fire. Golden chargers mirror flames, fireplaces cast a warm glow in the piano lounge and on the patio, and mesquite wood-fueled grills infuse dishes with smoke and char in the open kitchen.

As executive chef, Willard Thompson oversees all the culinary facets of the resort. "I love all the aspects—breakfast, lunch, buffets, the sports bar, and Ember, which is fine dining and more technical," he explains. "I bounce around and help where needed. It's a team effort, with the help of our talented chefs."

One such standout is executive pastry chef Jolie Skwiercz, who is known for desserts as delicious as they are inventive. "She's really amazing," Thompson agrees. Skwiercz describes her approach as "whimsical and artistic." At Ember, she reimagines traditional desserts, deconstructing them into colorful, textured creations. "I love incorporating seasonal ingredients in ways that paint a story."

For Thompson, these creative collaborations—and the camaraderie of a team with decades of dedication—are what make We-Ko-Pa special. "I walk around and meet people who have been here for twenty-five or thirty years, which says a lot about a place," he reflects. "We're a family."

CUCUMBER PICO DE GALLO

2 Roma tomatoes, core and insides removed, in ⅛-inch dice
1 medium red bell pepper, in ⅛-inch dice
1 English cucumber, in ⅛-inch dice
1 jalapeño, seeds removed, in ⅛-inch dice (or to taste)
6 Tbsp sherry vinegar
2 Tbsp canola oil
1 medium shallot, minced
1 Tbsp minced garlic
1 tsp kosher salt
½ tsp paprika
½ tsp ground cumin
¼ tsp chili flakes

AVOCADO MOUSSE

1 ripe avocado, halved and pitted
1–2 Tbsp lime juice, to taste
¼ cup sour cream
½ tsp kosher salt, plus more to taste

ASSEMBLY

1 lb yellowtail, sliced thin on a bias
Cucumber Pico de Gallo (see here)
1 Fresno chile, seeded and thinly sliced
Avocado Mousse (see here)
½ cup ponzu sauce
¼ cup micro cilantro or chopped cilantro, for garnish

Yellowtail Crudo with Cucumber Pico de Gallo, Avocado Mousse, and Ponzu

SERVES 4 This recipe is a nod to Willard Thompson's love for the coastal flavors of his youth. "Surfing all day and growing up in San Diego and traveling to Mexico, I've always loved seafood," he notes. Source fresh yellowtail (hamachi in Japanese cuisine) at quality markets such as Nelson's Meat + Fish (page 166) and find ponzu (a citrus-based Japanese condiment) in the Asian foods aisle of most grocery stores.

Cucumber Pico de Gallo Combine all ingredients in a mixing bowl. Cover and chill overnight for best results.

Leftover cucumber pico de gallo can be stored in the refrigerator for up to 3 days and used as a topping for grilled meats and fish, mixed into salads, added to tacos and sandwiches, or served as a dip with tortilla chips.

Avocado Mousse Scoop out avocado and add to a food processor, along with lime juice and sour cream. Blend until smooth.

Add salt and pulse blend for 30 seconds. Adjust lime juice and salt to taste.

Spoon into a plastic piping bag for plating. (If you don't have a piping bag, transfer to a zip-top plastic bag.)

Assembly Divide yellowtail among 4 plates. Arrange slices shingled and slightly overlapping in a straight line down the middle. For each serving, spoon 1 tablespoon of cucumber pico de gallo down the middle of the fish. Place 6 slices of Fresno chile on top of the pico de gallo. Using a piping bag (or zip-top bag with corner snipped), pipe 5–6 small dollops of avocado mousse around the plate. Spoon 2 tablespoons of ponzu sauce over the fish and garnish with cilantro.

PRICKLY PEAR JAM

6–8 prickly pears, for 2 cups blended prickly pear fruit (see Note)
1½ cups granulated sugar
2 Tbsp lemon juice
1 Tbsp Amaretto liqueur (optional)

PRALINE PECANS

2 cups water
½ cup granulated sugar
¼ cup Arizona desert blossom honey
1 cinnamon stick
¾ cup pecan pieces or halves
2 pinches fine sea salt

Desert Blossom Sticky Toffee Date Cake with Prickly Pear Jam, Blood Orange Semifreddo, and Praline Pecans

SERVES 6 "This is Arizona in a dessert," says executive pastry chef Jolie Skwiercz. "Many people don't realize that dates, pecans, prickly pears, and blood oranges all grow right here." Short on time to make all of the components? She suggests pairing the date cakes and toffee sauce with butter pecan ice cream.

Prickly Pear Jam Carefully rinse prickly pears under running water to remove any loose spines. Pat dry. Slice off both ends and make a shallow cut lengthwise down the body of the prickly pear. Using your fingers or the tip of a knife, lift the skin along the cut to peel it back. It should separate from the fruit in 1 piece.

Cut up pears, place in a blender, and blend on high speed for 3–5 minutes. Measure out 2 cups of purée and strain through a fine-mesh sieve over a pot. Add sugar, lemon juice, and Amaretto (if using), and stir to combine. Bring to a boil over medium-high heat.

Reduce heat to medium and simmer for 15–20 minutes until it has a jam-like consistency. Stir frequently to prevent scorching.

Allow to cool and transfer to a jar or other airtight container. Prickly pear jam can be stored in the refrigerator for up to 1 month.

Praline Pecans Preheat oven to 300°F. Line a baking sheet with parchment paper or a silicone mat.

In a saucepan, combine water, sugar, honey, and cinnamon stick. Bring the mixture to a boil over medium-high heat, stirring until sugar is dissolved. Stir in pecans and reduce heat to medium-low. Simmer, stirring occasionally, until mixture thickens to a syrup-like consistency, 10–15 minutes.

76 / Ember

BLOOD ORANGE SEMIFREDDO

2⅓ cups heavy cream

6 large egg yolks

1 cup granulated sugar

1½ tsp vanilla extract

¼ tsp kosher salt

2 blood oranges, zested and juiced

Orange cocoa butter velvet spray, to decorate (optional; see Note)

DATE CAKES

¾ cup pitted and chopped Medjool dates

1 cup water

2 tsp vanilla extract

½ tsp baking soda

1¾ cups all-purpose flour

1 tsp baking powder

Pinch of kosher salt

¼ cup (½ stick) unsalted butter, softened

¾ cup granulated sugar

1 large egg

Strain pecans and discard the cinnamon stick and excess syrup. Spread syrup-coated pecans onto the prepared baking sheet and sprinkle with salt.

Bake pecans for 15–20 minutes, stirring every 5 minutes, until crispy and fragrant.

Allow pecans to cool. Store in an airtight container for up to 1 month.

Blood Orange Semifreddo Line an 8½- × 5½-inch loaf pan with parchment paper.

Using a stand mixer fitted with a whisk attachment (or a hand mixer), whip cream to soft peaks. Transfer to a container and store in the refrigerator.

Bring a pot of water to a gentle simmer over medium-low heat.

Combine egg yolks, sugar, vanilla, salt, blood orange zest, and ¼ cup of blood orange juice in a heatproof bowl.

Set bowl over the pot of simmering water, ensuring bottom of bowl does not touch water (to prevent overheating). Whisk continuously until mixture is thick and creamy and reaches 160°F on an instant-read thermometer.

Transfer custard to a clean bowl for the stand mixer. Beat until thick and almost doubled in volume, about 5 minutes.

Gently fold whipped cream into custard using a rubber spatula.

Pour into the prepared loaf pan and use spatula to smooth top. Cover with plastic wrap or aluminum foil. Place in the freezer and chill for at least 4 hours, or until firm. Alternatively, you can use silicone sphere molds to shape semifreddo into balls. Pour semifreddo into molds, cover, and freeze for at least 4 hours, or until firm. Once frozen, unmold and place on a parchment-lined baking sheet. To decorate as oranges, spray with colored cocoa butter and return to the freezer.

Let sit at room temperature for a few minutes to soften slightly before serving.

Date Cakes Preheat oven to 350°F.

In a pot over medium-high heat, bring dates, water, and vanilla to a boil. Remove from heat and carefully stir in baking soda, as mixture will bubble. Continue stirring until bubbling subsides. Allow to cool. Blend cooled date mixture in a food processor until smooth and set aside.

DESERT BLOSSOM TOFFEE SAUCE
½ cup (1 stick) unsalted butter
½ cup light brown sugar
¼ cup honey, preferably Arizona desert blossom honey
1 cup heavy cream
1 tsp vanilla extract

ASSEMBLY
6 warm Date Cakes (see here)
Desert Blossom Toffee Sauce (see here)
Praline Pecans, for garnish (see here)
Prickly Pear Jam, to serve (see here)
Blood Orange Semifreddo, to serve (see here)
Fresh orange leaves, for garnish (optional)

In a bowl, sift together flour, baking powder, and salt, and set aside.

In a stand mixer fitted with the paddle attachment (or using a hand mixer), beat butter and sugar on medium speed until light and fluffy, 3–4 minutes.

Reduce speed to low and add egg. Next, add date mixture and sifted dry ingredients in alternating batches, mixing until just combined. Be careful not to overmix.

Grease 6 mini-bundt cake pans (or use a silicone muffin pan or lined muffin tray). Fill each pan three-quarters full with batter (you may have leftover batter). Bake for 16–18 minutes, or until cake springs back when touched.

Desert Blossom Toffee Sauce In a medium saucepan, combine butter, brown sugar, honey, and cream. Bring to a gentle boil over medium heat. Continue to cook for 5–7 minutes, stirring occasionally, until sauce thickens to the consistency of caramel. Remove from heat and stir in vanilla.

Toffee sauce can be prepared up to 2 weeks ahead and stored in the refrigerator. Reheat on low before serving.

Assembly To serve, place 1 date cake on each plate, coat with a generous amount of toffee sauce, and sprinkle with praline pecans. Serve with prickly pear jam and scoops, slices, or decorated balls of semifreddo garnished with orange leaves (if using). Alternatively, spread 1 tablespoon of prickly pear jam in a circle in the center of a dessert plate. Set 1 date cake on top and coat with toffee sauce. Top with a scoop of semifreddo and sprinkle with praline pecans.

NOTE Prickly pear fruit, also known as *tuna*, grows on the pads of the prickly pear cactus. In the Phoenix area, prickly pears are ready for harvest in late summer to early fall, when they can be found at local farmers' markets and Mexican grocers. Select firm, plump fruits with vibrant color for best quality.

Made from high-quality cocoa butter that is colored with food-safe pigments, these sprays come in a variety of colors. Available in spray cans for easy application, they are used to give desserts and confections a soft, matte finish with a velvety texture. You can find them at cake decorating stores such as ABC Cake Decorating Supplies, baking supply shops, and online retailers.

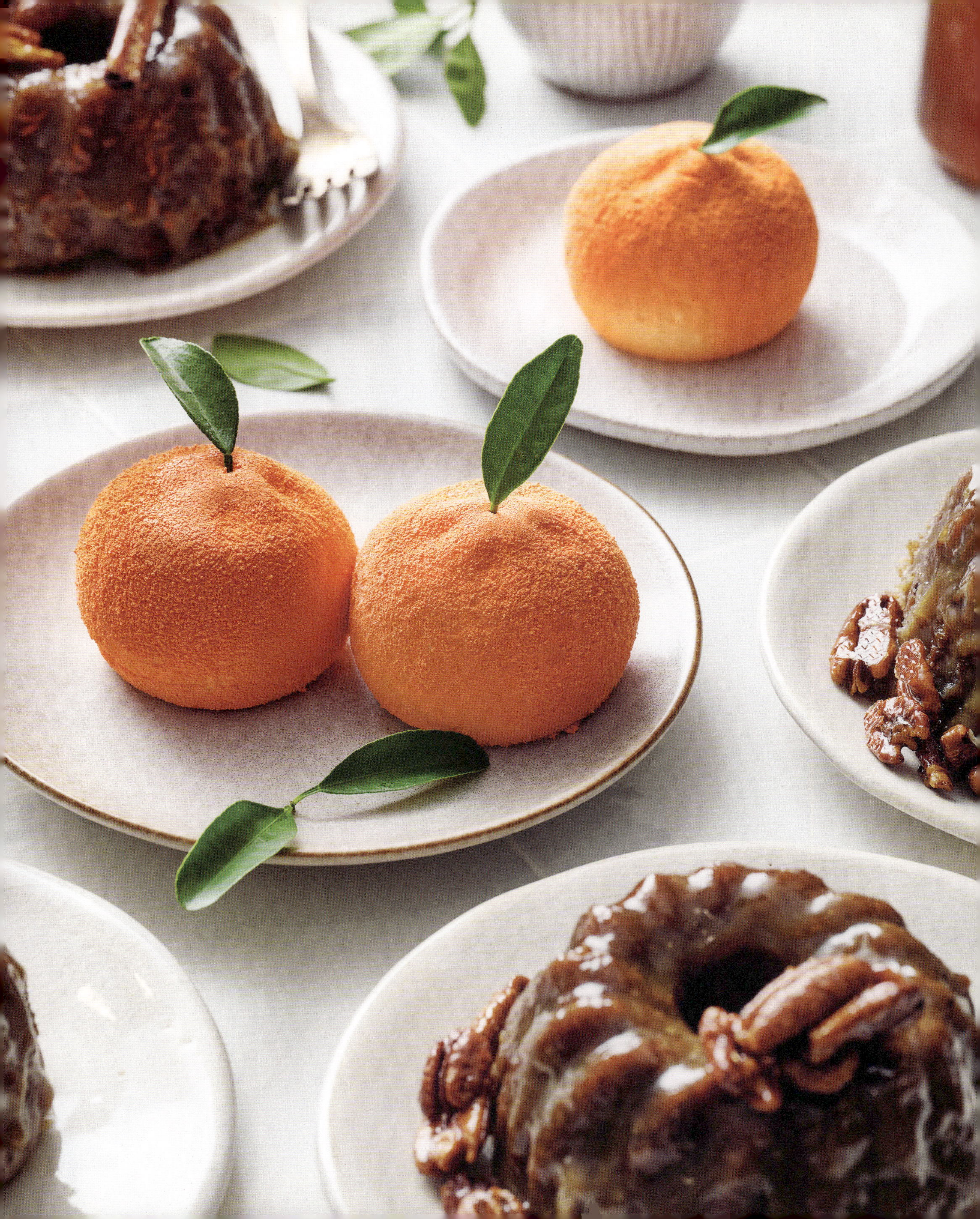

EVO

Saul Velazquez

EVO, Nick Neuman's popular gathering spot in Old Town Scottsdale, proved to be so popular that it spawned a second location, offering two unique experiences while maintaining its signature blend of Italian cuisine and casual sophistication. The Old Town original exudes a warm, rustic vibe with its dark wood and exposed brick walls, while its North Scottsdale sibling offers a more contemporary feel. Both share a commitment to great food and warm hospitality, setting themselves apart with late-night dining until 1:30 a.m. and seven-days-a-week happy hour specials.

"We're very neighborhood oriented, homey, and comfortable," says executive chef Saul Velazquez. At both locations, he draws the crowds in with dishes like crispy arancini and charred octopus with romesco sauce, alongside pizzas, handmade pastas, and signature plates of lobster gnocchi and chicken piccata. Velazquez believes in simplicity, letting ingredients take center stage. "My sous chefs laugh when I say this," says Velazquez, "but I tell them the carrot is just as important as the lobster that goes on the plate. Both need to be handled with love, and that's how I approach cooking—with an open mind and respect for each ingredient."

Beyond the kitchen, EVO's commitment to hospitality creates an inviting atmosphere that keeps diners returning. As Velazquez puts it, "I want people to remember not just the food but how our staff took care of them. I want them to say, 'You know what, I'm coming back here because I felt comfortable. I felt like I was at home. I felt like family.'"

▶ Striped Bass with Gremolata, White Bean Ragu, and Corn Nage

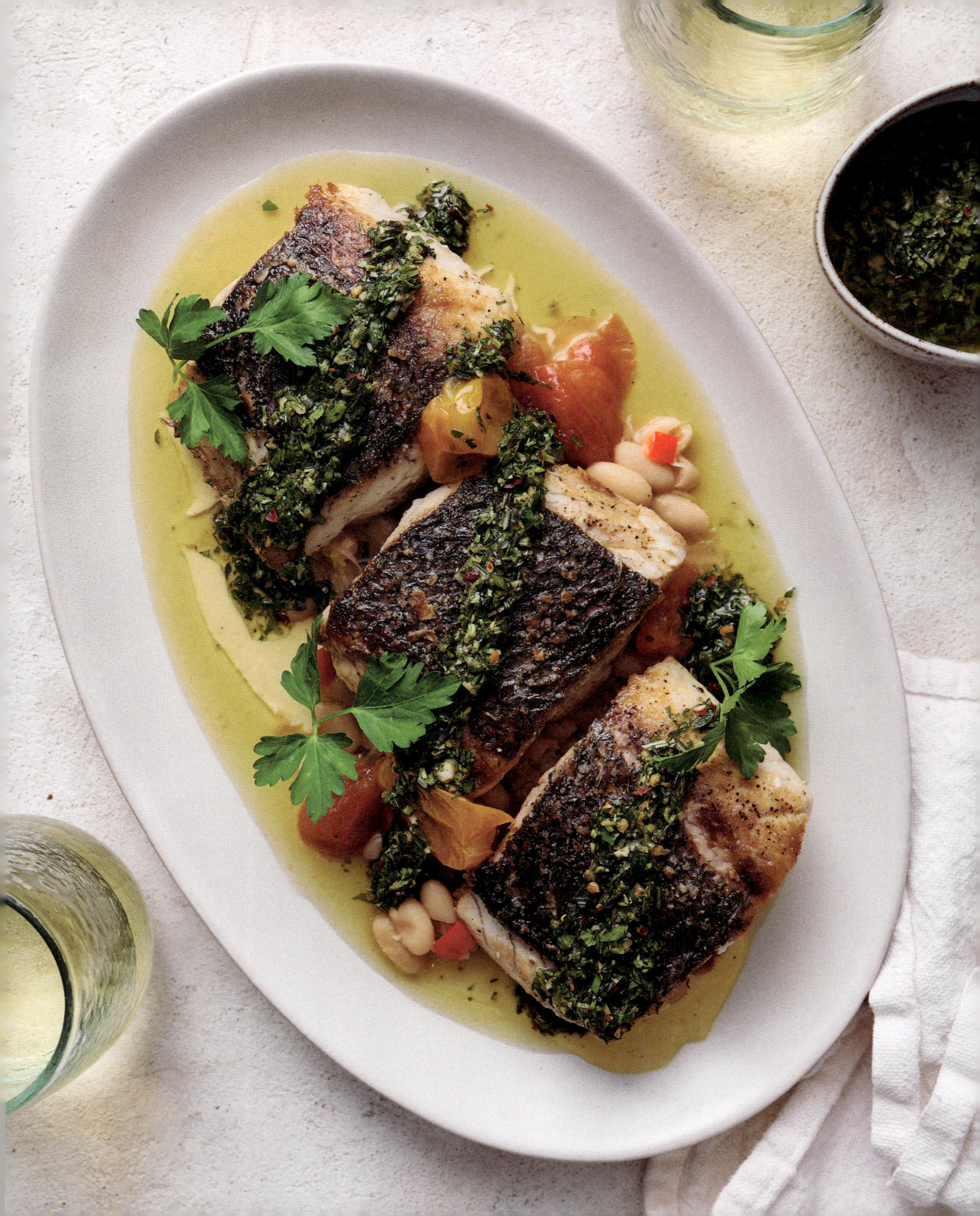

GREMOLATA
½ cup chopped flat-leaf parsley
1 Tbsp chopped oregano
1 Tbsp chopped rosemary
1 Tbsp lemon juice
¼ Tbsp lemon zest
¾ tsp chili flakes
1 clove garlic, chopped
¾ cup extra-virgin olive oil
¾ tsp kosher salt
½ tsp black pepper

CONFIT TOMATOES
8 oz (1 cup) grape tomatoes
1 sprig thyme
¼ cup granulated sugar
¼ Tbsp salt
1 Tbsp red wine vinegar
1 cup olive oil

WHITE BEAN RAGU
4 cups drained canned white beans
1 medium shallot, finely diced
2 Tbsp chopped garlic
¼ cup thinly sliced leeks (white and light green parts only)
¼ cup finely diced zucchini
1 medium red or yellow bell pepper, finely diced
¼ cup Confit Tomatoes (see here)
1–2 Tbsp olive oil
¼ cup (½ stick) unsalted butter

Striped Bass with Gremolata, White Bean Ragu, and Corn Nage

SERVES 4 Also known as rockfish or striper, striped bass is a saltwater fish prized for its flaky white meat and delicate flavor. Here, it's paired with a white bean ragu enriched with slow-cooked confit tomatoes and Parmesan, a creamy corn purée, and zippy gremolata. "I love the versatility of striped bass," says Saul Velazquez, "though we also make this dish with branzino. It's a delicious recipe that works year-round, regardless of the season."

Gremolata In a mixing bowl, combine all ingredients and stir until well blended.

Transfer to a container and refrigerate for up to 4 days.

Confit Tomatoes Combine all ingredients in a medium saucepan over medium-high heat. Bring just to a boil then reduce heat and simmer for 20 minutes, stirring occasionally, until tomatoes are soft and beginning to burst.

Remove from heat and discard thyme. Allow to cool.

Store in an airtight jar and refrigerate for up to 3 days. Leftover confit tomatoes can be used on bruschetta, in salads, or spooned over fish or chicken.

White Bean Ragu In a large bowl, combine beans, shallots, and garlic with the chopped vegetables and confit tomatoes. Set aside.

In a medium stockpot over medium heat, add enough oil to coat the bottom of the pan and prevent vegetables from sticking. Add bean mixture and sauté until vegetables are softened but not mushy, approximately 5 minutes.

Add butter and stock. Simmer, stirring occasionally, until butter is melted. Add Parmesan and stir. Cook until slightly thickened. Season with salt and pepper and set aside.

Ragu can be made 1 day ahead and refrigerated. Reheat on low, thinning with water or vegetable stock if needed.

½ cup vegetable stock
½ lb Parmesan, grated
Kosher salt and black pepper, to taste

CORN NAGE
½ Tbsp unsalted butter
1¼ cups corn kernels (preferably fresh off the cob, though frozen can be used)
1 Tbsp chopped celery
1 Tbsp chopped shallot
1 Tbsp chopped garlic

¾ Tbsp all-purpose flour
1 Tbsp white wine
1 cup vegetable stock
1 cup heavy cream
¾ tsp salt
¼ tsp black pepper

ASSEMBLY
3–4 Tbsp olive oil
4 (6-oz) striped bass fillets (skin on or off)

¼ cup (½ stick) butter, for basting
1½ cups Corn Nage (see here)
4 cups White Bean Ragu (see here)
1 cup Gremolata, for garnish (see here)
Flat-leaf parsley leaves, for garnish

Corn Nage Melt butter in a medium stockpot over medium heat. Add corn, celery, shallots, and garlic, and sauté until vegetables begin to soften, about 5 minutes. Stir in flour.

Add wine and simmer until reduced by half, 2–3 minutes. Add stock, cream, salt, and pepper, and stir to combine. Simmer for 20 minutes, or until mixture has thickened and vegetables are soft. Stir regularly to prevent cream from boiling over.

Remove from heat and allow to cool for 5 minutes (this prevents pressure buildup in the blender from hot steam).

Be careful when blending hot liquids: Remove cap on blender lid and cover with a folded dish towel to allow steam pressure to escape and catch any splashes. Purée the mixture in batches, being careful not to fill the blender more than halfway. Starting on low speed and gradually increasing to high, blend until smooth. Strain through a fine-mesh strainer into a bowl. Continue until all the nage is strained.

Nage can be made 2 days ahead and refrigerated. Reheat on low before serving.

Assembly Heat oil in a large sauté pan over medium-high heat. Add striped bass fillets. (If using skin-on fillets, place skin-side down into the pan. Press lightly to ensure the fish makes even contact with the pan to achieve crispy skin.) Cook for 2 minutes, then flip and cook for an additional minute. Add butter to the pan and baste for the last 30 seconds to 1 minute.

To serve, divide corn nage among 4 plates, spreading it in the center of each dish, and top each serving with 1 cup of ragu. Place fish on top (skin-side up if cooked skin-on). Garnish with gremolata and parsley.

To serve family style, spread corn nage in center of large platter and top with ragu. Place fish on top (skin-side up if cooked skin-on). Spoon gremolata onto fish, and garnish with parsley.

ORANGE WHIPPED CREAM

2 cups chilled heavy cream
¼ cup confectioners' sugar
1 orange, zested

ASSEMBLY

1¾ cups heavy cream
1¼ cups whole milk
¼ cup honey
7 large egg yolks
1 Tbsp granulated sugar
2 tsp vanilla paste, or 1 tsp vanilla extract
Orange Whipped Cream (see here)
Orange zest, for garnish
Mint, for garnish

Vanilla Pots de Crème

SERVES 4 "I love custards," explains Saul Velazquez. "To me, they're very comforting and very homey." Pot de crème, a rich and silky French custard, offers the perfect balance between ease of entertaining and elegance. "You can prepare them ahead of time and elevate the presentation with different types of serving jars and whipped creams."

Orange Whipped Cream Pour cream into the bowl of a stand mixer fitted with a whisk attachment. (If using a hand mixer, use a large mixing bowl.)

Begin mixing at low speed to avoid splattering. Gradually increase to medium-low as the cream starts to thicken. Slowly add confectioners' sugar. Once all sugar is blended in, turn off mixer and scrape down the sides of the bowl with a spatula.

Turn the mixer back on and whip at medium speed. Gradually increase to medium-high until the cream forms soft peaks that hold their shape but are not too stiff. Fold in zest.

Whipped cream can be made up to 3 hours ahead and refrigerated.

Assembly Preheat oven to 300°F.

In a saucepot, combine cream, milk, and honey. Heat over medium-low heat until honey fully dissolves, about 5 minutes. Do not let mixture boil. Remove from heat.

In a medium bowl, vigorously whisk together egg yolks and sugar until the mixture doubles in size and becomes a lighter shade of yellow, about 1 minute.

Gradually add ¼ cup of cream mixture to egg yolks, whisking continuously to temper eggs (to prevent scrambling). Continue adding cream mixture, a little at a time, until half is incorporated. Add vanilla and then the remaining cream mixture to the eggs, mixing well.

Divide custard evenly among four 6-ounce mason jars (or 6-ounce ramekins), filling them three-quarters full.

To stabilize jars and prevent sliding, place a wet kitchen cloth in the bottom of a large baking dish (for easier oven transport, place baking dish on a baking sheet). Arrange jars with 2 inches of space in between for even steaming.

Create a water bath by carefully pouring warm water into the baking dish until it reaches halfway up the sides of the jars.

Gently place the baking dish in the oven. Bake for about 40 minutes, or until the edges of the custard are firm but the centers jiggle slightly.

Remove from oven and let custards cool until warm to touch. Remove from water bath and completely cool at room temperature. Cover with plastic wrap and refrigerate for at least 3 hours, or overnight.

Remove pots de crème from the refrigerator 10 minutes before serving for custard to soften. To serve, top with whipped cream and garnish with orange zest and mint.

FABIO ON FIRE PIZZERIA ITALIANA

Fabio Ceschetti

At Fabio on Fire in Peoria, chef-owner Fabio Ceschetti serves up more than just delicious food—he brings generations of Italian tradition to every dish. A third-generation pizzaiolo, Ceschetti grew up steeped in the restaurant business. "My cooking style is traditional northern Italian with a bit of southern influence," he says. His roots trace back to Puglia, where his great-grandfather owned restaurants and a bakery before the family moved north to Domodossola, where Ceschetti was born and raised. From an early age, he learned the art of pizza-making, watching his grandfather perfect the dough at Il Barcantonio, their family pizzeria—the first in town.

Now, Ceschetti carries on that legacy, crafting everything in-house, from the pizza dough and pasta to pastries and gelato, using time-honored techniques and top-tier ingredients. "Our pastas are all handmade and we make all starters and bigas with organic flour from Molino Denti, a small mill in Bologna," he explains.

The heart of the kitchen is the Mugnaini wood-fired oven, turning out not just puffy, blistered pizzas, but also mouthwatering specialties like lamb and porchetta. The menu is filled with Italian classics, including a rich tagliatelle bolognese, an indulgent short rib tortelloni, and a seafood-packed cioppino (page 88). And don't forget dessert. Whether it's the creamy tiramisu, crispy cannolis, or seasonal indulgences like diplomatico, with its layers of puff pastry and Chantilly cream, you're in for a treat. Then there's the gelato. Ceschetti, who has nearly two hundred gelato recipes in his repertoire, rotates flavors like stracciatella, pistachio, and hazelnut alongside seasonal offerings such as lemon basil, peach, and strawberry.

"Quality is everything to us," Ceschetti says. "It's easy to buy ingredients, but when you make them yourself, you pour your love into it, and people can feel that."

SALSA DI POMODORO
2 Tbsp extra-virgin olive oil
¼ cup finely diced carrots
½ cup finely diced onions
½ cup finely diced celery
3 cloves garlic, minced
1 (28-oz) can whole peeled San Marzano tomatoes, crushed by hand
1 tsp granulated sugar, or to taste
Sea salt and black pepper, to taste

ASSEMBLY
2 medium Italian eggplants, each cut crosswise into 6 slices
Sea salt
Italian sunflower oil, or other neutral oil, for frying
Salsa di Pomodoro (see here)
¾ cup grated Parmigiano-Reggiano cheese
1 small bunch basil, leaves only
½ lb mozzarella di bufala, thinly sliced (see Note)
4 puccia buns, or focaccia buns

NOTE Mozzarella di bufala is a fresh Italian cheese made from the milk of water buffalo. Traditionally produced in southern Italy, it has a higher fat content than cow's milk mozzarella, for a softer, richer consistency. Look for imported mozzarella di bufala packed in brine or whey at grocery stores with well-stocked cheese departments, Italian specialty markets such as Dolce Vita Italian Grocery and Romanelli's Italian Deli, or online.

Eggplant Parmigiana Panini

SERVES 4 For his panini, Fabio Ceschetti uses puccia, a fluffy, wood-fired bread made from 72-hour fermented dough and a 110-year-old wild yeast hand-carried from Italy. You can purchase puccia buns at Fabio on Fire Panini & Gelateria, or use focaccia as an alternative. "Our eggplant panini is a traditional eggplant parmigiana," explains Ceschetti. "When we get an order, we warm a piece in the wood-fired oven and melt mozzarella on top. It's out of this world."

Salsa di Pomodoro Heat oil in a large saucepan over medium heat. Add carrots, onions, and celery. Sauté until vegetables are soft, 10–15 minutes. Add garlic and sauté for 1–2 minutes, until fragrant. Add crushed tomatoes, stirring to combine.

Reduce heat to medium-low and bring to a simmer. Add sugar and continue to simmer, uncovered, for 30–45 minutes, stirring occasionally. Season with salt and pepper to taste.

Assembly In a large strainer over a bowl, arrange eggplant slices in 2 layers, sprinkling each layer lightly with salt. Lay a plate over the eggplant and weigh down with cans to press out excess moisture. Let drain for 2 hours, then pat dry.

Preheat oven to 350°F.

Heat ¼ cup of oil, or enough to coat bottom of a large sauté pan, over medium heat. Fry eggplant until golden brown and crispy, 1–2 minutes per side. You may need to add more oil as you cook. As slices are fried, remove and drain on paper towel–lined plates.

Spread a thin layer of salsa di pomodoro in the bottom of an 8- × 8-inch baking dish. Add a layer of eggplant, enough sauce to cover, ¼ cup of Parmigiano-Reggiano, a few leaves of basil, and 3–4 slices of mozzarella, repeating for a total of 3 layers. Bake for 30 minutes.

Let cool 20–30 minutes and cut into four 4- × 4-inch squares. Stuff each puccia (or focaccia) bun with a square of eggplant parmigiana and serve immediately.

10 medium-sized mussels

10 littleneck clams

½ cup extra-virgin olive oil, plus more for garnish

2 cloves garlic, minced

Pinch of chili flakes

2 Tbsp white wine

4 large sea scallops

4 large (16/20) prawns, peeled and deveined

4 (5-inch) calamari, cleaned and sliced into rings (see Note)

Pinch of sea salt, plus more to taste

2 cups Salsa di Pomodoro (page 87)

1 Tbsp chopped flat-leaf parsley, plus more for garnish

Black pepper, to taste

Cioppino

SERVES 2 For this rustic fisherman's stew, "the ingredients are what matters most, so the seafood has to be fresh and never frozen," says Fabio Ceschetti, who sources his from Chula Seafood. "When you use food fresh from the ocean, all you need is a splash of tomato sauce, a bit of parsley and garlic, and a touch of white wine. Give it all a little love, and the result is amazing."

This cioppino is perfect on its own, but for a heartier version it can also be served with grilled bread brushed with olive oil, or over pasta.

Assembly Scrub mussels and clams under cold running water. Check any open shellfish by gently tapping them. If they do not close after tapping, discard. Set mussels and clams aside.

Heat oil in a large pan over medium heat. Add garlic and chili flakes and sauté for about 1 minute, until fragrant. Add white wine and all of the seafood and bring to a simmer. Cover pan and simmer for 5–7 minutes, or until clams and mussels open.

Stir in salt, salsa di pomodoro, and parsley and simmer for 3–5 minutes, allowing flavors to meld. Season with salt and pepper to taste.

Divide cioppino into serving bowls and garnish with parsley and a drizzle of oil.

NOTE To clean calamari, pull to separate head and tentacles from the body tube. Cut head and innards from tentacles and discard. Remove and discard the beak at the base of the tentacles and the transparent quill of cartilage inside the body. Peel off purple skin and then rinse under cold water. You can also have your fishmonger do this for you, or purchase calamari already prepared.

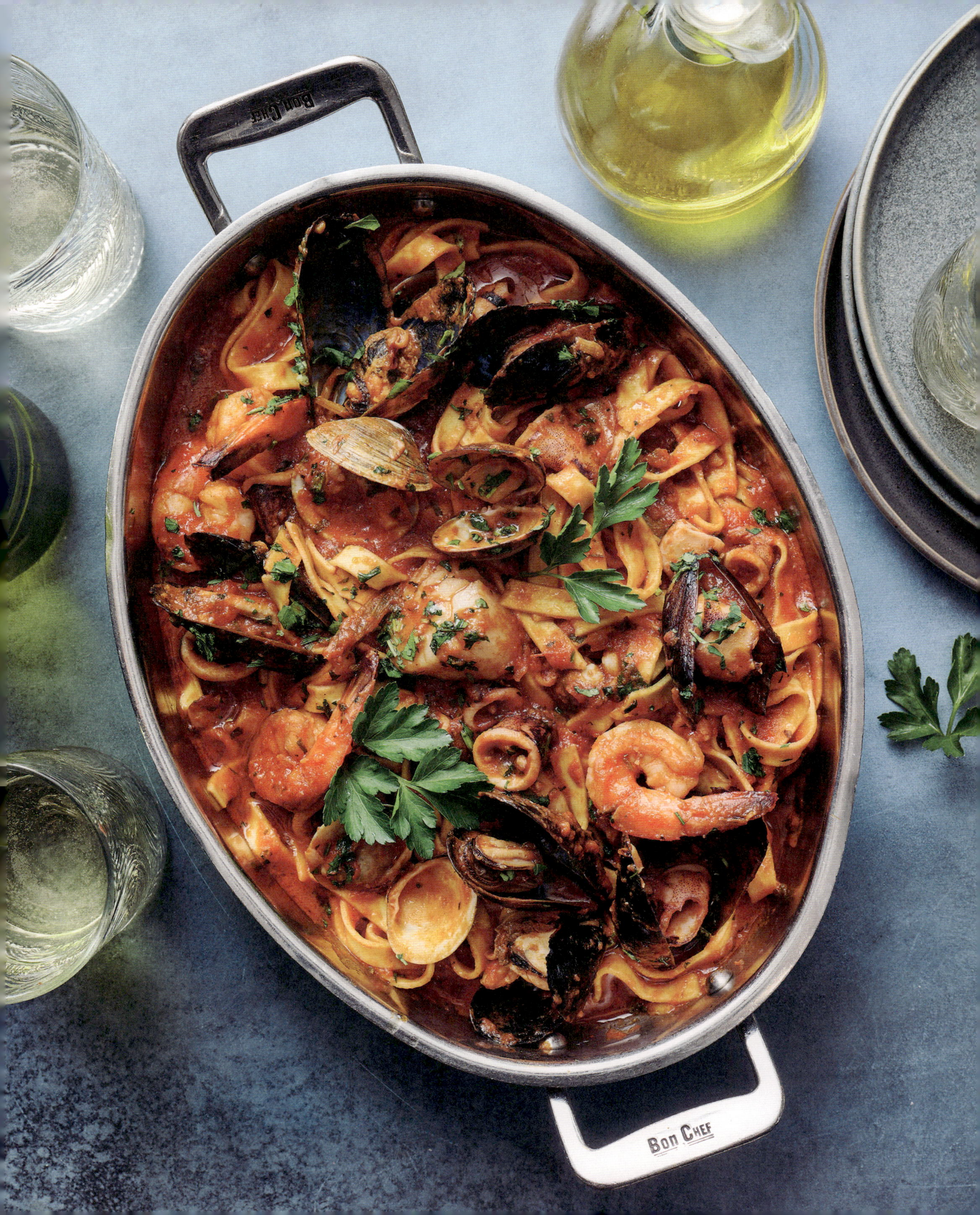
Bon Chef

FIRE AT WILL

Dom Ruggiero

In 2022, Fire at Will joined the success story that began when chef-owner Dom Ruggiero debuted award-winning Hush Public House in 2019. While both are beloved neighborhood gathering spots in Scottsdale, differences start with the decor. "Hush is more minimalist in black and white, so we made Fire at Will darker and moodier with richer colors," says Ruggiero of its sultry interior, where burgundy tiles play against brick walls, and the black ceiling is punctuated by a striking light fixture draped in greenery.

While Hush centers around shareable courses, Fire at Will entices guests with elevated comfort food classics such as bolognese with Sonoran Pasta Co. spaghetti, pan-roasted half chicken marsala, and the famous Hush Burger, once a weekly special and now a permanent fixture thanks to its cult-like following. "Originally, the menu was planned to be more 'chef-y,'" explains Ruggiero, "but the neighborhood told us what they wanted—something more casual and approachable. So, over the years we've shifted to more staples like steak, pasta, and mac and cheese, but you'll also see things like Iberico ham croquettes (page 94) and stacked enchiladas (page 92) to give it a little different flair."

It's a reflection of Ruggiero's philosophy that restaurants succeed by building connections with their neighborhoods. "While both restaurants are in strip malls, they don't feel like they are," he says. "You might think you're in a cool, hip restaurant in New York or San Francisco. You're going to get some new and exciting flavors, enjoy the space, the food and the staff, and just have a great time."

▸ Stacked Enchiladas

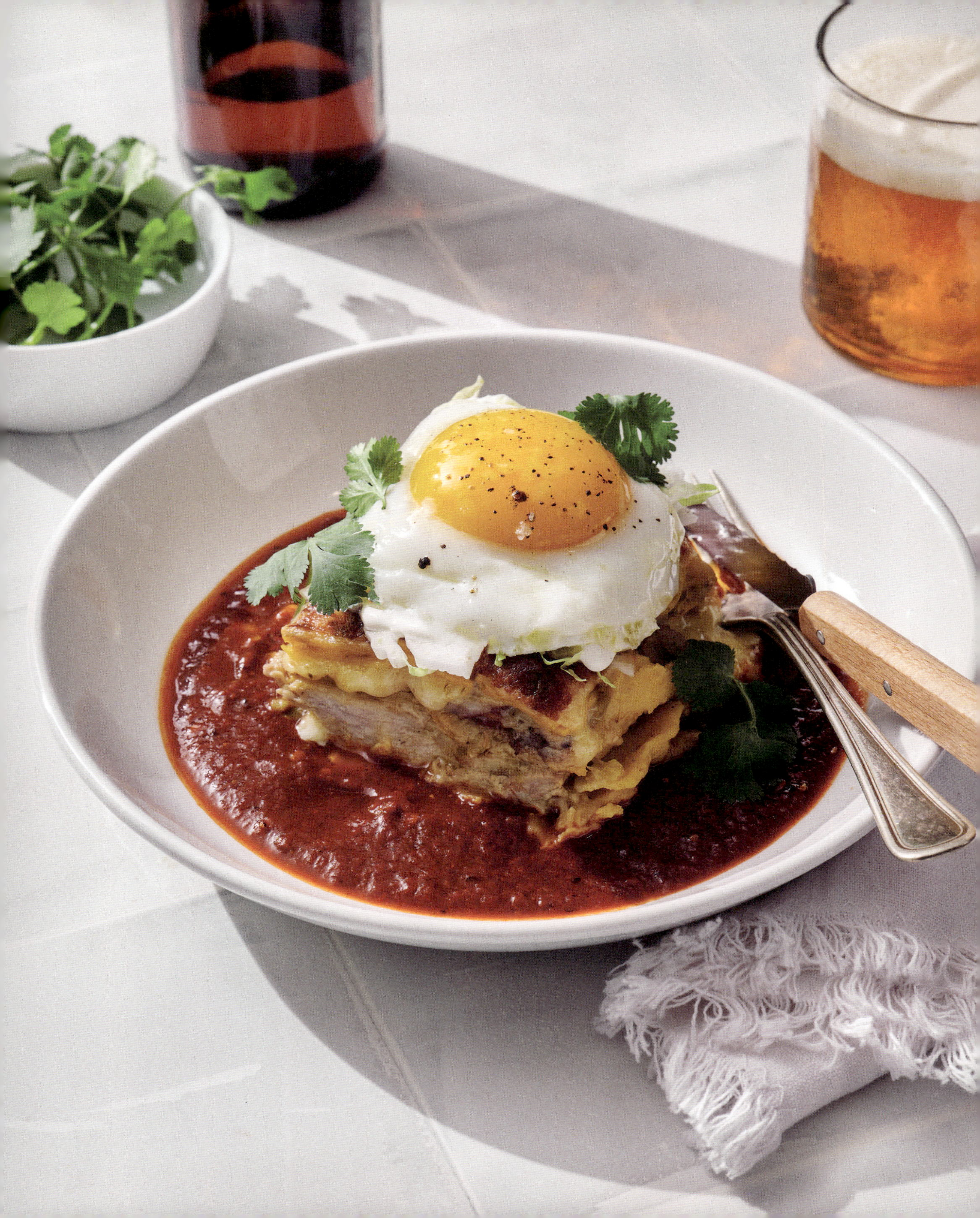

GREEN CHILE SAUCE

2 lbs Anaheim chiles

5 Tbsp (½ stick + 1 Tbsp) unsalted butter

1 medium yellow onion, diced

1 cup minced serrano chiles

3 Tbsp all-purpose flour

1 cup chicken stock

Pinch of baking soda

1 tsp extra-virgin olive oil

Kosher salt, to taste

SALSA ROJA

4 dried guajillo chiles, stemmed and seeded (see Note)

1 dried ancho chile, stemmed and seeded (see Note)

2 Tbsp canola–olive oil blend

1 small yellow onion, chopped

4 cloves garlic

1 Fresno chile, stemmed, seeded, and diced

¾ tsp smoked paprika

1¼ cups chicken stock

1 (14.5-oz) can peeled tomatoes, puréed in a blender or food processor

¾ tsp honey

Kosher salt and black pepper, to taste

Stacked Enchiladas

SERVES 12 "I created this originally for a video promotion for Green Mountain Grills," says Dom Ruggiero. "I took one of my favorite things—smoked pork—and put it in a New Mexico–style enchilada. With the layers of cheese and sauces, it's like a Mexican lasagna." Both the green chile sauce and the salsa roja can be made ahead of time to save time on assembly.

Green Chile Sauce Roast Anaheim chiles over an open flame or under a broiler, turning until all sides are blistered. Place in a plastic bag or covered bowl for 10 minutes to loosen skin. Peel chiles, remove stem and seeds, and dice. Set aside.

Melt butter in a skillet over medium heat. Add onions and sauté until browned, 6–8 minutes. Add serrano chiles and cook for 2–3 minutes, until softened. Sprinkle with flour and stir for 2–3 minutes, until roux turns a light blond color.

Gradually add stock, whisking continuously for 10 minutes, until thick and smooth.

Remove from heat and fold in Anaheim chiles, baking soda, and oil. Season with salt to taste. Chile sauce can be made ahead and refrigerated for up to 1 week.

Salsa Roja Preheat oven to 350°F.

Place guajillo and ancho chiles on a baking sheet and toast for 3–5 minutes, checking frequently to avoid burning as they darken quickly. Set aside.

Heat oil in a pot over medium heat. Add onions, garlic, Fresno chiles, and paprika and sauté until onions are softened, 5–7 minutes. Add chicken stock, scraping up any browned bits, then tomatoes and toasted chiles. Simmer until sauce is reduced by a quarter and chiles have softened, about 10 minutes. Let cool for a few minutes before transferring to a blender.

Be careful when blending hot liquids: remove cap on blender lid and cover with a folded dish towel to allow steam pressure to escape and catch any splashes. Purée the mixture in batches if needed, being careful not to fill the blender

ASSEMBLY

2 lbs pulled smoked pork shoulder (from your favorite recipe or BBQ spot)

6 cups Green Chile Sauce, divided (see here)

18 (4½-inch) yellow corn tortillas

2½ lbs 50/50 mix white cheddar and Oaxaca cheese, shredded

1–2 Tbsp canola–olive oil blend

12 large eggs

Flaky sea salt and fresh cracked black pepper, to taste

3 cups Salsa Roja (see here)

1½ cups Mexican crema, or sour cream thinned with cream or milk

4 cups shredded Napa cabbage

Cilantro, for garnish

---

more than halfway. Starting on low speed and gradually increasing to high, blend until smooth.

Stir in honey and season with salt and pepper to taste.

Assembly Preheat oven to 350°F.

In a large bowl, combine pulled pork with 2 cups of green chile sauce. Set aside.

Warm tortillas in the oven for 5 minutes and remove, leaving oven on.

Spread ½ cup of green chile sauce on the bottom of a 9- × 13-inch casserole dish. Layer 6 tortillas, half of the pork, and a third of the cheese. Repeat with another layer of tortillas, pork, and cheese. Top with final layer of tortillas. Pour remaining sauce over tortillas and sprinkle with remaining cheese. Gently press down to remove air gaps.

Bake uncovered (preferably in a convection oven) for 20 minutes until cheese is lightly golden. If you don't have a convection oven, bake for 5–10 minutes longer. Remove from oven, compress again, and allow to rest for 20 minutes.

Before serving, heat oil in a skillet over medium heat. Fry eggs for 4–5 minutes for sunny-side-up, and season with salt and pepper.

To plate, cut stacked enchiladas into 12 equal pieces. For each serving, pour ¼ cup of salsa roja on the plate, place 1 piece of stacked enchiladas on top, and top with a dollop of crema, ⅓ cup of cabbage, and a fried egg. Garnish with cilantro and season with salt and pepper.

NOTE Guajillo chiles are deep red with smooth skin, and have a fruity moderate heat. Ancho chiles are dark reddish-brown and wrinkled, with a sweet and smoky mild heat. These whole dried Mexican chiles are available at Mexican markets like Food City and Los Altos Ranch Market, at Sprouts and other specialty grocers, or online. For best quality, look for chiles that are pliable and glossy.

HARISSA

2 dried chiles de árbol, stemmed and seeded (see Note)
1 small dried ancho chile, stemmed and seeded (see Note)
1 small dried guajillo chile, stemmed and seeded (see Note)
½ tsp cumin seeds
¼ tsp coriander seeds
1 small clove garlic, chopped
1 Tbsp lemon juice
½ tsp red wine vinegar
½ tsp tomato paste
½ tsp smoked paprika
¼ tsp kosher salt
3 Tbsp canola–olive oil blend

HARISSA AIOLI

1 cup aioli (store-bought or favorite recipe, or substitute mayonnaise)
¼ cup Harissa (see here)

Iberico Ham Croquettes with Harissa Aioli and Manchego Cheese

SERVES 2 Every Spanish tapas bar boasts its own croquetas de jamón, but Dom Ruggiero elevates tradition with Manchego cheese and a bed of aioli spiked with homemade harissa—a North African chili paste that adds smoky, tangy heat. Ideal for entertaining, "you can keep the croquettes in the freezer and bread and fry them when you're ready," says Ruggiero.

Harissa Preheat oven to 350°F.

Place chiles on a baking sheet and toast for 3–5 minutes, checking frequently to avoid burning as they darken quickly.

Remove chiles from oven, place in a pot, and cover with water. Bring to a boil, then reduce heat and simmer until chiles are soft, 10–15 minutes.

Meanwhile, in an unoiled pan over medium heat, toast cumin and coriander seeds until fragrant, 3–5 minutes. Finely grind in a spice grinder.

Strain chiles, reserving chile water.

To a blender, add chiles, ground spices, and remaining ingredients, except oil. Blend into a smooth, thick paste, adding a little reserved chile water as needed.

Continue to blend, slowly adding oil in a thin and steady stream, until thickened and emulsified.

Transfer to an airtight container or glass jar. Harissa will keep refrigerated up to 1 week or frozen up to 3 months.

Leftover harissa can be used as a marinade, sauce, or seasoning for any number of dishes.

Harissa Aioli In a large mixing bowl, whisk aioli (or mayonnaise) and harissa until smooth and well blended.

CROQUETTES

2 Tbsp butter

2 Tbsp extra-virgin olive oil

¼ cup finely diced yellow onion

¼ lb Iberico ham, finely diced

1¼ cups all-purpose flour, divided

2 cups whole milk, room temperature

Pinch of grated nutmeg

Kosher salt and black pepper, to taste

4 large eggs, beaten

1½ cups panko breadcrumbs

ASSEMBLY

Neutral high-temperature oil, for frying

8 Croquettes (see here)

½ cup Harissa Aioli (see here)

8 thin (1- × 2-inch) slices Manchego cheese

Thinly sliced scallions, or scallion curls, for garnish

NOTE Ancho chiles are dark reddish-brown and wrinkled, with a sweet and smoky mild heat. Guajillo chiles are deep red with smooth skin, and have a fruity, moderate heat. Dried chiles de árbol are bright red and smaller, with a spicy lingering heat. These whole dried Mexican chiles are available at Mexican markets like Food City and Los Altos Ranch Market, at Sprouts and other specialty grocers, or online. For best quality, look for chiles that are pliable and glossy.

Croquettes Melt butter with oil in a saucepan over medium heat. Add onions and cook until soft and translucent (do not brown), 5–7 minutes. Add ham and cook for another 1–2 minutes. Sprinkle with ¼ cup of flour and stir for 2–3 minutes, until it turns a light blond color.

Gradually add milk, stirring constantly to avoid lumps. Increase heat, bring to a boil, and stir until smooth. Turn off heat, stir in nutmeg, and season with salt and pepper to taste.

Transfer to a container, allow to cool, and refrigerate until cold. As it chills, béchamel batter will thicken and firm up.

Line a baking sheet with parchment paper. Using a 1-ounce ice cream scoop, portion batter into balls and set on the prepared sheet, then chill in the freezer for 20–30 minutes. You should have 8 croquettes.

Set up a breading station with remaining 1 cup of flour, beaten eggs, and breadcrumbs in separate pans. Roll each frozen croquette in flour, dip in eggs, and coat with breadcrumbs. Chill in the refrigerator. (Preparation to this step can be done up to 3 days in advance.)

Assembly In a cast-iron skillet over medium-high heat, add enough oil to submerge croquettes. When oil reaches 350°F, fry croquettes, turning occasionally, until golden brown on all sides, 4–5 minutes.

Using a slotted spoon or strainer, remove croquettes to a paper towel–lined plate and pat dry.

To serve, spread ¼ cup of harissa aioli in a circle on each serving dish. Arrange 4 croquettes in a spaced square on top of the aioli.

In between the croquettes, insert upright pieces of Manchego. Garnish with scallions.

FIRST & LAST

Robb Hammond, Delena Humble-Fischer

Step into First & Last in downtown Phoenix and you'll discover a love story, a piece of history, and a celebration of community. Housed in the historic 1925 Gold Spot building, it embodies Robb and Ashley Hammond's vision to honor the building's roots while creating a space for locals to connect over food, drinks, and hospitality.

Ashley leads front-of-house operations and oversees the beverage program alongside beverage director Delena Humble-Fischer, while executive chef Robb brings three decades of culinary expertise to the ever-changing menu. "It reflects the Mediterranean palate through Spanish, French, and Italian influences with an emphasis on seasonality," notes the Michigan native. "I grew up in an agrarian place where farming was part of life and love the care and attention it takes for a farmer to produce even one leaf of spinach. There's a lot to be said about that."

This connection to the land mirrors their connection to the community. "We have a lot of regulars and that's so important to us," notes Robb. "We live just a mile down the road so we're part of a community that goes back to the '30s. We love being a bridge between the old and the new."

The name "First & Last" likewise celebrates relationships—it's the couple's affectionate shorthand for thinking of one another. As Robb reflects on their successful venture: "I'm very proud to share this experience with my wife, and I'm proud of the work we do to make things just a little bit better every day."

▶ Albacore Tuna Tartare Toast and Verde de la Vida

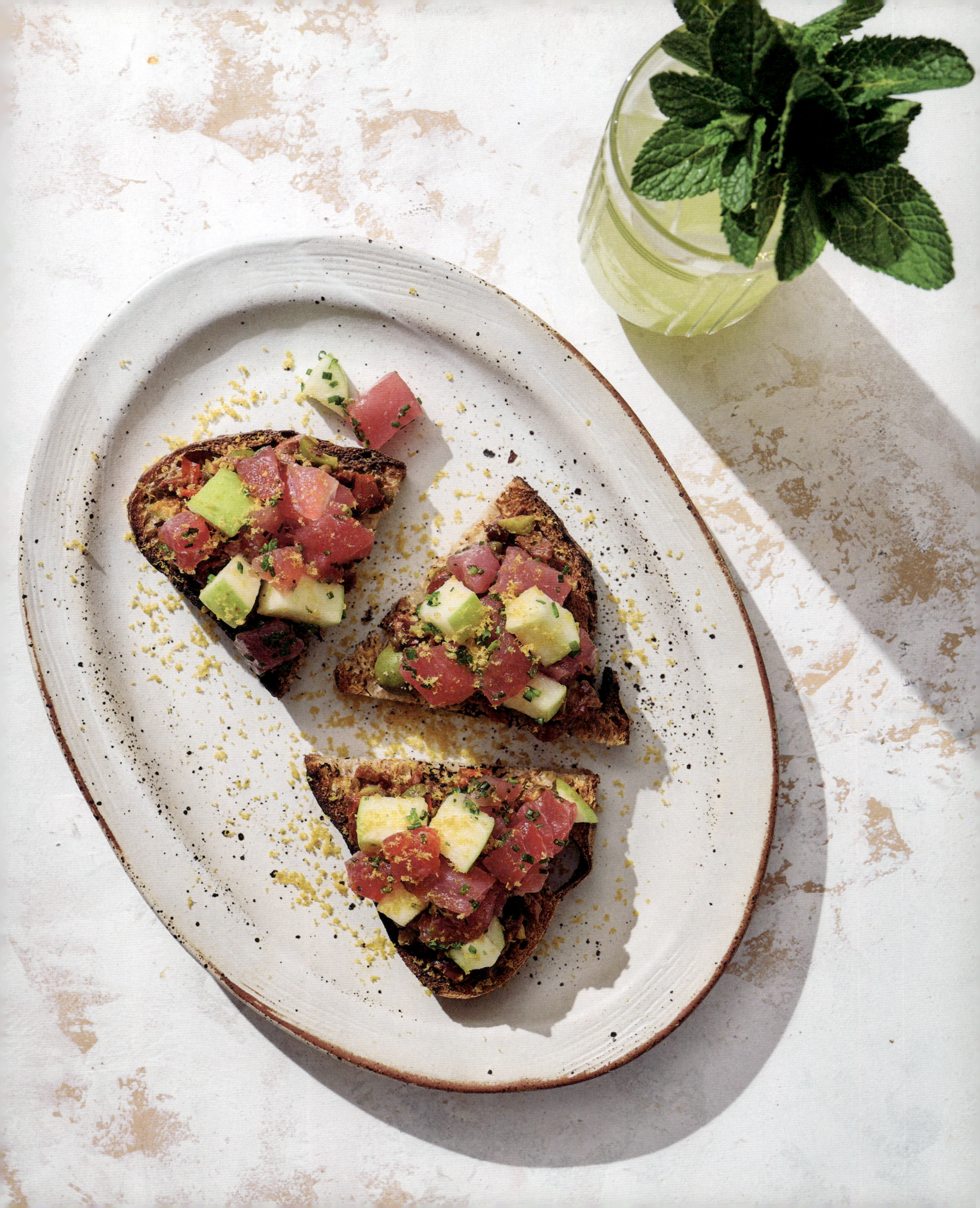

TAPENADE

½ cup pitted mixed olives
2 anchovy fillets, rinsed
2 cloves garlic, minced
1 Tbsp capers (preferably salt packed and rinsed)
4 basil leaves
1 Tbsp lemon juice
¼ cup extra-virgin olive oil

ASSEMBLY

12 oz albacore tuna, cut into ½-inch cubes
1 Granny Smith apple, cored and cut into ½-inch cubes
1 Tbsp minced chives
1 tsp cider or pear vinegar
2 Tbsp extra-virgin olive oil, divided
Salt, to taste
4 slices sourdough or rustic loaf
½ cup Tapenade (see here)
Bottarga, for garnish (optional)

Albacore Tuna Tartare Toast

SERVES 4 A fan favorite, "this is the only dish that has stayed on our menu since opening night," says Robb Hammond. "A playful take on a raw niçoise salad, Granny Smith apple adds the perfect tang, and bottarga is a fantastic option if you can find it." Bottarga, a dried and cured fish roe sold grated or as firm, waxy whole lobes, adds an umami richness to any number of dishes. Both the tuna and bottarga can be sourced at local fishmongers like Chula Seafood and Nelson's Meat + Fish (page 166). If albacore tuna isn't available, bluefin tuna is a suitable substitute.

Tapenade Place all ingredients, except oil, in a food processor and pulse 10 times. Slowly drizzle in oil until tapenade reaches your desired consistency (smooth or chunky but spreadable).

Tapenade can be refrigerated for up to 1 week.

Assembly Combine tuna, apples, chives, vinegar, 1 tablespoon of oil, and salt in a bowl. Mix well and refrigerate for at least 15 minutes, and up to 1 hour.

Heat grill to medium-high heat or turn on broiler.

Drizzle remaining oil lightly over bread slices. Grill or broil until toasted to preference.

Spread 1–2 tablespoons of tapenade over toasted bread. Top with ¼–⅓ cup of the tuna tartare mixture. Use a microplane or fine cheese grater to add a dusting of bottarga, if using, over the top.

RICH SIMPLE SYRUP

2 cups granulated sugar

1 cup filtered water

VERDITA

½ English cucumber, peeled, seeded, and chopped

1 jalapeño, seeded and sliced

½ Granny Smith apple, cored and sliced

¼ cup mint leaves

2 cups pineapple juice

Pinch of kosher salt

ASSEMBLY

1½ oz Verdita (see here)

¼ oz Rich Simple Syrup (see here)

1½ oz G4 blanco tequila

¼ oz Bordiga Centum Herbis, or Green Chartreuse

½ oz fresh lime juice

1 mint bouquet, for garnish

Verde de la Vida

SERVES 1 "This patio-pounder is what every agave lover will reach for in the Phoenix heat," says Delena Humble-Fischer. "It's vegetal, herbaceous, and bright. Want more heat? Add extra jalapeños. Love cucumbers? Toss in a few more. With fresh green vegetables, ethically made tequila, and a touch of acid and spice, this drink will have you wondering, 'Will I ever want to drink a margarita again?'"

Rich Simple Syrup In a saucepan over medium heat, combine sugar and water. Stir regularly until all sugar is dissolved. Do not let the syrup boil.

Remove from heat and allow to cool, then bottle and store in the refrigerator for up to 2 weeks.

Syrup can also be used to sweeten coffee and desserts.

Verdita Add all ingredients to a blender and blend on high for 2–3 minutes, or until ingredients break down completely into a smooth and homogenous mixture.

Once blended, strain using a fine-mesh strainer and discard pulp.

Pour into a bottle or airtight container and refrigerate until ready to use. Verdita will keep in the refrigerator for up to 5 days. It is also delicious in mocktails with simple syrup, lime, and sparkling water.

Assembly Pour all ingredients, except mint garnish, into a Boston shaker. Add ice and shake vigorously for 12–15 seconds.

Using a hawthorn strainer, strain into a Collins glass filled with fresh ice.

Garnish with the mint bouquet and serve with a straw.

FRASHER'S STEAKHOUSE AND LOUNGE

George Frasher

Originally from St. Louis, chef-restaurateur George Frasher (pronounced "Frazier") has introduced a taste of his heartland hospitality to the Arizona dining scene. What started with the original (now closed) Frasher's Steakhouse on Scottsdale Road has blossomed into a culinary trifecta: Mrs. Chicken, a fast-casual spot specializing in Nashville hot chicken; Frasher's BBQ and St. Louis Pizza, formerly Frasher's Smokehouse, a beloved BBQ joint; and the current iteration of Frasher's Steakhouse and Lounge in Old Town, which opened in 2020 as Frasher's Tavern.

At his eponymous steakhouse, Frasher's menu draws inspiration from traditional chophouses while adding those distinctive touches that make it uniquely his. Alongside ribeye steaks and rack of lamb, diners find hometown treasures like toasted ravioli and Mayfair salad. But Frasher's influence extends beyond savory dishes; he has also been acknowledged for popularizing gooey butter cake, a St. Louis classic that quickly captured local hearts. His dessert version (page 104), introduced twenty-five years ago, became so popular that other restaurants added their takes on the treat. "My mom thought I was crazy when I first said I was going to serve it as a dessert," he says with a laugh, "because in St. Louis it's served as a coffeecake or breakfast cake. I was the first restaurant to have it on my dessert menu, and now you see it all over."

For Frasher, however, success isn't measured just in satisfied appetites—it's found in the relationships he's built. "I love my employees, and I love our customers," he says. "Just last night, a couple drove two hours from Tucson to celebrate a birthday with our St. Louis pizza. Nothing beats putting smiles on people's faces through great food."

2 Tbsp cracked peppercorns, plus more for garnish
2 tsp dried thyme
2 tsp dried rosemary
1 bay leaf
⅔ cup brandy
1 cup (2 sticks) + 3 Tbsp unsalted butter, divided
1 cup diced onions
¾ cup diced celery
2¾ cups chicken stock
2 tsp jarred beef base (see Note)
1 cup all-purpose flour
2 cups whole milk
1⅓ cups heavy cream
4 tsp corn or vegetable oil
1¾ lbs beef tenderloin, cut into ½-inch cubes
Kosher salt, to taste
Chopped flat-leaf parsley, for garnish

Peppercorn Steak Soup

SERVES 4–6 This genius twist on steakhouse flavors was born out of a customer's request for peppercorn sauce. "It's now our signature soup," says George Frasher about this creation, which has garnered a cult following. "It's amazing served so many ways: with good bread for dunking, on top of noodles like stroganoff, or—my favorite—over mashed potatoes."

Assembly In a small saucepan over medium heat, combine peppercorns, thyme, rosemary, bay leaf, and brandy. Simmer until reduced and syrupy, 10–15 minutes. Strain through a fine-mesh sieve and set aside.

In a large stockpot, melt 3 tablespoons of butter over medium heat. Add onions and celery and cook until softened, about 10 minutes. Stir in stock, beef base, and brandy reduction. Keep warm.

In a separate pot, make a roux by melting 1 cup of butter over medium heat, then gradually whisking in flour. Cook until light golden, 3–5 minutes. Gradually whisk in milk and cream, and simmer, continuously whisking, until thick and smooth, 10–15 minutes. Add to stockpot, stirring to combine. Continue to simmer, stirring occasionally.

Meanwhile, heat oil in a large skillet over medium-high heat. Sear beef tenderloin until evenly browned on all sides, about 5 minutes. Add beef to stockpot and simmer for an additional 10 minutes. Season to taste with salt.

Divide into serving bowls and garnish with parsley and cracked peppercorns.

NOTE Beef base is a concentrated paste made from roasted beef, vegetables, and seasonings. Unlike bouillon cubes or powder, which can be saltier and more processed, beef base offers a more robust, natural flavor. Common brands like Better Than Bouillon can be found in the soup aisle of grocery stores, and online.

Peppercorn Steak Soup and Gooey Butter Cake

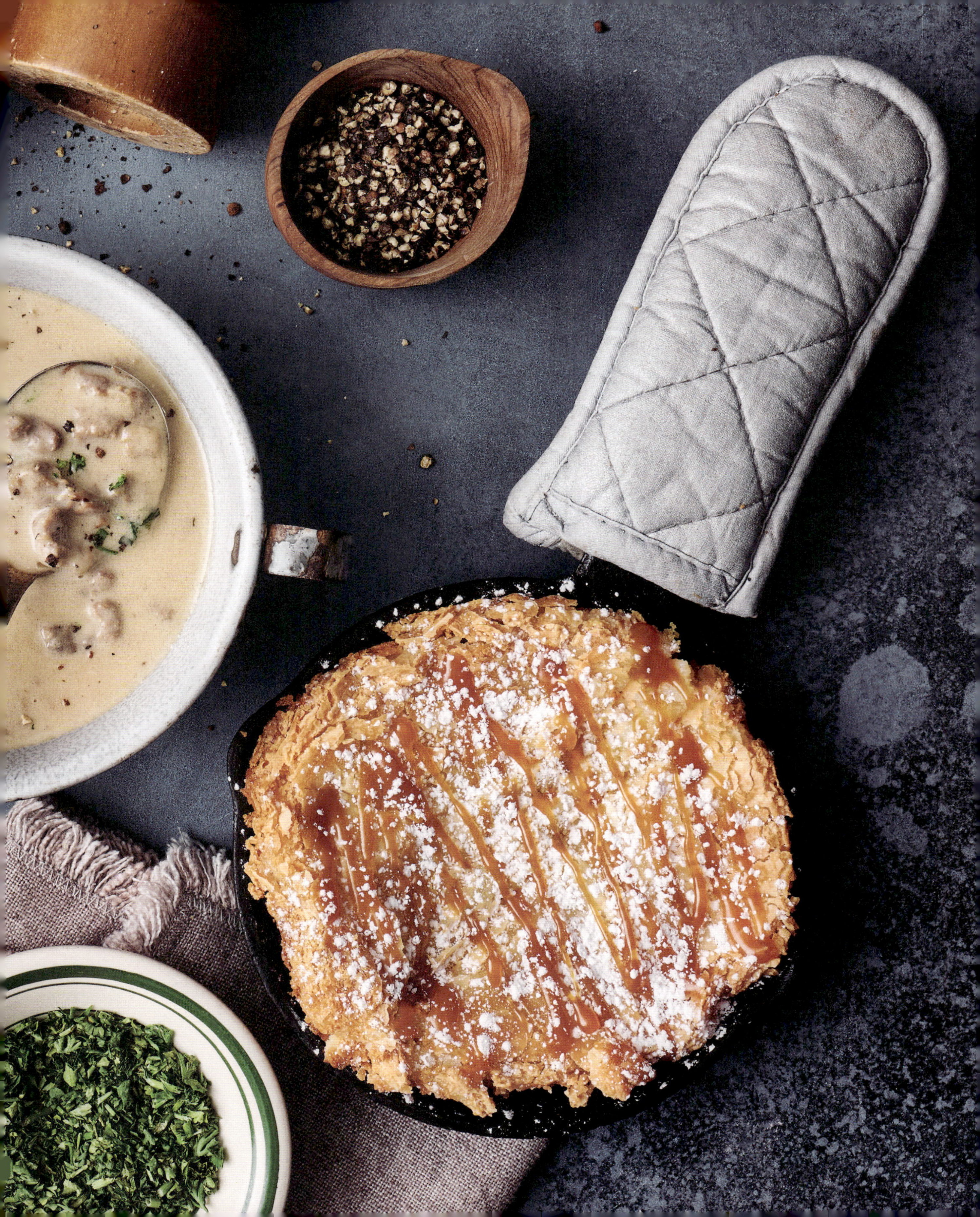

BAILEYS BUTTERSCOTCH CARAMEL
¼ cup corn syrup
¼ cup water
1 cup granulated sugar
1½ tsp lemon juice
6 Tbsp heavy cream
1½ tsp cornstarch
2 Tbsp Butterscotch Schnapps
¼ cup Baileys Irish Cream

ASSEMBLY
Cooking spray
½ cup (1 stick) butter, softened
4 large eggs, divided
1 box yellow cake mix
8 oz cream cheese, softened
1 lb confectioners' sugar, plus more for garnish
Baileys Butterscotch Caramel (see here)

Gooey Butter Cake

SERVES 10–12 George Frasher, a St. Louis native, brought Phoenicians a dessert that has since become a cult favorite. The rich indulgence dates back to the 1930s in St. Louis when a baker's ingredient mishap created a gooey, buttery cake with a cheesecake layer over a yellow cake base. Frasher's version is topped with a decadent Baileys butterscotch caramel and finished with a sprinkle of powdered sugar.

Baileys Butterscotch Caramel In a large saucepan over medium-low heat, whisk together corn syrup, water, sugar, and lemon juice. Stirring often, cook until mixture darkens to a golden caramel color, about 20 minutes. Watch carefully, as caramel can burn quickly. When the color is right, remove immediately from heat.

In a separate saucepan over medium-low heat, whisk together cream and cornstarch until smooth. Cook, stirring continuously, until cream thickens. Remove from heat and allow to cool for 5 minutes. Stirring gently but continuously, slowly add cream to caramel. Gradually stir in Butterscotch Schnapps and Baileys Irish Cream until combined.

Return to medium heat and bring mixture to a gentle boil, stirring constantly, until slightly thickened to a caramel consistency.

Remove caramel from heat and pour through a fine-mesh strainer into a heatproof bowl. Strain once more to ensure caramel is velvety smooth and free of clumps.

Assembly Preheat oven to 350°F.

Coat a 9- × 13-inch baking pan with cooking spray.

Using a stand or hand mixer, beat butter and 2 eggs until smooth. Add yellow cake mix and beat until combined.

Press yellow cake mix evenly into bottom of baking pan.

In a separate bowl, beat cream cheese, confectioners' sugar, and the remaining 2 eggs until smooth, 2–3 minutes. Spread cream cheese filling evenly over yellow cake crust in prepared pan.

Place in oven on center rack and bake for 17 minutes. Rotate pan and bake for another 17 minutes. Remove cake from oven and allow to cool in pan.

To plate, cut into serving pieces. Garnish with Baileys butterscotch caramel sauce and sprinkle with confectioners' sugar.

HONEY + VINE

Adam Rzeczkowski

Meet Adam Rzeczkowski, the talent bringing fresh flavors to Arizona's gaming scene. As corporate executive chef, Rzeczkowski oversees all culinary operations across the state's Gila River Resorts & Casinos, including their newest picturesque property, Santan Mountain. As part of this ambitious $180-million development, Honey + Vine aligns with the casino's aesthetic, which breaks from tradition with a light and bright design of floor-to-ceiling windows, white marble floors, and a refined neutral color palette.

"Honey + Vine is casual, lively, and upbeat; we don't take ourselves too seriously," explains Rzeczkowski, who most recently helmed kitchens at Hawaii's Merriman's restaurant and the Grand Wailea Waldorf Astoria. "But it's still an upscale elevated experience that's approachable to everyone. There's a lot of retirement communities nearby, but at the same time, neighborhoods with younger families."

Open for lunch and dinner, the diverse menu reflects a Mediterranean influence that also incorporates ingredients sourced from the farms of the Gila River Indian Community. At the heart of the kitchen, a rotisserie works its magic on juicy prime rib and spiced chicken shawarma. Handcrafted pastas and shareable plates complete the experience, including the restaurant's signature whipped feta with honey (page 108). "It was one of the first dishes we created when we opened," explains Rzeczkowski. "With the restaurant's name, we wanted to highlight honey in one of the staple dishes, and it's been really popular."

Rzeczkowski credits the restaurant's success to more than just standout dishes. "We've built a phenomenal team and every day we're coming up with new outlets and new concepts," he muses. "It's really kind of mind-blowing to see what can be achieved when everyone comes together, and a lot of fun."

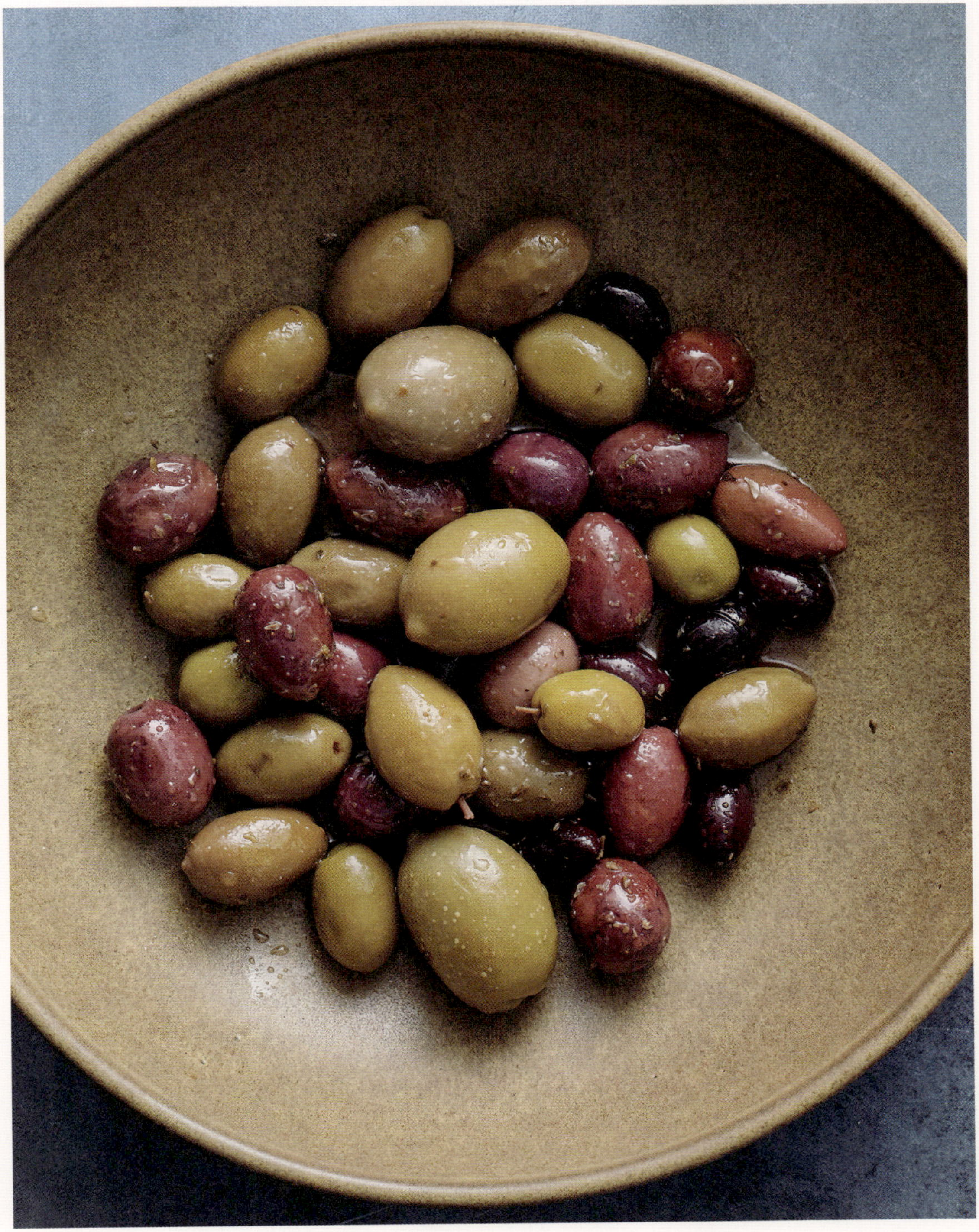

HONEY WHIPPED FETA

8 oz feta cheese, broken up into pieces

3 oz cream cheese, room temperature

2 Tbsp honey

½ tsp cracked black pepper

1 tsp za'atar spice (see Note)

ROASTED OLIVES

3 cups mixed olives, pitted

¼ cup extra-virgin olive oil

6 cloves garlic, crushed

1 shallot, cut in quarters lengthwise and julienned

1 small lemon, cut into ¼-inch slices

3 sprigs thyme

3 sprigs oregano

½ tsp chili flakes

ASSEMBLY

Honey Whipped Feta (see here)

Roasted Olives (see here)

Extra-virgin olive oil, for garnish

Cracked black pepper, for garnish

6–8 slices sourdough bread, toasted, to serve

Honey Whipped Feta with Roasted Olives

SERVES 2–4 Adam Rzeczkowski recommends using high-quality Greek brands of feta like Dodoni, Greco, or Kourellas, which can be found at your local deli counter, specialty grocers such as Whole Foods and AJ's Fine Foods, and Middle Eastern markets. "These brands follow traditional methods using 70% sheep's milk, 30% goat milk, sea salt, cheese cultures, and rennet enzymes," he explains. "If options are limited, avoid pre-crumbled varieties and look for feta packed in brine."

Honey Whipped Feta Combine feta, cream cheese, and honey in a food processor and pulse until smooth. Stir in pepper and za'atar. Set aside.

Roasted Olives Preheat oven to 450°F.

In a baking dish, combine olives with remaining ingredients and fold all components together until thoroughly incorporated. Bake for 12 minutes until olives, garlic, and shallots begin to caramelize. Cool for 10 minutes before serving.

Assembly Divide whipped feta among individual serving dishes or serve family style by placing whipped feta in the center of a large serving bowl or platter. Use a spoon to spread it out, creating a slight depression in the middle. Mound warm olives in the center of the whipped feta.

Garnish with a drizzle of oil and pepper, and serve with toasted sourdough.

NOTE Za'atar is a Middle Eastern spice blend typically made with dried thyme, oregano, sumac, and toasted sesame seeds. Look for it in the spice aisle of most grocery stores, specialty markets like Baiz Market and Caspian Food Market, or online.

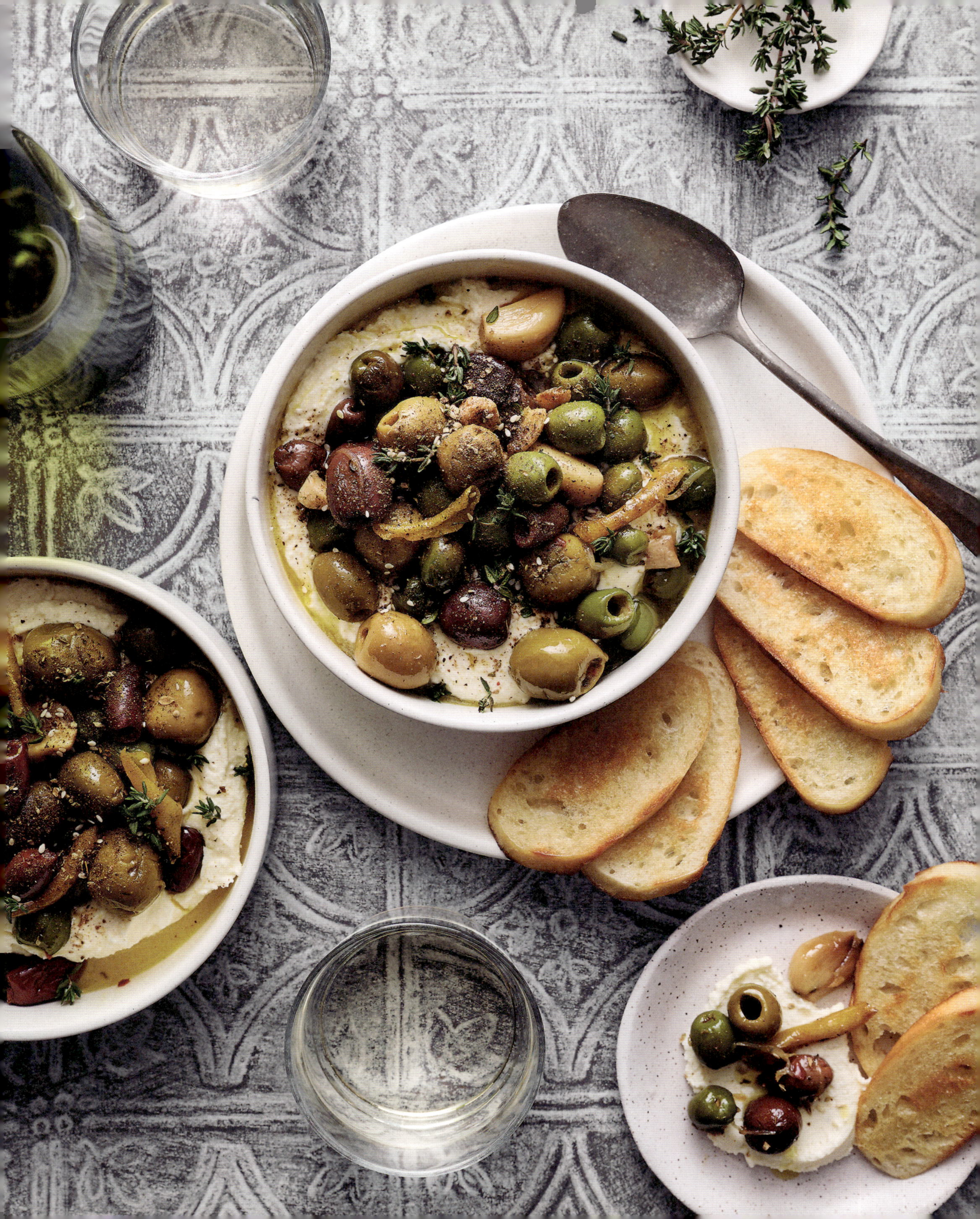

WHIPPED RICOTTA

2 cups ricotta cheese, strained (see Note)

1 Tbsp finely chopped flat-leaf parsley

WAGYU MEATBALLS

¼ cup light olive oil

1 yellow onion, finely diced

1 lb ground beef (85/15 preferred, or 80/20)

1 lb ground Wagyu beef

1 lb ground pork

2 Tbsp chopped garlic

1 Tbsp kosher salt

1 tsp chili flakes

2 cups grated Parmesan

2 large eggs, beaten

2 cups ricotta cheese, strained (see Note)

1 Tbsp dried basil

2 Tbsp thinly sliced flat-leaf parsley

2 cups panko breadcrumbs

1 cup whole milk

Wagyu Meatballs with Pomodoro Sauce and Whipped Ricotta

SERVES 4 Adam Rzeczkowski sources his beef from Legacy Prime Farms, a family-owned operation that employs regenerative practices and specialized feeding methods on their sixth-generation Arizona farm. "They grow their own feed, and finish their Wagyus just east of Sedona," he explains.

Whipped Ricotta Using a stand mixer with the paddle attachment, whip ricotta on medium speed until light and aerated, about 3–4 minutes. Stir in parsley.

Transfer to a container, cover, and refrigerate until ready to use.

Wagyu Meatballs In a large sauté pan, heat oil over medium heat. Add onions and sauté until translucent (do not allow to caramelize), 5–7 minutes. Remove from heat.

In a stand mixer fitted with the dough hook attachment, mix ground meats until combined. Add sautéed onions, garlic, salt, chili flakes, and Parmesan. Mix on low speed until incorporated.

Add eggs, strained ricotta, basil, parsley, and breadcrumbs. Continue to mix on low speed until incorporated.

Slowly add milk until mixture is moist (you may not need the full amount of milk).

Form mixture into 2-ounce meatballs (about ⅓ cup each) and place on a large baking sheet lined with parchment paper. Cover and refrigerate until ready to use.

Recipe yields approximately 2 dozen meatballs; extra meatballs can be frozen.

ASSEMBLY

¼ cup extra-virgin olive oil, plus more for garnish
2 sprigs flat-leaf parsley
2 sprigs oregano
1 sprig rosemary
2 sprigs basil, plus more for garnish
1 small yellow onion, diced
4 cloves garlic, sliced very thin
1 tsp chili flakes
2 (28-oz) cans whole peeled San Marzano tomatoes, crushed by hand
1–2 Tbsp kosher salt, to taste
1 tsp cracked black pepper
16 Wagyu Meatballs (see here)
2 cups Whipped Ricotta (see here)
Grated Parmesan, for garnish

Assembly Heat oil in a large saucepot over medium heat. Add the sprigs of parsley, oregano, rosemary, and basil to flavor the oil. Cook for 4–5 minutes, or until herbs become crisp. Remove herbs and discard.

Add onions, garlic, and chili flakes and stir to combine. Cook until onions are translucent, 5–7 minutes, reducing heat if necessary to prevent browning. Add crushed tomatoes, salt, and pepper and stir to combine.

Add raw meatballs to sauce and simmer for 30–40 minutes, or until sauce thickens and meatballs are cooked thoroughly, stirring occasionally.

For each serving, spoon ½ cup of whipped ricotta into bottom of bowl. Top with 4 meatballs and ¾ cup of tomato sauce, or to taste.

Drizzle with oil and garnish with grated Parmesan and torn basil leaves.

NOTE To strain ricotta, place a strainer over a bowl and line it with cheesecloth. Spoon ricotta onto cheesecloth, then gather edges of cheesecloth together and tie with kitchen twine or a rubber band to form a bundle. Refrigerate for 2–3 hours. Squeeze out any remaining liquid.

THE HOUSE BRASSERIE

Drew Hatfield, Dustin Wheeler, Joe Ieraci

Ensconced in a 1939 bungalow in Old Town Scottsdale, The House Brasserie offers an enchanting escape under the stewardship of managing partner Joe Ieraci and his wife, Julie. Inside this charming hideaway, antique chandeliers, damask wallpaper, and vintage accents create a warmth that's effortlessly elegant. Outside, a white picket fence outlines a lush patio with a retractable canopy that keeps things comfortable year-round. And then there's what may be the city's most romantic table for two set in front of a cozy brick fireplace, making it feel like your own private garden party.

"We have such a unique setting and can create a more personalized experience—something that will wow people and make them want to tell their friends about it," says Ieraci, who has assembled a passionate, like-minded team who share his vision.

In the kitchen, executive chef Dustin Wheeler draws inspiration from Arizona's agricultural bounty, frequenting local farmers' markets so he can weave ingredients like mesquite, chufa, moringa, and sorghum into his spectacular dishes.

Complementing Wheeler's prowess is a cocktail program curated by beverage director Chad Whittington with lead bartender Drew Hatfield showcasing vibrant flavors using house-made syrups, freshly squeezed juices, and unique ingredients straight from the kitchen. Standouts include the Green Lantern, where honeydew melon and serrano chiles mingle with gin and cracked black pepper, as well as a signature rye sour elevated with the zing of grapefruit and ginger (page 116).

The collaboration of kindred spirits, combined with culinary innovation and historic ambiance, sets the House Brasserie apart. "People can tell that we're a family here," Ieraci reflects, "and that translates into every aspect of our guests' experience."

The House Brasserie / 113

PICHUBERRY CHUTNEY

1 cup pichuberries (see Note)
2 Tbsp golden raisins
½ cup orange juice
2 Tbsp simple syrup (1:1 ratio of granulated sugar dissolved in water)
1 cinnamon stick
3 juniper berries
⅛ tsp Espelette pepper

MUSHROOM CARAMEL

3 Tbsp unsalted butter
4 medium cremini mushrooms, thinly sliced
4 shiitake caps, thinly sliced
½ cup heavy cream
2 Tbsp honey
1 Tbsp water
1 tsp tamari
⅛ tsp fish sauce, preferably whisky barrel–aged, like Haku Iwashi brand

ASSEMBLY

2 (2-oz) slices refrigerated foie gras (see Note)
¼ cup Mushroom Caramel (see here)
2 (2-inch-thick) slices brioche, toasted
Pichuberry Chutney (see here)
Bordelaise sauce, for garnish
Edible flowers, for garnish
Popped sorghum, for garnish

Foie Gras on Brioche with Pichuberry Chutney and Mushroom Caramel

SERVES 2 Inspired by his frequent farmers' market visits, Dustin Wheeler built this dish around discoveries like locally grown pichuberries (tart, golden fruit native to South America), foraged mushrooms, and sorghum from nearby grain farmers. Both popped sorghum and bordelaise, a rich reduced sauce, can be found at gourmet grocers and online retailers.

Pichuberry Chutney Place all ingredients in a pot over medium heat. Simmer, gently stirring occasionally, until the liquid has evaporated and the pichuberries are soft, about 15 minutes.

Mushroom Caramel In a medium saucepot, melt butter over medium heat.

Add mushrooms and sauté for about 8–10 minutes, stirring constantly. You want mushrooms to develop a crispy texture and a slight char.

Add cream, honey, water, and tamari. Stir the mixture well to combine all ingredients. Simmer, stirring occasionally, until reduced by half, about 5 minutes.

Transfer sauce to a blender and add fish sauce. Blend until smooth, beginning on low speed and gradually increasing to high.

Assembly Heat a dry, heavy sauté pan over high heat. Using a sharp knife and shallow 1/16-inch cuts, score the top of each piece of foie gras in a crosshatch pattern.

Place foie gras scored side down and allow its fat to render for 1 minute. Flip and sauté, using a spoon to baste foie gras in its own fat, until medium rare, about 3 minutes. Be careful not to overcook, as foie gras can render into fat if cooked too long.

The House Brasserie

For each serving, spread 2 tablespoons of mushroom caramel in a circle in the center of the plate. Place a piece of toasted brioche on top. Spread chutney on the brioche and lay the foie gras on top of the chutney.

Drizzle with bordelaise sauce, and garnish with edible flowers and popped sorghum.

NOTE Look for pichuberries at local farmers' markets and specialty grocers such as AJ's Fine Foods and Whole Foods. Choose fruit that is plump, firm, and vibrant in color. You'll want to remove the husks and give the pichuberries a quick rinse to wash off any residual stickiness. If unable to find pichuberries, substitute with seasonal fruit like strawberries or blackberries, adjusting simple syrup as needed.

You can find pre-portioned foie gras in gourmet specialty shops, or source online from sellers like D'Artagnan Foods and Hudson Valley Farms. Thaw if frozen, but keep chilled in the refrigerator until preparing to serve.

The House Brasserie / 115

GINGER SIMPLE SYRUP

1 cup granulated sugar
¼ cup raw sugar
¾ cup peeled and chopped fresh ginger
1 small serrano chile, sliced
Peel from half an orange, removed with a vegetable peeler to avoid white pith

ASSEMBLY

2 oz rye whisky
¾ oz fresh pink grapefruit juice
½ oz fresh lemon juice
½ oz Ginger Simple Syrup (see here)
1 small egg white
Angostura bitters, for garnish
1 sprig rosemary, for garnish

Grapefruit-Ginger Rye Sour

SERVES 1 This cocktail balances the spicy warmth of rye whisky with bright citrus and ginger syrup infused with serrano chile and orange peel. The rich, concentrated syrup is made without water, relying instead on the liquids released as the sugars dissolve into the ginger's juices. To achieve the meringue-like foam that distinguishes a sour, a technique called dry shaking is used to emulsify the egg white.

Ginger Simple Syrup Combine all ingredients in a saucepan over medium heat. Bring to a gentle boil, stirring as sugar dissolves into syrup. Reduce heat to a simmer and continue to stir for 10–15 minutes, until all sugar is dissolved. Remove from heat and allow to cool for 1 hour. Stir to combine, then strain through a fine-mesh strainer or cheesecloth into a glass bottle or container, discarding solids.

Ginger simple syrup can be stored in the refrigerator for up to 2 weeks.

Assembly Combine all ingredients, except garnishes, in a cocktail shaker.

Vigorously dry shake without ice for 15–20 seconds.

Add ice and shake vigorously for an additional 15 seconds.

Double strain (pour through the shaker strainer and then through a fine-mesh strainer) into a chilled coupe glass. Garnish with Angostura bitters and rosemary sprig.

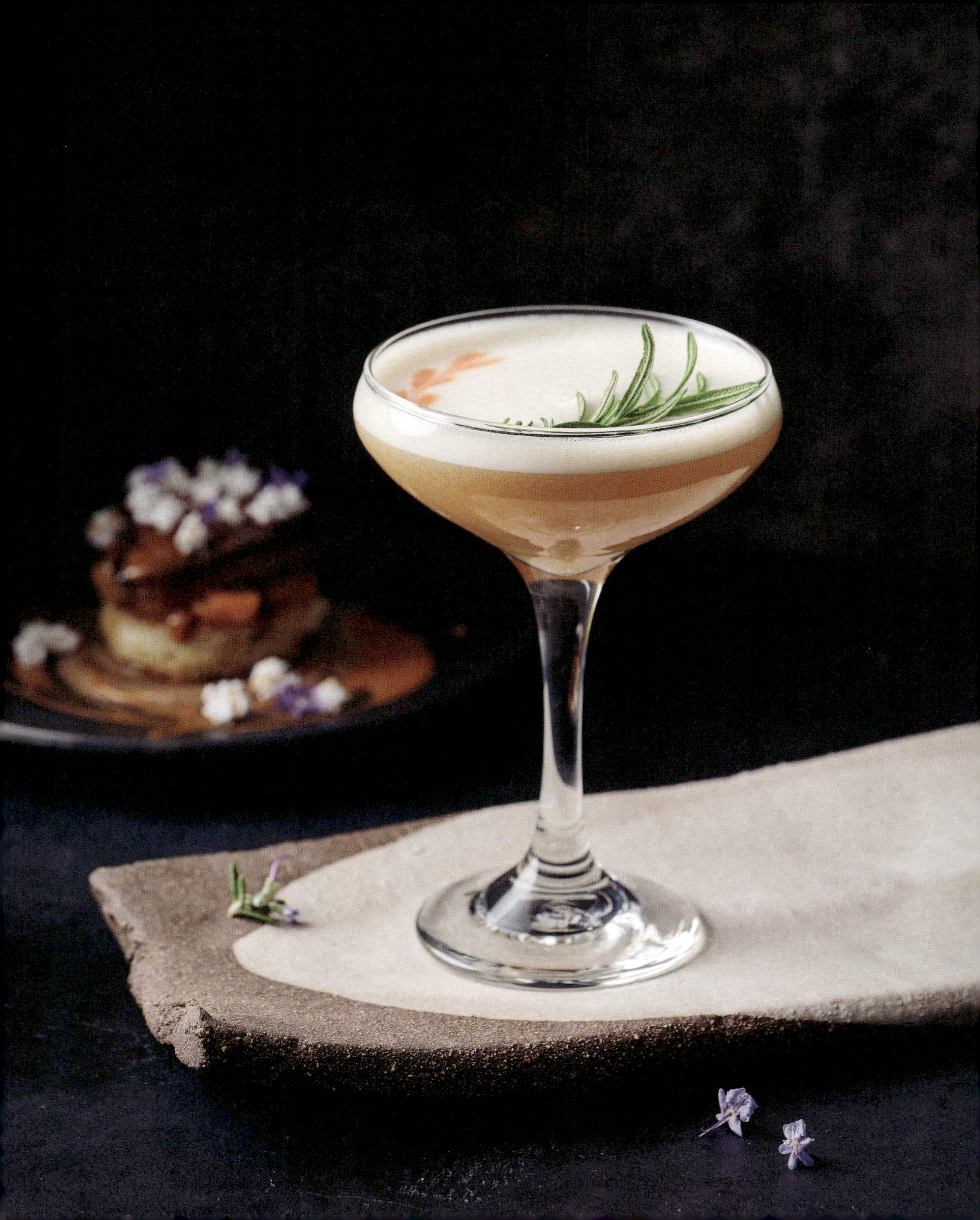

THE ITALIAN DAUGHTER

Vittorio Colafranceschi

Family recipes and traditions hold a special place in shaping culinary concepts, especially when they connect us to our heritage. For Melissa Maggiore Meyer, her restaurants—the Italian Daughter, helmed by executive chef Vittorio Colafranceschi, and Patricia's Pizza, named in honor of her mother—are heartfelt tributes to her family, blending nostalgia, legacy, and the flavors of home.

"I grew up in the restaurant business," she explains. "And while I always used my father's teachings and family recipes as the backbone for my other concepts, I never really brought everything completely back to my roots." When her father fell ill and passed away, it sparked a moment of reflection. "When you go through something like that, you take a look at your life," Maggiore recalls. "I realized that what truly represented me was being an Italian daughter. My father taught me my love affair with food and wine and the beauty and joy that a good meal can bring to one's life."

Maggiore's fondest memories center around family meals, and her vision for the Italian Daughter was simple but meaningful: to re-create those precious moments. "I wanted to bring that joy back," she explains. For example, "one of our signature dishes is my father's cioppino," she shares, "and people really love our bolognese, which is my grandmother's recipe."

At Italian Daughter, guests experience the same warmth and tradition that defined her upbringing. "The dishes are classic dishes done my father's way," she continues. "I wanted to share the genuine, comforting Italian food I grew up with in hopes that others can make their own memories around the table, too."

2 cups grape tomatoes
2 cloves garlic
1 cup blanched almonds
2½ cups basil leaves
3 mint leaves (optional, but traditional)
⅔ cup extra-virgin olive oil, plus more if needed
⅔ cup grated Pecorino Romano, or Parmigiano-Reggiano, plus more to taste
Pinch of chili flakes (optional)
Kosher salt and black pepper, to taste
1 lb casarecce pasta, or other curly short pasta, such as busiate or fusilli

Casarecce Trapanese (Pasta with Sicilian Pesto of Trapani)

SERVES 4 "My father made this dish for family gatherings so the taste brings back so many memories," recalls Melissa Maggiore Meyer. "And when we visited Sicily, my nonna would always make extra pesto because I would spread it on bread for breakfast or put it on top of grilled shrimp and fish. It's so light and refreshing."

Assembly Bring a large pot of water to a rolling boil over high heat. Prepare an ice bath by filling a large bowl with ice and cold water. Boil tomatoes until skins crack. Using a slotted spoon, immediately transfer tomatoes to the ice bath. Cool, peel, and set aside.

In a food processor, pulse garlic and almonds into a coarse paste. Add basil, mint (if using), peeled tomatoes, and oil and pulse to combine. Add Pecorino Romano (or Parmigiano-Reggiano) and chili flakes (if using). Pulse again, drizzling in more oil as needed for a coarse but silky pesto. Taste and season with salt and pepper.

Cook pasta according to package directions. Strain, reserving 1 cup of pasta water, and place pasta in a serving bowl.

Blend small increments of pasta water into the pesto to make it creamy, but still thick and not too loose.

Add pesto to the serving bowl and stir until pasta is well coated, adding more cheese if desired.

- 2–3 Tbsp olive oil
- 2 medium to large zucchini, cut into ¼-inch rounds
- 3 cups arborio rice
- 6 cups warm vegetable or chicken stock, plus more as needed
- 2 Tbsp unsalted butter
- 2 Tbsp freshly grated Parmigiano-Reggiano
- Kosher salt and black pepper, to taste
- 1 small zucchini, cut lengthwise into thin slices and sautéed, for plating (optional)
- Grated Provolone del Monaco, for garnish (see Note)
- Basil leaves, torn, for garnish
- Microgreens, for garnish (optional)

NOTE Provolone del Monaco is a semi-hard, aged provolone from Campania with a nutty, buttery flavor. Alternatives include aged provolone, provolone picante, and caciocavallo. Look for imported Italian cheeses at grocers with well-stocked cheese sections, local specialty markets such as Andreoli Italian Grocer and Romanelli's Italian Deli, and from online purveyors such as Buona Italia and Dolceterra.

Risotto alla Nerano

SERVES 4 "My mother's family is from near Naples, and one of my favorite Amalfi Coast dishes is spaghetti alla Nerano," shares Melissa Maggiore Meyer. In this humble yet elegant dish, which originated in its namesake seaside village, spaghetti is combined with zucchini, starchy pasta water, and Provolone del Monaco, made from the milk of cows grazing in the Lattari Mountains. For this version, Maggiore trades out the pasta for arborio rice.

Assembly Heat oil in a heavy sauté pan over medium-high heat.

Fry zucchini until golden brown on both sides with curled edges. Remove and place on a paper towel–lined plate, reserving pan.

Mash half of the fried zucchini into a paste using a mortar and pestle. Set aside.

Reduce heat to medium. Add rice to same pan, stirring constantly until lightly toasted and edges are translucent.

Add stock a ladle at a time, stirring and allowing each addition to be nearly absorbed before adding more. Rice should be tender but with a slight firm bite in the center of each grain. This process should take 12–15 minutes.

At 9–10 minutes, add butter, Parmigiano-Reggiano, and zucchini paste and stir to combine. Season with salt and pepper to taste.

Continue to cook and stir until risotto is creamy and tender to the bite.

Divide risotto among serving plates. Garnish each plate with fried zucchini slices, Provolone del Monaco cheese, basil, and microgreens (if using).

Alternatively, for a more formal presentation, line a 3-inch ring mold with thin lengthwise slices of sautéed zucchini, slightly overlapping them around the inner circumference. Fill with risotto, pressing gently. Remove mold by lifting straight up. Repeat for the other servings of risotto, then top with fried zucchini slices, Provolone del Monaco cheese, basil, and microgreens (if using).

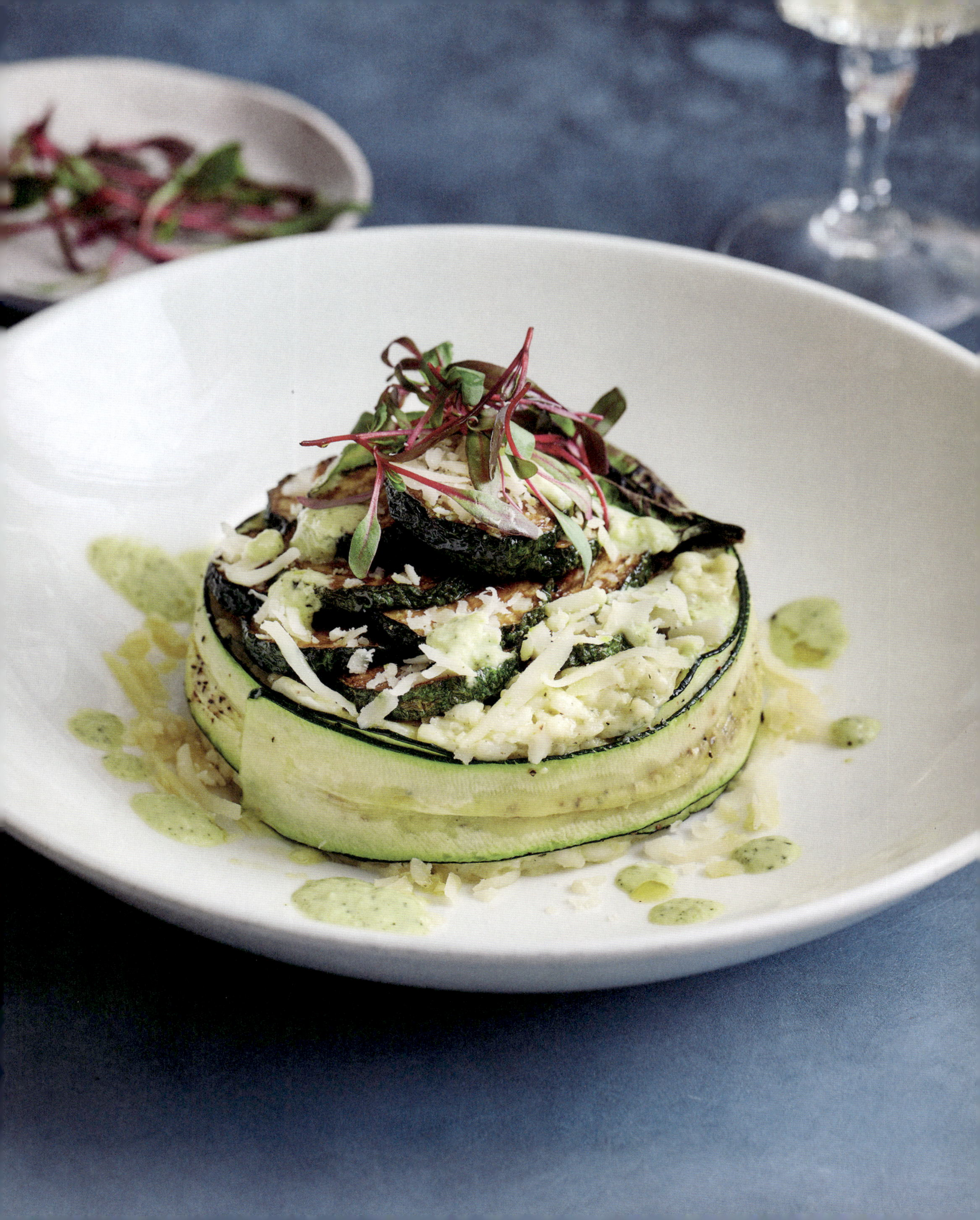

JOE'S FARM GRILL

Tim Peelen

Joe's Farm Grill in Gilbert is more than just a beloved neighborhood hangout—it's a tribute to history, family, and an authentic farm-to-table lifestyle. It's located within Agritopia, an agricultural residential community founded by Joe Johnston to blend urban life with farming traditions. As befits its setting, fresh ingredients, many grown right on Agritopia's farm, take center stage.

"Our slogan is 'Common food done uncommonly well,'" says Tim Peelen, who, along with his brother Tad, is Johnston's partner in both Joe's Farm Grill and Joe's Real BBQ. "Joe and I have been in the restaurant business since we opened Coffee Plantation in 1988," he recalls. Together, they've cultivated a space where the community can gather, not only for great food but to experience a deeper connection to the land.

Adding to the restaurant's charm is its location in Johnston's childhood home, built in 1966. The former bedrooms now house the kitchen, while the original kitchen and dining area has been transformed into a sunny atrium. "You'll see family photos in the main dining room, which was the Johnstons' living room," says Peelen, and in a playful nod to the home's '60s roots, "we have *The Jetsons* and *Jonny Quest* playing on a continuous loop in the restrooms."

"For a first-time visitor, it's an unexpected oasis in the desert," he continues. "We're literally nestled in a twelve-acre urban farm with hundred-year-old trees, orchards, and date palms in the midst of historic farmland. When you sit at our picnic tables, you're looking out at the farm, and if we can exceed expectations with every bite, then we've achieved our goal."

▶ Grilled Wedge Salad

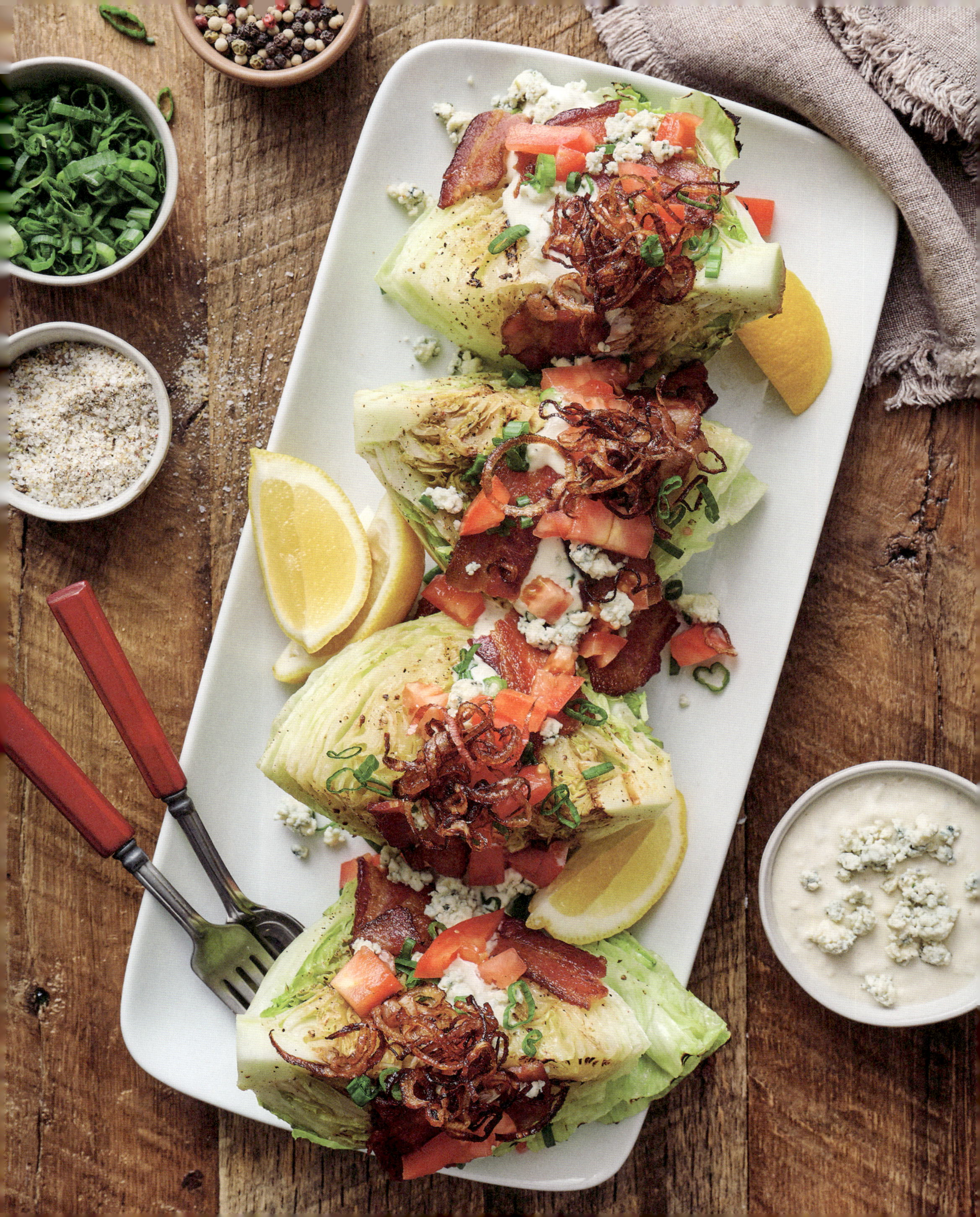

BURGER SHAKE SEASONING

1 Tbsp kosher salt

1 tsp ground peppercorn medley (any combination of black, white, green, red, pink), or black pepper

1 tsp dried Greek oregano (see Note)

1 tsp granulated garlic, or ¼ tsp garlic powder

BLUE CHEESE DRESSING

1 cup mayonnaise

1 cup sour cream

1 tsp Worcestershire sauce

½ tsp dry mustard

½ tsp kosher salt

½ tsp granulated garlic, or ¼ tsp garlic powder

¼ tsp ground peppercorn medley (any combination of black, white, green, red, pink), or black pepper

1¼ cups crumbled high-quality blue cheese

Grilled Wedge Salad

SERVES 4 This smoky twist on the classic comes loaded with blue cheese dressing, bacon, tomatoes, and crispy shallots. "I love wedge salads and we have a great blue cheese dressing that I worked really hard to create," Tim Peelen says. "It's grilled just long enough to give it a bit of char. We ran it as a special, but it was so popular, we couldn't take it off the menu."

Burger Shake Seasoning In a small bowl, combine all ingredients. Transfer seasoning to an airtight container.

Seasoning will keep for 3 months. Recipe can be scaled up for a versatile all-purpose seasoning for eggs, potatoes, meat, poultry, and vegetables.

Blue Cheese Dressing In a mixing bowl, whisk together all ingredients, except blue cheese, until smooth.

Using a spatula, fold in blue cheese until well combined.

Transfer dressing to a container and store in the refrigerator for at least 3 hours and up to 7 days.

ASSEMBLY

4 strips bacon

1 medium shallot, thinly sliced

1 medium head iceberg lettuce, as firm (dense) as possible

2 Tbsp olive oil, or your favorite salad oil

Burger Shake Seasoning (see here)

1 cup Blue Cheese Dressing (see here)

1 fresh Roma tomato, diced

4 Tbsp crumbled blue cheese

1 Tbsp finely chopped scallion tops

1 lemon, cut into quarter wedges, to serve

NOTE Greek oregano, with its intense, earthy flavor and peppery bite, is more pungent than its Mexican or Italian counterparts. Find dried Greek oregano at Mediterranean markets, specialty spice shops, or well-stocked grocery stores.

Assembly Preheat grill to medium-high to high heat.

In a sauté pan over medium heat, fry bacon until crisp. Remove bacon, leaving residual fat in pan. Chop bacon and set aside.

In the same pan, crisp-fry shallots in bacon drippings over medium heat. Remove shallots and set aside.

Remove outer leaves of iceberg lettuce, but do not remove core or stalk. Cut head into 4 equal wedges, making sure to cut through the core so wedges hold together. Brush cut sides with oil and sprinkle with burger shake seasoning.

Place lettuce wedges cut-side down on the grill and cook for about 30 seconds per side, until grill marked but still cool and crisp on the inside.

To serve, arrange iceberg quarters on a decorative platter or individual serving plates. Top each wedge with ¼ cup of blue cheese dressing. Garnish with bacon, tomatoes, blue cheese crumbles, crispy shallots, and scallions. Accompany each serving with a lemon wedge.

FRESH HERB RANCH DRESSING

1 cup mayonnaise
½ cup sour cream
½ cup buttermilk
1 tsp white wine vinegar
1 tsp dried Greek oregano (see Note)
1 small clove garlic, minced
1 tsp finely minced flat-leaf parsley
½ tsp finely minced fresh dill
½ tsp finely minced onion
¼ tsp Tabasco
¼ tsp kosher salt, plus more to taste
¼ tsp ground peppercorn medley (any combination of black, white, green, red, pink), or black pepper, plus more to taste

Goat Cheese–Stuffed Lamb Burgers

SERVES 4 These juicy lamb burgers, stuffed with tangy goat cheese and fragrant herbs, offer a gourmet twist on classic cookout fare. "The lamb makes it a little more 'special occasion' for a barbecue," says Tim Peelen. "Serve it with a salad (like Grilled Wedge Salad, page 124) or corn on the cob for a wonderful outdoor meal."

Fresh Herb Ranch Dressing Place all ingredients in a small mixing bowl and stir until well combined. Season with more salt and pepper to taste.

Refrigerate for at least 2–3 hours, or preferably overnight, to allow flavors to meld. Store in the refrigerator for up to 7 days. Extra dressing can be used as a dip, salad dressing, or sandwich spread.

Assembly Combine basil and mint in a small bowl and set aside.

Divide ground lamb into four 8-ounce balls. Shape each ball into a 1-inch-thick patty, making a shallow well in the center of the burger with a spoon or your thumb. Place 1 slice of goat cheese and 1 teaspoon of herbs into each well.

Fold edges of each patty over the goat cheese and herbs, making sure the filling is completely enclosed. Gently flatten to ensure an even ½-inch-thick patty.

Heat a large skillet (or BBQ grill) over medium-high heat. If using a skillet, add 1–2 tablespoons of butter or oil. Sauté (or grill) onion slices, keeping rings intact. Cook until each side is slightly browned and onions are firm-tender. Set aside.

ASSEMBLY

1 Tbsp chopped basil
1 Tbsp chopped mint
2 lbs ground lamb
1 (4-oz) goat cheese log, sliced into 4 pieces
4–5 Tbsp butter or oil of choice, divided
4 (¼-inch-thick) slices red onion
3 Tbsp Burger Shake Seasoning (page 124)
4 brioche buns, or your favorite hamburger buns
1 cup arugula leaves
2½ Tbsp Fresh Herb Ranch Dressing (see here)
4 (¼-inch-thick) slices beefsteak tomato
2 Tbsp crumbled feta cheese
Sliced pickles, to serve (optional)

If using a skillet, heat another 1–2 tablespoons of butter or oil in the same pan. Season each side of all 4 patties with approximately 1 teaspoon of burger shake seasoning. Pan-fry (or grill) patties for about 4 minutes per side, adjusting time for desired level of doneness. A still-juicy medium-well is recommended.

Meanwhile, brush butter or oil on each bun surface. Griddle (or grill) over medium heat until light golden brown, a little crispy, and warmed through.

To assemble each burger, place ¼ cup of arugula leaves on the bottom bun. Drizzle with 1 teaspoon of ranch dressing, and place patty on top. Top with another teaspoon of ranch dressing, followed by a slice of tomato, a slice of grilled onion, and a quarter of the feta cheese. Serve with sliced pickles, if using.

NOTE Greek oregano, with its intense, earthy flavor and peppery bite, is more pungent than its Mexican or Italian counterparts. Find dried Greek oregano at Mediterranean markets, specialty spice shops, or well-stocked grocery stores.

THE JOY BUS DINER

Jennifer Caraway

Chef Jennifer Caraway's career as a restaurant owner took an unexpected turn when her close friend Joy Seitz-Butz was diagnosed with ovarian cancer. Seeing the vital role of nutritional food during her treatment inspired Jennifer to found The Joy Bus in 2011, a nonprofit organization delivering healthy meals to homebound cancer patients. Originally it was a one-woman operation, with Caraway delivering the meals she prepared in her home kitchen. However, as word spread, volunteers joined her cause, expanding its reach across Phoenix.

In 2015, Jennifer advanced her vision by opening The Joy Bus Diner, where 100% of the proceeds fund the charity's delivery program. "My intent was to create a kitchen to prepare meals while raising funds," she explained. "But now it's turned into a community. It's so rad. You get to see the client meals being packed into their beautiful bags, the florist adding her bouquets of flowers, and the pastries made by a local mother and daughter team."

The diner, open for breakfast and lunch, hums with purpose as the staff, which includes volunteers, serves up signature dishes like chorizo made with Caraway's unique spice blend, a Reuben stacked with fifteen-hour smoked brisket, and chilaquiles topped with a smoky guajillo and pasilla chile sauce she whipped up on her winning Food Network *Chopped* episode.

"I don't know of another place where everyone who comes in feels such ownership of the food and the mission," she says, her voice filled with gratitude. "I'm so lucky that this is what I get to do, and that these are the people I get to know."

The Joy Bus Diner

- 10 dried guajillo chiles, stemmed and seeded (see Note)
- 8 dried pasilla chiles, stemmed and seeded (see Note)
- 2 dried chiles de árbol, stemmed and seeded (see Note)
- 6 cups chicken stock
- 1 large white onion, peeled and halved
- 5 tomatoes, chopped
- 10 cloves garlic, crushed (divided)
- 2 Tbsp dried Mexican oregano
- 1 Tbsp ground cumin
- 1 tsp dried marjoram
- 5 black peppercorns, crushed
- ¼ tsp grated ginger
- 3 lbs bone-in goat meat, cut into 4-inch pieces
- 4 Tbsp vegetable oil
- 2 dried bay leaves
- 1 cinnamon stick
- Kosher salt, to taste
- Toasted sesame seeds, for garnish
- Chopped white onion, for garnish
- Cilantro, for garnish
- 2 limes, cut into wedges, for garnish
- Flour or corn tortillas, warmed, to serve
- Chile de árbol salsa, to serve

Jennifer's Famous Birria de Chivo

SERVES 6 "I started making this when I owned a restaurant in Puerto Vallarta in Jalisco, Mexico," says Jennifer Caraway. "I use goat because that's how it's meant to be made, and it has such a unique richness and depth of flavor you can't get from beef." She recommends sourcing young goat meat from Middle Eastern grocers like Baiz Market, and fresh chile d'árbol salsa from your favorite carnicería.

Assembly Preheat oven to 350°F.

Place chiles in a single layer on a baking sheet and toast for 3–5 minutes, checking frequently to avoid burning as they darken quickly. Remove from oven and allow to cool.

In a pot over medium-high heat, bring chicken stock, onions, tomatoes, and 5 crushed garlic cloves to a boil. Reduce heat and simmer for 20 minutes. Set aside.

Place toasted chiles in another pot and add at least 2 cups of water (more if needed to cover chiles). Bring to a boil over high heat, then reduce heat and simmer until chiles are soft, about 15 minutes. Strain, reserving 2 cups of chile water.

In a blender, combine chiles, oregano, cumin, marjoram, crushed peppercorns, ginger, and the remaining 5 crushed garlic cloves and blend, adding reserved chile water as needed, to form a smooth paste.

Place goat meat in a container. Strain 1 cup of blended chile paste through a fine-mesh strainer over the goat meat, discarding solids. Stir to ensure the meat is coated in the paste. Cover and refrigerate for 24 hours to marinate.

Working in batches, ladle the warm chicken stock and vegetables from the pot into the blender with the remaining chile paste and purée until smooth. Strain chile sauce through a fine-mesh strainer into a separate container and refrigerate until needed.

When ready to prepare birria, heat oil in a large sauté pan over medium-high heat.

Sear marinated goat on all sides, avoiding overcrowding to ensure even browning.

Transfer goat to a large stockpot. Add chile sauce, bay leaves, cinnamon stick, and enough water to cover the meat by 10 inches. Bring to a boil over high heat, then reduce heat and simmer for 3½ hours, or until meat is tender and falls off the bone (skim off any floating fat and add water as needed to maintain 10 inches covering the meat while simmering). Remove and discard bones, then add salt to taste.

To serve, ladle birria into 6 bowls. Garnish with sesame seeds, onions, cilantro, and limes, and serve with warm tortillas and salsa.

NOTE Guajillo chiles are deep red with smooth skin, and have a fruity, moderate heat. Pasilla chiles are dark and wrinkled, with a rich, earthy flavor. Dried chiles de árbol are bright red and smaller, with a spicy lingering heat. These whole dried Mexican chiles are available at Mexican markets like Food City and Los Altos Ranch Market, at Sprouts and other specialty grocers, or online. For best quality, look for chiles that are pliable and glossy.

SALSA A LA HUANCAÍNA
2 Tbsp canola oil
½ lb queso fresco, broken up into chunks
4 Tbsp ají amarillo paste (see Note)
1 clove garlic
¼ cup chopped white onion
¼ cup evaporated milk
2 saltine crackers

ASSEMBLY
6 lbs Yukon Gold potatoes, peeled and diced into ½-inch cubes
2 cloves garlic
3 limes, juiced
¼ cup mayonnaise
3 Tbsp ají amarillo paste (see Note)
Kosher salt, to taste
6 leaves butter lettuce
2 avocados, thinly sliced
1 (3-lb) rotisserie chicken, meat pulled off the bone and shredded
1 cup Salsa a la Huancaína (see here)
3 black olives, halved
3 quail eggs, soft boiled and halved
¾ cup (½ pint) cherry tomatoes, halved

Causa Rellena de Pollo with Salsa a la Huancaína

SERVES 6 "It's so easy but looks so creative and beautiful," Jennifer Caraway says of this chilled Peruvian dish of golden mashed potatoes layered with colorful fillings. "I was inspired after a trip to Peru to hike Machu Picchu with my daughter Areli. When I got back, I made it for patient meals and events and everyone loved it! Now it's part of the regular rotation."

Salsa a la Huancaína Place all ingredients in a blender and purée until smooth.

Salsa can be made ahead and refrigerated for up to 1 week. Any extra salsa would also be delicious as a dip, sandwich spread, or a sauce for grilled meats and roasted vegetables.

Assembly Bring potatoes to a boil over high heat in a pot of water. Cook for 10–12 minutes, until soft, adding garlic to the pot about halfway through the cooking time.

Drain potatoes and garlic and push through a ricer into a large bowl. (If you don't have a ricer, you can push the potatoes through a fine-mesh strainer using the back of a spoon.) Add lime juice, mayonnaise, and ají amarillo paste and stir until smooth. Add salt to taste, and allow to cool to room temperature. Potatoes can also be prepared ahead, refrigerated, and served chilled.

Place a leaf of butter lettuce on each plate. For each serving, set a 4-inch metal ring mold on the lettuce. Spoon a thick layer of potato mixture into the ring and press down gently. Add a layer of avocado, then a layer of chicken. Top with a thinner layer of potato and smooth evenly. Remove ring mold and spread a thin layer of salsa a la huancaína on top. Garnish with half a black olive and half a quail egg on top, and a few cherry tomato halves to the side.

NOTE Ají amarillo paste is a vibrant yellow-orange medium-heat paste made from the ají amarillo chile, which is native to South America. Commonly sold in jars, you can find it at Latin American markets, or order online from specialty stores.

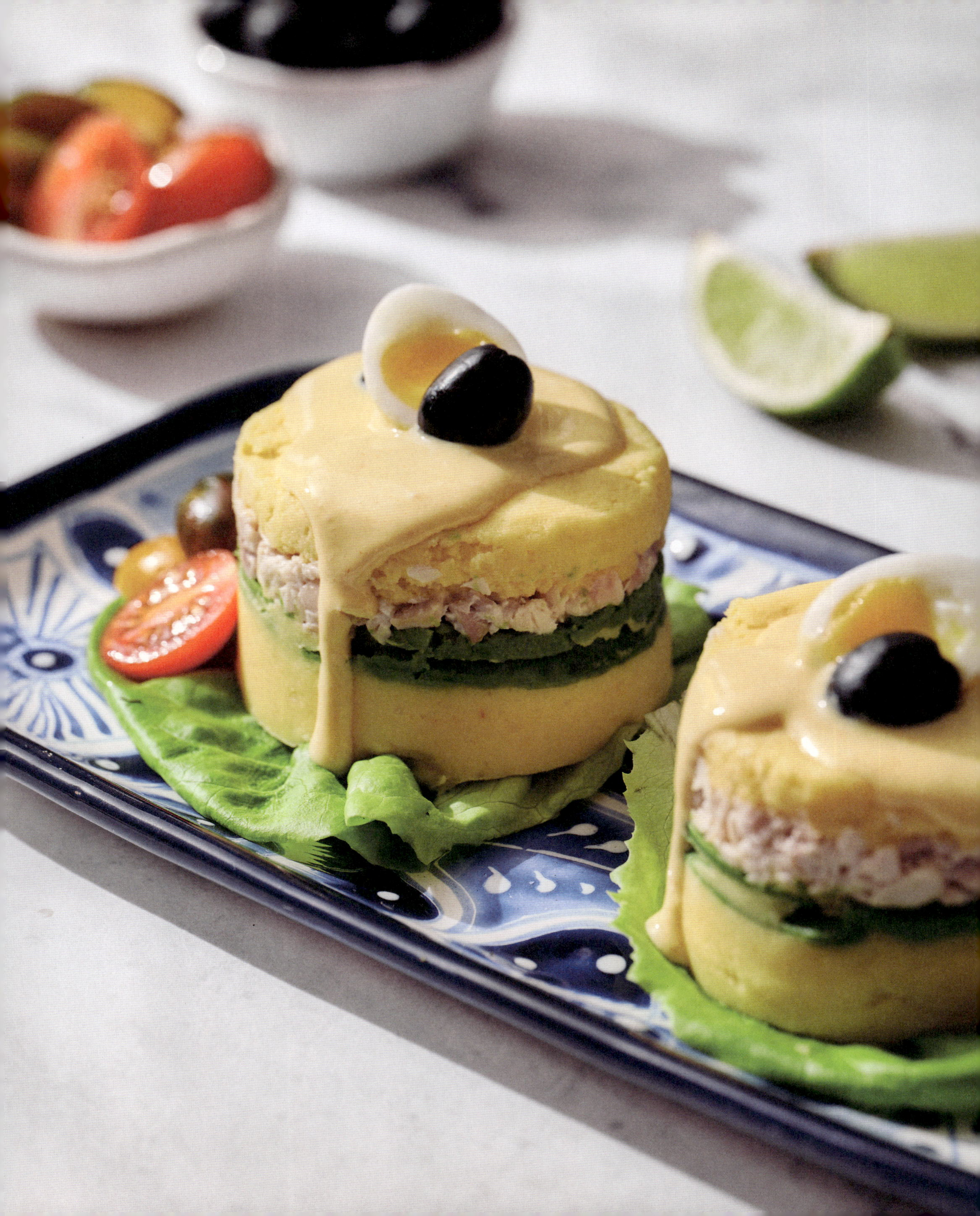

J.T. PRIME KITCHEN & COCKTAILS

Alex Trujillo

At first glance, J.T. Prime blends in with the unassuming row of businesses on Brown Avenue in Old Town Scottsdale. But step closer and you'll find a secret escape. Within a brick-lined, lantern-lit alleyway, the entrance beckons to this sultry forty-seat hideaway, with its dim lighting, provocative artwork, and velvet-draped walls.

Chef-owner Alex Trujillo's restaurant is a creative leap from its humble roots as J.T. Bros Handcrafted Sandwiches in Yuma (named for his sons' shared initials). What began as impromptu fine-dining pop-ups in the evenings soon evolved into something bigger. "We started out doing private dinners for friends and special guests," says Trujillo, whose résumé includes various Four Seasons resorts across the western U.S. "We would serve a fine-dining menu, block out the windows with velvet drapes, and turn up the music." The transformation became so popular that J.T. Bros shifted its schedule to accommodate both concepts. "Now, we close at 3:00 p.m., which gives us time to open the cocktail lounge for happy hour and reset the room with tablecloths and glassware."

A loyal customer planted the seed for expansion, which led to a Scottsdale debut in 2022. Here, Trujillo's handmade pastas, fresh seafood, and juicy steaks share a stage with signatures like short rib ravioli enrobed in Gorgonzola sauce (page 136) and the Del Mar duo featuring Portuguese octopus and Sea of Cortez shrimp infused with chile de árbol and garlic.

"It's the perfect size," says Trujillo of the intimate space. "A smaller footprint means our service is more personal and we can take better care of our guests."

CHIPOTLE AIOLI

½ cup mayonnaise (homemade, or your favorite brand)

1 canned chipotle chile pepper in adobo sauce, finely chopped (see Note)

1 tsp adobo sauce from canned chipotles

1 clove garlic, minced

1 Tbsp lime juice

Sea salt, to taste

ASSEMBLY

12 jumbo organic Medjool dates, pitted

3 oz blue cheese, such as Point Reyes, crumbled

6 slices bacon, cut in half

Chipotle Aioli, to serve (see here)

Bacon-Wrapped Dates with Chipotle Aioli

SERVES 4 These bacon-wrapped stuffed dates are the ultimate sweet-and-salty party starter. "We've been making them for as long as I've been catering—almost fourteen years—and it's our number one appetizer for weddings," says Alex Trujillo. "They're great for entertaining because you can keep them in the freezer."

Chipotle Aioli Combine all ingredients in a bowl, mix until smooth, and season with salt to taste.

Cover and refrigerate until ready to serve. Aioli can be made 1 day ahead.

Assembly Preheat oven to 375°F.

Stuff each date with ½ tablespoon of crumbled blue cheese, ensuring it is well-packed but not overflowing.

Wrap each date with half a slice of bacon and secure with a toothpick. Dates can be prepared up to 3 days ahead and refrigerated, or frozen for up to 3 months. If frozen, thaw for 30 minutes before baking.

Place bacon-wrapped dates seam-side down on a baking sheet lined with parchment paper or aluminum foil.

Bake for 20–25 minutes, or until the bacon is medium crisp, turning once halfway through for even cooking. Remove from oven and allow to cool slightly before serving.

To serve, arrange warm bacon-wrapped dates on a serving platter and serve with chipotle aioli for dipping.

NOTE Canned chipotle peppers in adobo sauce are dried, smoked jalapeños packed in a tomato-based sauce with garlic, vinegar, and spices. You'll find them in the international aisle or Mexican foods section of grocery stores, at Mexican markets, and online. Unused peppers and sauce will keep in the refrigerator for 2–3 weeks, or purée the peppers and sauce together and freeze for later use.

BRAISED SHORT RIB FILLING

2 lbs boneless beef short ribs
Kosher salt and black pepper, to taste
2 Tbsp extra-virgin olive oil
1 medium onion, diced
2 medium carrots, diced
2 stalks celery, diced
10 cloves garlic
1 cup sun-dried tomatoes (not oil packed), thinly sliced
2 cups dry red wine, such as Bordeaux
2 sprigs thyme
1 sprig rosemary
1 bay leaf
2 cups beef stock, or enough to cover short ribs

BEEF SHORT RIB RAVIOLI

2 cups all-purpose flour
3 large eggs
1 Tbsp extra-virgin olive oil
½ tsp kosher salt
Braised Short Rib Filling (see here)
1 large egg, beaten, for egg wash

Beef Short Rib Ravioli with Gorgonzola Cream Sauce

SERVES 4 Born from creative ingenuity, this dish shows how a sandwich ingredient became a fine-dining star. Wine-braised beef prepared for the Vallarta Especial at J.T. Bros—a torta stacked with fork-tender short rib and crispy pork belly—finds an elevated new home stuffed into silky homemade pasta draped with a velvety Gorgonzola cream sauce.

Braised Short Rib Filling Preheat oven to 300°F.

Season short ribs generously with salt and pepper on all sides.

Heat oil in a Dutch oven or heavy-bottomed pan over medium-high heat. Sear ribs on all sides until browned, about 4 minutes per side. Remove and set aside.

In same pan, reduce heat to medium and add onions, carrots, and celery. Sauté until soft and translucent, about 8 minutes. Add garlic and sun-dried tomatoes and cook for an additional 2 minutes.

Pour in red wine and deglaze by scraping up browned bits from the bottom. Simmer for 3–4 minutes to reduce slightly.

Return ribs to the pan, and add thyme, rosemary, bay leaf, and enough beef stock to cover the ribs. Bring to a simmer, cover, and braise in oven for 2½ to 3 hours, or until fork tender. Remove ribs, shred meat, and set aside.

Discard herbs from braising liquid. Strain through a fine-mesh strainer and return liquid to the pan, reserving vegetable mixture. Skim off excess fat, if necessary.

Simmer braising liquid over medium heat until reduced by half. It should be thick and flavorful.

In a mixing bowl, combine shredded beef with reserved vegetables and enough braising liquid reduction to moisten. The mixture should be thick but not too wet. Taste and adjust seasoning.

Any leftover braising liquid reduction can be used as a soup base or as gravy or sauce.

CRISPY CARROT SHAVINGS
1 medium carrot
2 cups neutral oil, for frying
Sea salt, to taste

GORGONZOLA CREAM SAUCE
1 Tbsp extra-virgin olive oil
½ cup fresh baby spinach
1 cup heavy cream
½ cup crumbled Gorgonzola cheese
8 cherry tomatoes, halved
Sea salt, to taste

ASSEMBLY
12 Beef Short Rib Ravioli (see here)
Gorgonzola Cream Sauce (see here)
Balsamic reduction, for garnish
Crispy Carrot Shavings, for garnish (see here)

Beef Short Rib Ravioli On a clean surface, mound flour, making a well in the center. Crack eggs into the well and add oil and salt. Using a fork, whisk eggs while gradually incorporating flour from edges of the well until dough forms.

Knead dough for 8–10 minutes, or until smooth and elastic. Wrap in plastic wrap and allow to rest at room temperature for 30 minutes.

Divide dough into 4 portions. Working one portion at a time, roll dough out using a pasta machine or rolling pin to a 1/16-inch thickness. Cut dough into 3-inch squares (or use a round cutter for circular ravioli).

Place 1½ tablespoons of short rib filling in center of each square.

Brush edges of dough with egg wash, then top each square with a second piece of dough. Press firmly around the filling and along the edges to seal.

Crimp edges with a fork or a ravioli cutter. Transfer ravioli in a single layer to a baking sheet lined with parchment paper. Repeat with remaining dough and filling.

Cover the ravioli with plastic wrap and refrigerate until ready to cook.

Crispy Carrot Shavings Peel carrot into thin shavings with a vegetable peeler. Pat dry.

Heat oil in a small pot over medium-high heat. Add carrot shavings and fry, stirring occasionally, until crispy, 1–2 minutes.

Remove carrot shavings with a slotted spoon or strainer and drain on a paper towel–lined plate.

Sprinkle with sea salt.

Gorgonzola Cream Sauce Add oil to a sauté pan over medium heat. Cook spinach for 1–2 minutes, just until spinach wilts. Add heavy cream and bring to a simmer.

Reduce heat to low and add Gorgonzola cheese. Stir or whisk continuously until cheese is completely melted and sauce is smooth, about 3–4 minutes. Stir in tomatoes.

Season with salt to taste. Keep warm.

Assembly Bring a large pot of salted water to a boil over high heat.

Cook ravioli until they float to the surface, about 3–4 minutes, then drain.

To serve, place 3 ravioli on each plate. Spoon ½ cup of cream sauce over the ravioli. Drizzle with balsamic reduction and garnish with carrot shavings.

▸ Beef Short Rib Ravioli with Gorgonzola Cream Sauce

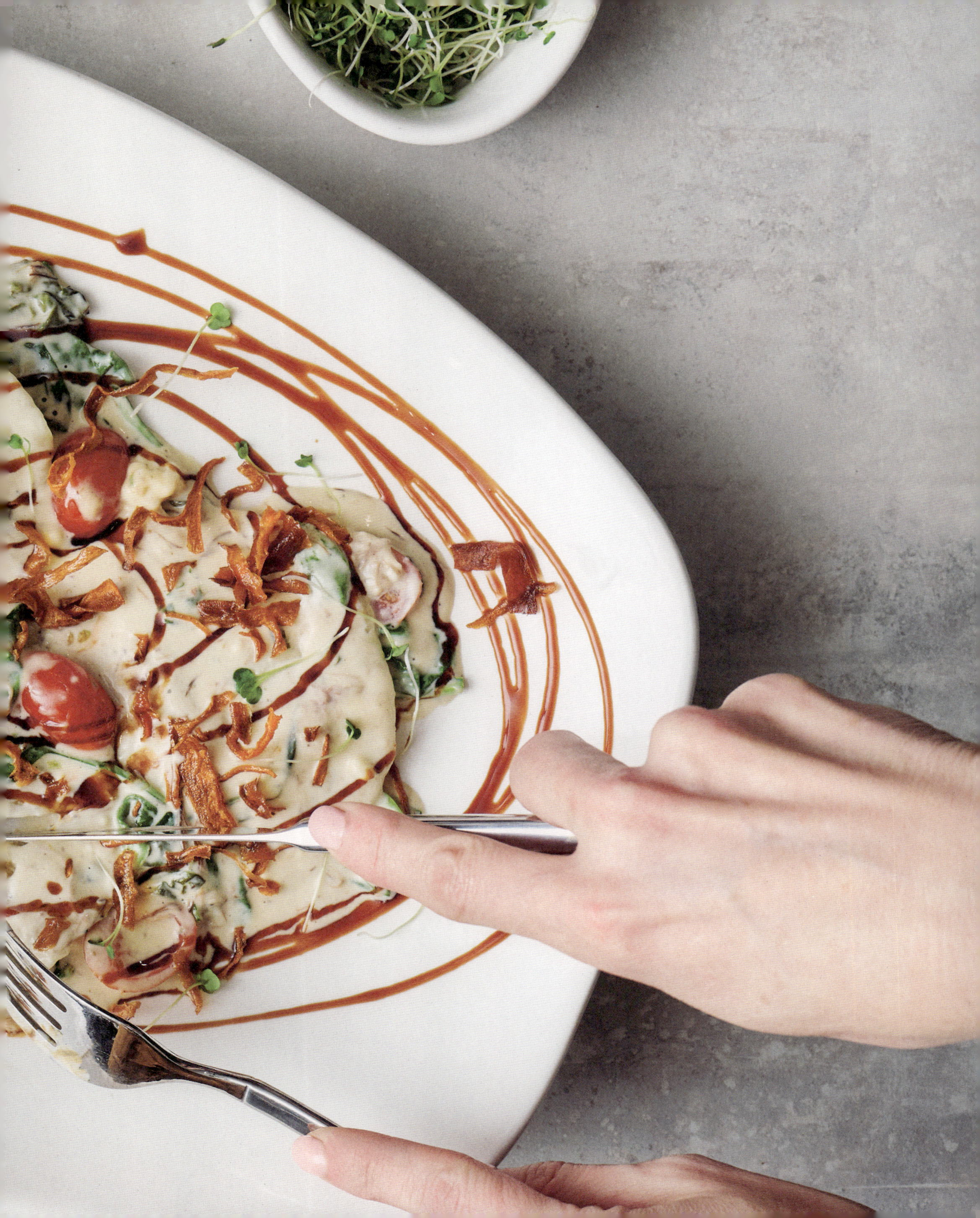

LITTLE RITUALS

Aaron DeFeo

There's a reason Little Rituals has amassed an array of accolades, including recognition by the James Beard Foundation and the Spirited Awards. Located on the fourth floor of the Residence Inn Phoenix Downtown, it's an intimate gem that offers sweeping views of the city's skyline along with some of the most inventive drinks you'll find in the Southwest.

"I would describe it as a modern interpretation of a classic hotel bar," says co-owner Aaron DeFeo, who opened the spot in 2019 alongside Ross Simon, of Bitter & Twisted Cocktail Parlour (page 32). "There's both a retro and a futuristic vibe to it that we hope makes guests feel like they could be in any major city in the world." A striking mural, however, reminds guests of where they are. As DeFeo explains, "While we wanted to transport people away from Phoenix, we also want to remind them of our roots." The colorful artwork illustrates iconic landmarks, natural wonders like Picacho Peak, and famous Arizonans. "There's Steven Spielberg, Emma Stone, and Wonder Woman Linda Carter," adds DeFeo. "And Alfred Hitchcock, because parts of *Psycho* were filmed in downtown Phoenix."

Rather than a traditional menu, guests are invited to flip through a book of cocktail drawings tucked into old-school photo corners. "Since our concept is all about the rituals in life, that includes how people collect memories," explains DeFeo. "We designed the menu as if you were looking through an old photo album or scrapbook."

It's part of the goal to turn every visit into a story worth sharing. "We want people to have a personal connection," reflects DeFeo. "We want them to leave here excited to tell everyone they know about us, yet still feel like Little Rituals is their own private secret."

POMEGRANATE GRENADINE

2½ cups pomegranate juice
2 cups organic cane sugar
1 dash rose water
1 dash orange flower water
1 tsp citric acid (see Note)

LIME LEAF MEZCAL

1 (750-mL) bottle of mezcal (preferably espadín)
10–12 large makrut lime leaves, roughly chopped (see Note)
1 Tbsp coriander seeds, lightly crushed

ASSEMBLY

1½ oz Lime Leaf Mezcal (see here)
½ oz Martini & Rossi Riserva Speciale Rubino Vermouth
¼ oz Ruccolino Amaro
¾ oz Pomegranate Grenadine (see here)
¾ oz fresh lime juice
1 makrut lime leaf, for garnish
Pomegranate seeds, for garnish

Pleasure Island

SERVES 1 Aaron DeFeo's cocktail draws inspiration from the Mexican Firing Squad, a drink first documented in Charles H. Baker Jr.'s 1939 classic *The Gentleman's Companion: Being an Exotic Drinking Book; Or, Around the World with Jigger, Beaker, and Flask*. "The components of mezcal, lime, and pomegranate are buoyed by rich, aromatic vermouth and arugula amaro from Italy—taking the place of traditional Angostura bitters," DeFeo explains.

Pomegranate Grenadine Gently warm pomegranate juice and sugar in a saucepan over low heat, stirring just until sugar dissolves. Do not let boil; the less heat, the better.

Remove saucepan from heat and stir in rose water, orange flower water, and citric acid.

Transfer grenadine to a container and place in a larger bowl filled with ice and a little water to cool as quickly as possible.

Once cool, bottle the grenadine and store it in the refrigerator for up to 1 month.

Lime Leaf Mezcal Add all ingredients to an airtight container and allow to infuse at room temperature for 3 to 5 days.

Strain through a coffee filter into the original mezcal bottle. Infused mezcal will keep indefinitely in a cool, dry place or the refrigerator (preferred), although flavor may change over time.

Assembly In a cocktail shaker, combine mezcal, vermouth, amaro, grenadine, and lime juice with ice. Shake vigorously for 10–12 seconds.

Fill a chilled double old-fashioned glass with ice or, preferably, with one large cube. Strain cocktail through a fine-mesh strainer into glass.

To garnish, float lime leaf on surface of cocktail and top with pomegranate seeds.

NOTES Citric acid is a natural acid found in citrus and provides a balanced tartness that enhances the flavor profile of cocktails. Look for citric acid in the baking section of grocery and health food stores, or online.

Makrut lime leaves, commonly used in Thai and Southeast Asian cuisine, have a pronounced floral and citrus flavor. Packages of fresh leaves can be found in the produce section of Asian markets, as well as from specialty grocers or online.

MACADAMIA NUT–BARLEY BREAKFAST BAR

1 cup macadamia nuts
½ tsp neutral oil
1 tsp ground cinnamon
6 cups Grape-Nuts cereal
4 cups dried blueberries
1 cup macadamia nut butter
1 cup honey
½ cup dried plums
4 Tbsp brown sugar
1 Tbsp vanilla extract
1 tsp fine sea salt
1 cup white chocolate baking chips
¼ cup whole milk

ASSEMBLY

1 oz Glenfiddich 12 Year Amontillado Finish Single Malt Scotch Whisky
¾ oz R. Jelínek Slivovitz Plum Brandy
¾ oz Lustau Vermut Rojo vermouth
¼ oz Trader Vic's Macadamia Nut Liqueur
¼ oz Drambuie liqueur
1 Macadamia Nut–Barley Breakfast Bar, for garnish (see here)

Breakfast of Champions

SERVES 1 This ingenious creation by bartender Frank De La Cruz proves that the best drinks don't always require laborious house-made ingredients. While experimenting with flavor profiles, De La Cruz came up with a Bobby Burns variation that surprisingly evokes breakfast flavors—think granola bars, barley cereal, and dried fruit. For a fun flourish, it's garnished with a no-bake breakfast bar created by executive chef Mike Williams that can be made in batches and stored in the freezer.

Macadamia Nut–Barley Breakfast Bar Preheat oven to 375°F.

Toss macadamia nuts with oil and cinnamon and spread on a parchment-lined baking sheet. Roast for 7 minutes, or until golden brown. Keep a close eye on them to avoid burning. Let cool, then finely chop.

Line the baking sheet with fresh parchment paper and lightly coat with nonstick spray.

Combine macadamia nuts and all other ingredients, except white chocolate chips and milk, in a bowl. Press the granola mixture evenly onto the baking sheet.

Place another piece of sprayed parchment paper on top, sprayed-side down, then another baking sheet. Freeze overnight with a weight (such as skillets or cans) on top to compress bars.

To decorate bars, place white chocolate chips and milk in a saucepot over medium-low heat, stirring frequently until chips melt and chocolate is smooth. Transfer to a squeeze bottle.

Remove baking sheet from the freezer. Allow to soften slightly and cut into approximately 3- × 1½-inch bars. Drizzle white chocolate over the top in a zigzag pattern. Store the bars in the freezer for up to 3 months. Bars are best served directly from the freezer as the macadamia nut butter will soften at room temperature.

Assembly Add all ingredients, except breakfast bar, to a stirring vessel full of ice cubes, and stir for 15–20 seconds.

Strain over fresh ice cubes into a chilled double old-fashioned glass.

Garnish with the breakfast bar.

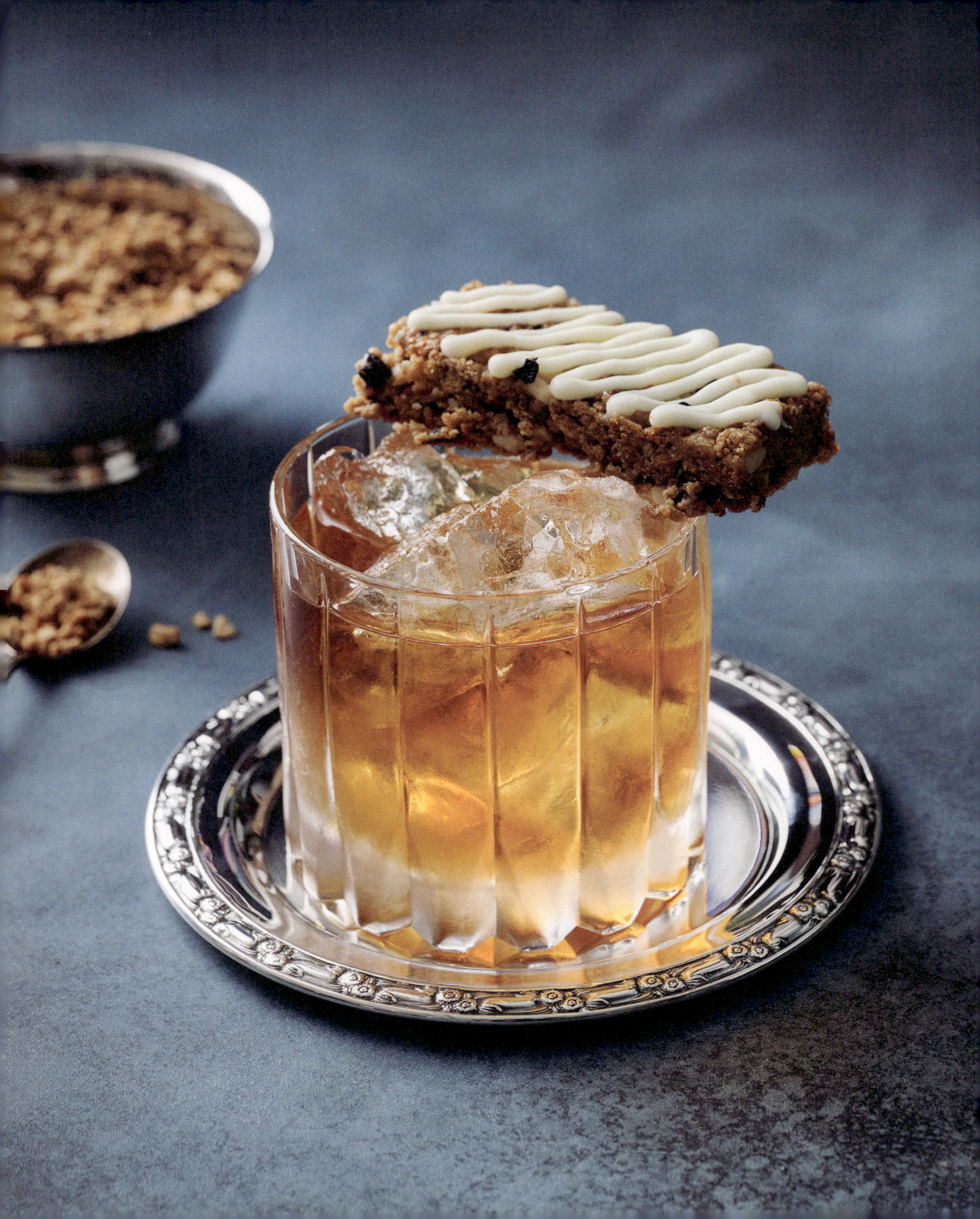

MELINDA'S ALLEY

PJ Vader Baron

Hidden in the basement of the Renaissance Phoenix Downtown Hotel, Melinda's Alley is a speakeasy that whisks its patrons back to an era of clandestine gatherings. To find this elusive gem, look for a seventy-foot mural of a fiery-haired woman in the alley behind the hotel between Central Avenue and First Street. Hidden in the artwork is a camouflaged door lit with a glowing red light, a nod to its notorious past.

The cocktail destination is a tribute to Malinda Curtis, though the first article written about the hotel misspelled her name as "Melinda," and the spelling stuck. A colorful figure in Phoenix's history and a purported madame, "Malinda was an African-American business owner in the 1800s known for taking care of everybody regardless of their race or circumstance," explains bar manager PJ Vader Baron. "She was a community leader in the founding of this great city and has been a real inspiration to us."

Step inside the dimly lit, narrow space and you'll notice period furnishings that capture the Prohibition era. On a wall, Melinda's House Rules include the warning "Smokin', cussin', fightin', breakin' bottles and overall unpleasantness will get you thrown in the alley!" A chalkboard lists four rotating creations that join their mainstay old-fashioned, while exposed brick walls and a moody red glow furthers the speakeasy vibe. "We want guests to feel like they're a part of our history," Baron explains.

"My style of cocktail recipe creation and style of hospitality are one and the same," he continues. "It's all about the narrative: here's why it's special, and here's why you'll connect with it."

▶ First Street Last Word

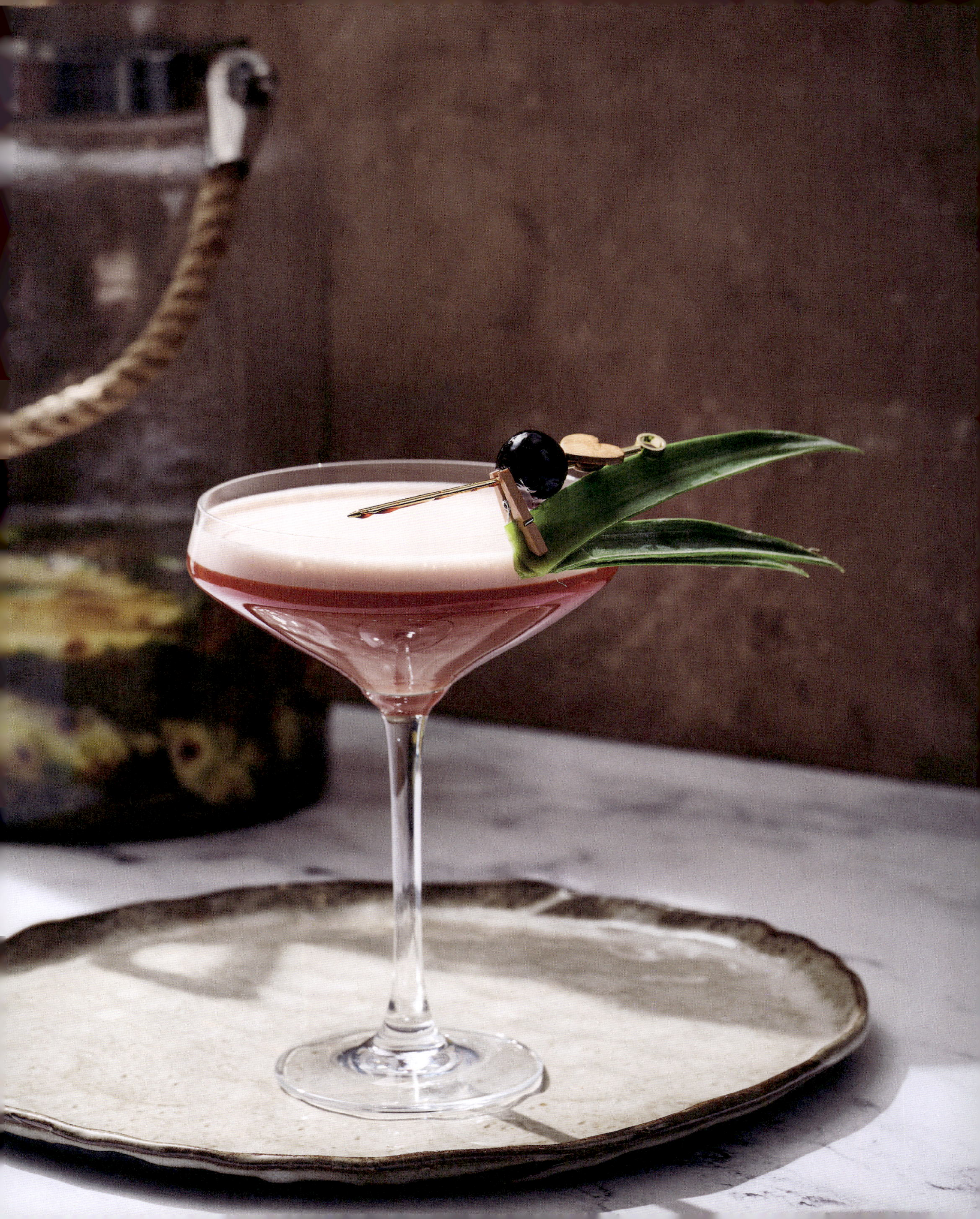

CARAMELIZED PINEAPPLE PURÉE

¾ cup (200 g) white miso (Baron suggests Eden brand shiro miso)

½ cup packed (100 g) light brown sugar

1 whole fresh pineapple

TEPACHE

½ tsp instant yeast, such as Fleischmann's RapidRise

1 liter hot (not boiling) water, divided

¼ cup light brown sugar

Pineapple peels, reserved from making purée (see here)

1 cinnamon stick

1 clove

1 pod star anise

1 splash Red Light Melinda Ale, or other ale

Special equipment: 1½-liter fermentation jar (see Note)

First Street Last Word

SERVES 1 Named for the speakeasy's location and its storied past, this cocktail memorializes Malinda, whose legend was twisted by time. While tales claim she stabbed a customer over a bowl of noodles, "it was really about protecting her staff from possible future mistreatment," explains PJ Vader Baron. "So literally, geographically, over noodles, Phoenix's first lady of the night got the last word... on First Street."

Caramelized Pineapple Purée Preheat grill to medium-high.

In a mixing bowl, combine miso and brown sugar to form a smooth glaze.

With a sharp heavy knife, remove the crown of the pineapple and discard, saving fronds for drink garnish. Slice off pineapple peel in strips from top to bottom, reserving for tepache (see here).

Cut pineapple lengthwise into 8 long, thin pieces and coat each piece with miso glaze.

Grill pineapple, turning occasionally, for approximately 10 minutes, or until pieces are evenly charred but not blackened.

Remove pineapple from grill and process through a cold-press masticating juicer. (Alternatively, blend in a blender until smooth.)

Leftover purée can be refrigerated for up to 1 week or frozen for up to 3 months. Use it as an ice cream or breakfast topping or in smoothies and other drinks, such as espresso martinis and carajillos.

Tepache In a gallon pitcher, combine yeast and ½ cup of hot water, stirring gently to combine. Toss in a pinch of brown sugar and stir. Allow 5 minutes for yeast to activate.

Add remaining water and the rest of the ingredients to the pitcher, ensuring all solids are fully submerged. Cover loosely with plastic wrap.

Allow to ferment for 3 days at room temperature, continually checking to ensure airflow and that it doesn't bubble over. Skim white foam off top when necessary.

After 3 days, skim all foam, strain out solids, and transfer to your fermentation jar. Monitor water level in the jar's airlock seal, as this allows carbon

ASSEMBLY
1 oz Zephyr Gin
¾ oz Joshua Tree Distilling Tobalá Maguey Blanco agave spirit
¾ oz CHELLY Modernized Limoncello
¼ oz Brucato Amaro Chaparral
½ oz Monin Tart Cherry Syrup
½ oz Tepache (see here)
½ oz fresh lemon juice
1 oz Caramelized Pineapple Purée (see here)
1 large egg white, or 1 oz liquid egg whites
1 Luxardo cherry, for garnish (see Note)
3 pineapple fronds, reserved from making purée, for garnish (see here)

dioxide to escape and prevent the jar from exploding due to pressure buildup.

Ferment for 3 more days at room temperature (you should see bubbling). Transfer to the refrigerator to chill.

Once chilled, transfer tepache to bottles with pour spouts, but not airtight corks or seals, as fermentation will slow, but not stop. Keep refrigerated.

Tepache will keep for up to 1 week, and can be used in glazes, marinades, and sauces, or enjoyed on its own as a refreshing drink. (For a delicious low-ABV chiller, Baron recommends combining with local Big Marble Tonic.)

Assembly Combine all ingredients, except egg white and garnishes, in a Boston shaker. Add ice and shake vigorously for 15–20 seconds to combine, chill, and dilute.

Double strain (pour through shaker strainer and then through a fine-mesh strainer) out of the shaker into a separate container, discarding ice. Pour mixture back into shaker.

Add egg white and dry shake (without ice) vigorously for 30–40 seconds to emulsify egg white, creating a frothy texture.

Double strain into a coupe or martini glass.
Garnish with cherry and pineapple fronds.

NOTE Fermentation jars have airtight lids with grommets for airlocks to allow carbon dioxide to escape. If you already have a large mason jar, airlocks can be purchased separately. Look for airlocks and fermentation jars in grocers with well-stocked canning aisles or online. (Alternatively, spring-top jars or bottles can be used, but "burp" daily and monitor for excessive bubbling to prevent pressure buildup and glass breakage.)

Originally created by the Luxardo family in Croatia, these marasca cherries are candied in a rich syrup made from the fruit's own juices. Darker and denser than standard maraschino cherries, Luxardo cherries have notes of almond and chocolate and are used in cocktails and desserts. Find them at specialty grocers such as AJ's Fine Foods and Whole Foods, liquor stores like Total Wine & More and BevMo, or online.

HONEY BUNCH SYRUP

½ cup water
½ cup raw cane sugar
1 Tbsp orange blossom honey
1 Tbsp saba (see Note)

HEART OF GOLD BITTERS

12 oz mesquite-smoked high-proof distillate like Whiskey Del Bac Old Pueblo, or Everclear
2 cinnamon sticks
2 bird's eye chiles
2 pecans
3 Tbsp dried hibiscus flowers
2 Tbsp gentian root pieces (see Note)
1 Tbsp toasted green cardamom pods
1 Tbsp whole cloves
1 rose petal

Heart of Gold Old-Fashioned

SERVES 1 "For our signature old-fashioned, incorporating influences from Northern Arizona to the southern border and beyond, the key is to be preparation-heavy and execution-friendly," says PJ Vader Baron. "We use our own private barrel Redwall Distillery grain-to-glass bourbon made with pure Sedona spring water, but use whatever you love," he says. "Uncle Nearest 1884 is a nice connection to whisky's history and Carefree Spirits makes great bourbon if you're keeping it local. Or treat yourself to a Sedona trip for your own bottle of Redwall bourbon. The distillery tasting room is one of the best places to watch the sunset."

Honey Bunch Syrup Heat water in a pot on medium-high until it is just below boiling. Stir in sugar until fully dissolved.

Remove from heat and immediately add the honey and saba, stirring until dissolved.

Place syrup in the refrigerator, uncovered, to cool. Syrup will keep refrigerated for up to 10 days.

Heart of Gold Bitters Combine all ingredients, except the rose petal, in a 16-ounce mason jar. Seal and allow to infuse for 5 days at room temperature, agitating the jar once or twice a day. Add the rose petal and infuse for 2 more days, again agitating once or twice a day. After 7 days, strain the mixture through a fine-mesh sieve into an airtight container and discard aromatics. Bitters are shelf stable and will last indefinitely in a cool, dry place.

ASSEMBLY

2 oz Redwall Distillery Sedona Small Batch Bourbon

½ oz Honey Bunch Syrup (see here)

3 dashes Heart of Gold Bitters (see here)

1 orange peel, cut into a 1-inch-wide strip with minimal white pith, for garnish

Assembly Combine bourbon, syrup, and bitters in a mixing glass with ice. Stir for 20 seconds to chill and dilute.

Strain over a large ice cube in a 14-ounce double old-fashioned glass.

Express the orange peel over the drink and skewer it for garnish. (To express, hold peel over the glass with outer side facing down and give it a gentle squeeze to release the oils onto the surface of the drink.)

NOTE Saba is a rich, sweet Italian syrup made by reducing the fresh juice (must) of grapes. Look for saba at Italian markets like Andreoli Italian Grocer and Romanelli's Italian Deli, gourmet grocers such as AJ's Fine Foods and Whole Foods, or online sources.

Gentian root is an alpine herb used in cocktail bitters and aperitifs to provide an earthy, bitter structure to other botanicals. Dried gentian root is packaged as woody brown pieces and can be found at specialty herb shops, well-stocked brewery supply stores, and online retailers. Avoid gentian powders and tinctures.

THE MEXICANO

Rigo Martinez

At the Mexicano, prepare to celebrate every day as a lively fiesta under the creative vision of restaurateur Joey Maggiore and the culinary skills of corporate chef Rigo Martinez. Its roots trace back to an unexpected source of inspiration. "In the early years, we had a chef working at one of our restaurants whose name was Balthazar," Maggiore recalls. "He made the most amazing pastas, but at three o'clock, we would have family meal and it was always Mexican food; we became huge fans. My dad always teased that we should open a Mexican restaurant."

In the kitchen, Martinez channels his Mexican heritage into the menu. The Jalisco native, who has been with Maggiore for over a decade, draws inspiration from his regional travels across Mexico, from Sinaloa to Puebla. "We change the menu every two to three months," Martinez says. "We're always coming up with ideas and trying new things." As a result, his dishes have earned a devoted following. "Since day one, the molcajetes (page 152) have sold like crazy," Maggiore adds. "And the birria tacos are our number one selling taco. You put Rigo's birria on anything and it will sell."

Maggiore, whose restaurant empire includes The Sicilian Butcher, The Sicilian Baker, Hash Kitchen, and The Italiano, has a flair for creating dynamic spaces. At The Mexicano, DJs spin their turntable and folklórico dancers in their charro suits and swirling skirts weave between tables. "It's a Mexican club vibe," says Maggiore. "It's upscale, entertaining, and wild. You can come here and have a beautiful dinner, or feel like you're at a nightclub with your friends."

▶ Sonoran Molcajete

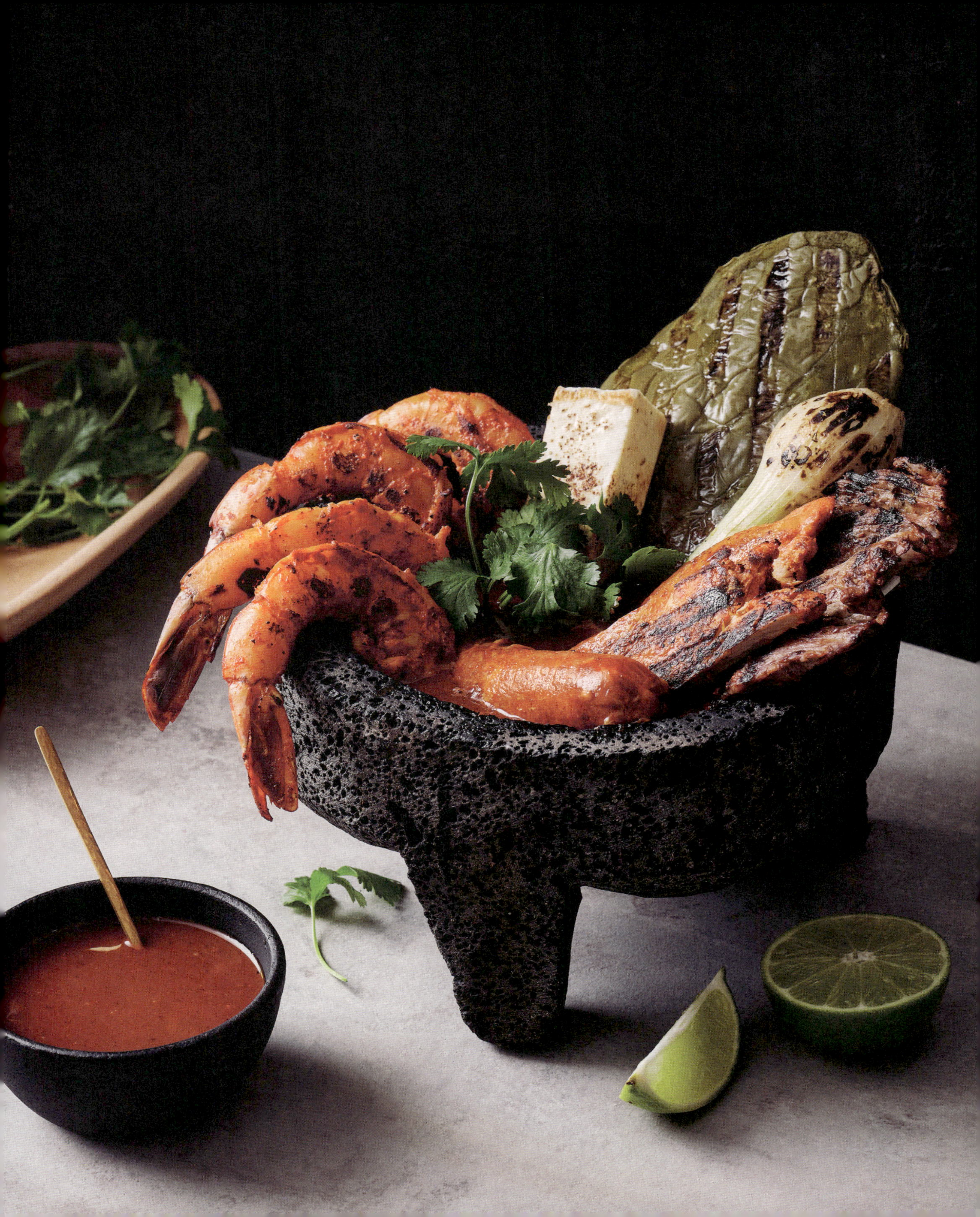

MAFIOSA SAUCE

1 oz dried morita chiles
1 oz dried pasilla chiles
1 oz dried guajillo chiles
1 oz dried chiles de árbol
1 oz dried cascabel chiles
½ cup extra-virgin olive oil
1 cup fresh Roma tomatoes, chopped
1 tsp minced white onion
1 tsp minced garlic
1 Tbsp jarred chicken base (see Note)
1 cup water
1 Tbsp adobo sauce from canned chipotle peppers in adobo sauce
1 Tbsp Maggi seasoning
2 Tbsp honey
¼ cup lime juice

Sonoran Molcajete

SERVES 2 A volcanic stone mortar, or molcajete, becomes a sizzling vessel for this Sonoran feast. "It's a very popular dish, not only in the restaurant, but in Mexican culture," says Rigo Martinez. In this recipe, grilled meats, seafood, cheese, and cactus nestle around the rim of bubbling "mafiosa" sauce, a playful fusion nod to Maggiore's heritage. Whole dried chiles, canned chipotles in adobo, and molcajetes can be found at Mexican markets like El Rancho Market, Food City, and Los Altos Ranch Market, and online.

Mafiosa Sauce Preheat oven to 350°F.

Remove stems from dried chiles. Spread chiles out on a baking sheet and toast them in oven for 3–5 minutes, until fragrant, checking frequently to avoid burning as they darken quickly. Remove from oven and set aside.

Heat oil in a pot over medium heat. Add tomatoes, onions, and garlic and cook until onions are translucent, 5–7 minutes.

Add in the chicken base and water and stir until chicken base is dissolved. Add toasted chiles and cook until softened, 5–10 minutes.

Transfer to a blender. Be careful when blending hot liquids: Remove cap on blender lid and cover with a folded dish towel to allow steam pressure to escape and catch any splashes. Purée the mixture in batches if needed, being careful not to fill the blender more than halfway. Starting on low speed and gradually increasing to high, blend until smooth.

Transfer to a container and stir in adobo sauce, Maggi seasoning, honey, and lime juice.

Mafiosa sauce can be made up to 5 days ahead and stored in the refrigerator. Reheat before serving. Recipe makes about 3 cups. Leftover sauce can be used for any dishes that call for salsa, such as tacos and burritos, or mixed into eggs, rice, or beans. It can also serve as a braising liquid for beef, pork, or chicken, or a flavorful base for stews and soups.

MARINATED BEEF, CHICKEN, AND SHRIMP

¼ cup fresh lime juice
¼ cup fresh orange juice
1 tsp red wine vinegar
1 tsp adobo sauce from canned chipotle peppers in adobo sauce
1 tsp achiote paste
¼ cup chopped white onions
1 tsp fresh oregano leaves
¼ tsp kosher salt
¼ tsp black pepper

2 Tbsp canola oil
3 oz sirloin flap beef
3 oz boneless, skinless chicken breast (½ chicken breast)
4 extra-large (U12) shrimp

ASSEMBLY

1 medium nopal (cactus paddle; see Note)
2 Mexican green onions
1–2 Tbsp canola–olive oil blend
Kosher salt and black pepper, to taste
Marinated Beef, Chicken, and Shrimp (see here)
4 oz Mexican longaniza sausage
4 oz panela cheese
1 to 1½ cups Mafiosa Sauce (see here)
Cilantro, for garnish
6 corn or flour tortillas, warm, to serve

Marinated Beef, Chicken, and Shrimp In a bowl, combine all marinade ingredients. Add beef and chicken, cover, and marinate for 12 hours or overnight in the refrigerator. Add shrimp to the bowl and toss to coat 30 minutes before grilling.

Assembly Preheat grill to medium-high.

Heat a 12-ounce lava stone molcajete in a 350°F oven 15 minutes before serving. Once heated, handle with care using oven mitts as it will remain hot for an extended time.

In a bowl, toss nopal and green onions with oil, salt, and pepper to coat.

Grill beef, chicken, shrimp, nopal, green onions, and longaniza until cooked and lightly charred. Shrimp and longaniza will take approximately 2–3 minutes per side, nopal and green onions 3–4 minutes per side, beef 4–5 minutes per side (for medium-rare), and chicken 5–6 minutes per side.

To serve, arrange the beef, chicken, shrimp, nopal, longaniza, panela, and green onions around the edge of the hot molcajete. (Beef, chicken, nopal, and panela can be sliced before placing in molcajete, if you prefer). Pour mafiosa sauce into the center of the molcajete.

Garnish with cilantro and serve with warm tortillas.

NOTE Chicken base is a concentrated paste that has a more robust natural flavor than bouillon cubes or powder. Common brands like Better Than Bouillon can be found in the soup aisle of grocery stores.

Nopales (singular: nopal) are the edible pads of the prickly pear cactus with a texture similar to okra and a mildly tart flavor. Though spines are typically removed beforehand, some thorns may remain. Scrape them off with a knife or vegetable peeler, and rinse nopal under cold water.

BIRRIA BEEF

½ cup canola–olive oil blend
1 (5-lb) chuck roast
1 large white onion, chopped
¼ cup garlic, chopped
2 cups chopped Roma tomatoes
1 oz dried guajillo chiles
1 oz dried mulato chiles
4 cups water, plus more if needed (divided)
2 Tbsp beef bouillon
1 tsp chopped oregano
1 tsp ground cinnamon
1 tsp kosher salt
1 tsp black pepper
1 tsp ground cumin
1 tsp paprika

Quesabirria Tacos

SERVES 4 Birria's journey from Jalisco's festive gatherings to being a global phenomenon showcases Mexican slow-cooking as an art form rooted in tradition and community. Chiles, garlic, and spices infuse the meat during hours of braising, creating fork-tender beef and its own rich dipping broth, referred to as consomé. "You want that consomé flavorful and vibrant because you're dunking these beautiful tacos in it," says Joey Maggiore.

Birria Beef Heat oil in a large stockpot over high heat.

Once the oil is hot, sear beef on each side for about 3–4 minutes to form a deep brown crust.

Add onions and garlic and cook for 3–4 minutes, or until onions are translucent.

Add tomatoes and dried chiles, stirring everything together to allow tomatoes to break down slightly and the chiles to lightly toast, about 6–8 minutes.

Pour in 1 cup of water to deglaze the pot, scraping up the browned bits stuck to the bottom.

Add the remaining 3 cups of water, ensuring the beef is covered completely, along with all remaining ingredients, and stir to combine. Bring to a boil.

Reduce heat to low, cover, and allow to simmer for 3 hours, or until beef is fork tender. Keep lid slightly ajar, adding more water if necessary to keep the beef submerged.

Remove beef, reserving consomé. Shred beef, discarding any large pieces of fat, and place in a large pot. Strain the broth through a fine-mesh sieve, discarding solids, and pour consomé over the shredded beef.

Meat and consomé can be stored in an airtight container in the refrigerator for up to 5 days.

ASSEMBLY

Birria Beef and consomé (see here)

24 (6-inch) corn tortillas

1½ cups shredded queso menonita or Monterey Jack cheese

1 small white onion, chopped, for garnish

Chopped cilantro, for garnish

4 lime wedges, to serve

Assembly Skim the fat from the birria and transfer fat to a shallow bowl large enough to dip the tortillas in. In a pot over medium-low heat, warm birria and consomé. (If made in advance and birria is chilled, remove fat cap and transfer it to a small pot over low heat. In a separate pot, reheat birria and consomé.)

Heat a nonstick skillet or griddle over medium-high heat.

For each taco, dip 2 tortillas into birria fat, stack together, and place in the skillet (or on the griddle). Sprinkle a layer of queso menonita (or Monterey Jack) on one half of the tortilla and add about ¼ cup of shredded birria on top of cheese.

Fold the double tortilla over to create a taco, pressing gently to seal. Brown the taco for 1–2 minutes on each side, or until the shell becomes crispy and the cheese melts.

Repeat with remaining tortillas, birria, and cheese.

To plate, arrange 3 tacos on each plate. Garnish with onions and cilantro.

Serve with a lime wedge and a small bowl of warm consomé on the side for dipping.

The Mexicano / 155

THE MICK BRASSERIE

Brent Menke, Michael Winneker

Founded by friends John Krause and Brent Menke, The Mick brings a French brasserie vibe to Scottsdale, with a menu shaped by Menke's decade and a half as a chef on luxury yachts traversing the world. "I spent about fifteen years cooking for oligarchs and billionaires on motor yachts," Menke shares. He crafted dishes for clients as notable as U.S. presidents and the British royal family.

The Mick Brasserie features an award-winning wine program led by wine director Jeff Menzer, offering educational tastings, wine dinners, and special events, while the menu reflects French colonial influences, with shareable plates drawing cues from Vietnam to North Africa.

But Menke isn't ready to drop anchor just yet. His love for adventure has inspired a series of luxe food and wine tours across Europe, complete with glamorous villas and gourmet culinary experiences. With a second home in France, where his wife is from, Menke has carved out a new voyage leading food lovers through Provence and Italy. "We've practically become a travel business," he jokes, adding that while he's away, his talented chef de cuisine Michael Winneker keeps the kitchen running at full steam.

"Our guests like to call us an upscale Cheers," says Menke. "We get to know their names, and our team loves engaging with everyone. We have very loyal regulars, but there are always new people who say 'We didn't even know you were here!' I know we're a little hard to find, but once you do, we're going to make you a fan."

▶ Shrimp Tartine with Creole Butter Sauce and Escargot on Brioche with Brie and Bordelaise Sauce

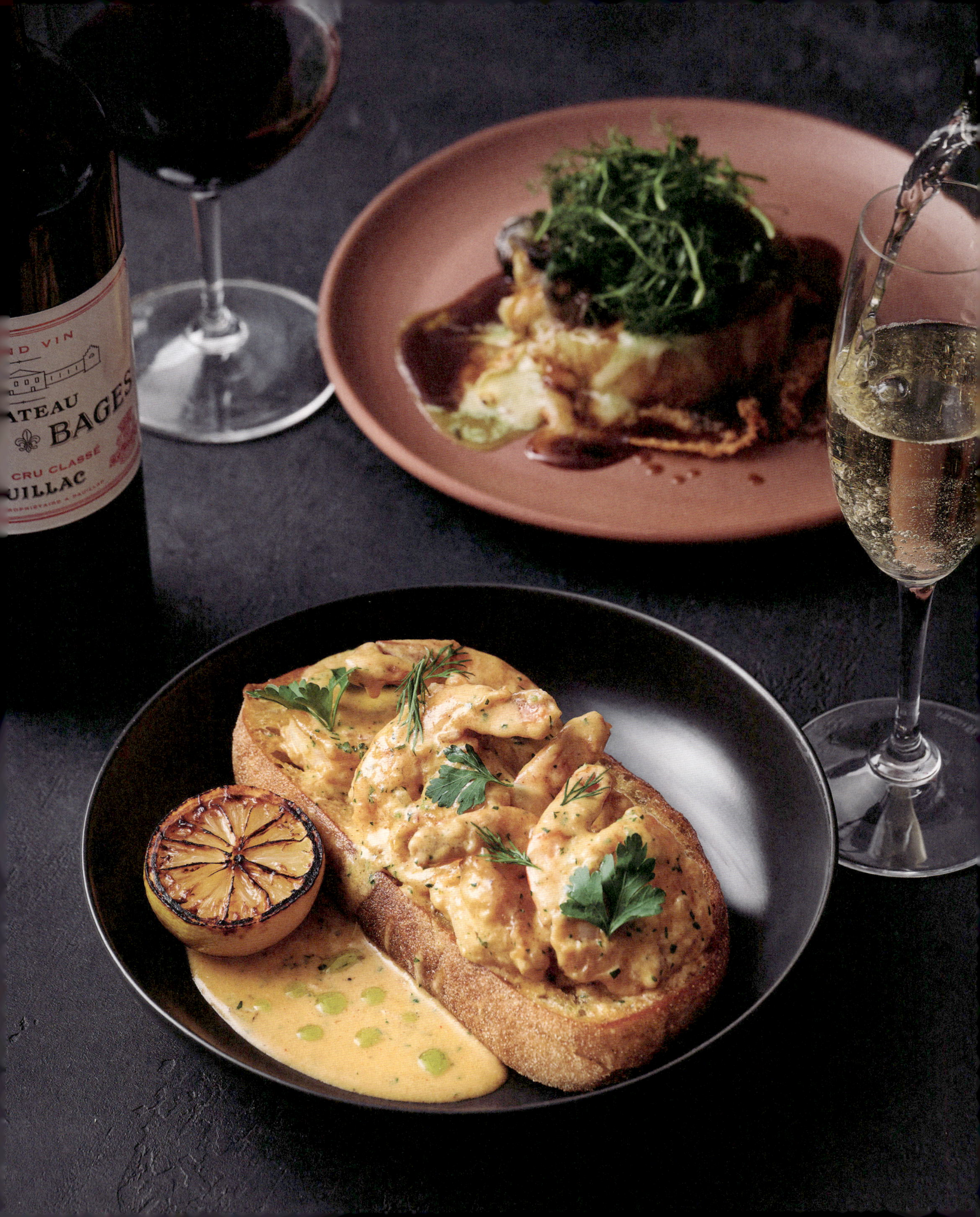
ND VIN
ATEAU
BAGES
CRU CLASSÉ
UILLAC

CREOLE BUTTER

½ lb (2 sticks) unsalted butter, softened
2 large cloves garlic, minced
1 Tbsp chopped thyme leaves
1½ tsp onion powder
1½ tsp granulated garlic
1½ tsp smoked paprika
½ tsp dried oregano
¼ tsp cayenne pepper, or to taste
½ lemon, zested and juiced
2 Tbsp Worcestershire sauce
Kosher salt and black pepper, to taste

SEASONED FLOUR

1 cup all-purpose flour
2 Tbsp kosher or sea salt
1 Tbsp smoked paprika
1 Tbsp granulated garlic
1 Tbsp onion powder
¼ tsp cayenne pepper

Shrimp Tartine with Creole Butter Sauce

SERVES 4 "I think if I were to take this off the menu, people would revolt," jokes Brent Menke of this fan favorite, which he serves with local Noble Bread. Inspired by classic New Orleans barbecue shrimp, his recipe yields extra Creole butter—a happy bonus, since it's also delicious with grilled meats, fish, and vegetables, and stirred into soups and pasta.

Creole Butter Place all ingredients in the bowl of a stand mixer fitted with the whisk attachment (or use a hand mixer). Whip on high speed until light and fluffy and almost doubled in volume, 3–4 minutes.

Leftover butter can be stored in the refrigerator for up to 2 weeks and used to season other dishes.

Seasoned Flour Combine all ingredients in a mixing bowl and mix until well blended.

Assembly Sear lemon halves using hot skillet over medium-high heat for 2–3 minutes, or until marked. Set aside for garnish.

Dredge shrimp in seasoned flour, shaking off any excess.

Heat oil in a stainless steel or nonstick skillet over medium-high heat. Add shrimp and cook for 1 minute per side.

Add garlic and shallots, cooking for 30–45 seconds to soften.

Deglaze pan with a splash of white wine, scraping up any browned bits. Once alcohol has cooked off (about 30 seconds), pour in cream and stir to combine. Simmer, stirring occasionally, until sauce reduces by one-third, 3–5 minutes.

ASSEMBLY

2 lemons, halved

20 extra-large (U13–U15) shrimp, peeled and deveined (about 1½ lbs)

Seasoned Flour (see here)

½ cup olive oil, plus extra for drizzling

4 tsp sliced garlic

4 tsp minced shallots

Dry white wine, for deglazing

4 cups heavy cream

½ cup Creole Butter (see here)

2 Tbsp chopped flat-leaf parsley

Kosher or sea salt, to taste

4 (1-inch-thick) slices ciabatta, toasted

Parsley leaves and dill sprigs, for garnish

Reduce heat to low. Gradually whisk in Creole butter until sauce is emulsified, smooth and thickened. Add the chopped parsley and season with salt to taste.

To serve, place a slice of toasted ciabatta in the center of each plate. Divide shrimp among servings and set on top of ciabatta. Pour sauce over shrimp tartines, and garnish with parsley, dill, and a drizzle of oil. Set a charred lemon half next to each tartine.

HERB BUTTER

1 small clove garlic
1½ tsp kosher salt
¾ tsp chopped flat-leaf parsley
¾ tsp chopped mint
¾ tsp chopped dill
¾ tsp chopped rosemary
¼ lb (1 stick) unsalted butter, softened

BORDELAISE SAUCE

5 lbs veal bones (see Note)
2 Tbsp avocado oil, or beef fat
2 medium white or yellow onions, chopped
4 medium carrots, peeled and chopped
½ cup tomato paste
4 cups Burgundy wine
8 quarts water
4 sprigs thyme
4 sprigs rosemary
1 Tbsp black peppercorns
Kosher salt, to taste

Escargot on Brioche with Brie and Bordelaise Sauce

SERVES 4 "I love escargot," says Brent Menke, "but instead of having snails simply swimming in garlicky butter, I wanted something that was a complete bite." Snails from France's Burgundy region (often labeled as *escargots de Bourgogne*) come cooked in cans and can be found at specialty grocers like AJ's Fine Foods and Whole Foods, or gourmet food shops online.

Herb Butter Place garlic, salt, and herbs in a food processor and blend until finely minced, scraping the sides as needed. Add butter and blend on high until well combined and smooth.

Bordelaise Sauce Preheat oven to 425°F.

Bring a large pot of water to a boil over high heat and add veal bones. Boil for 5 minutes to blanch and remove impurities. Using tongs, remove bones and place on a baking sheet. Roast for 15 minutes, or until golden brown.

While bones are roasting, heat oil (or beef fat) in a large stockpot over medium heat. Add onions and carrots, and cook, stirring occasionally, until caramelized and slightly browned, 10–15 minutes. Stir in tomato paste and cook for an additional 5 minutes.

Pour in wine, scraping up any flavorful bits stuck to the bottom of the pot. Add the water, thyme, rosemary, peppercorns, and roasted veal bones.

Reduce heat to a low simmer and simmer stock for up to 14 hours, skimming off any fat or impurities that float to the top.

Strain stock through a fine-mesh sieve or cheesecloth to remove all solids. Return stock to a clean pot over medium heat and simmer until the sauce reaches a consistency that will coat the back of a spoon (nappe). This process can take several hours, depending on how much liquid is left after straining. Season with salt to taste.

You should have approximately 1 quart of bordelaise sauce. Leftover sauce can be frozen for up to 3 months. When ready to use, thaw the sauce in the refrigerator overnight and reheat gently on the stovetop.

ASSEMBLY

4 (1-inch-thick) slices brioche, cut into 3-inch rounds

2–3 Tbsp unsalted butter, softened

1 (4.4-oz) can cooked Burgundy snails

6 oz double cream brie, cut into ¼-inch-thick slices

4 Tbsp Herb Butter (see here)

Bordelaise Sauce (see here)

Microgreens or frisée lettuce, for garnish

Assembly Preheat oven to 425°F.

Spread each piece of brioche with a thick layer of butter and place on a baking sheet. Arrange 6 snails on top of each one and cover evenly with brie. Bake for 5 minutes, or until brie is golden brown and melted.

To plate, spread 1 tablespoon of herb butter in the center of each dish. Place brioche with escargot and melted brie on top. Spoon a generous amount of bordelaise sauce over and around brioche. Garnish with microgreens or frisée.

NOTE Veal bones provide the necessary gelatin and richness to make a silky bordelaise, a classic French sauce from the Bordeaux region. Check with local purveyors including The Meat Market, Arcadia Meat Market, and Nelson's Meat + Fish (page 166) for sourcing veal bones, or ask your favorite butcher to special order them.

MIRACLE MILE DELI

Josh Garcia

A Phoenix institution since 1949, Miracle Mile Deli was born when Brooklyn native Jack Grodzinsky brought East Coast flavors to the desert. In 1965, the deli expanded from its original McDowell Road and Sixteenth Street location to the Chris-Town Mall, where busboy George Garcia met Jill Grodzinsky, Jack's daughter. The two eventually married, and George became president of the family business. Today, the Garcias' son Josh represents the third generation in continuing the family's legacy. "I started working in the business when I was eleven, serving coffee on Saturday mornings, standing on a milk crate because I couldn't see over the counter," he recalls.

In 2015, Miracle Mile Deli relocated to its current location at Sixteenth Street and Campbell Avenue, where it maintains the tradition of hearty meals served with a side of family pride. Here, crowds still clamor for family recipes handed down through generations, such as Hungarian stuffed cabbage (page 163), beef stew, and matzo ball soup. However, the undisputed stars are corned beef, brisket, and navel pastrami, cut from the richly marbled belly instead of the more common brisket. "We sell over 4,000 pounds of pastrami a month," says Garcia with well-earned pride.

But it's not just recipes that have stood the test of time. With two head chefs each celebrating over thirty-seven years and an employee turnover rate below 8%, Miracle Mile has mastered the recipe for success. "We take care of our employees and they enjoy being a part of the Miracle Mile family," says Garcia. "In turn, that gives the customer a great experience that they want to come back and enjoy again."

STUFFED CABBAGE FILLING

2 Tbsp vegetable oil
1 cup finely chopped yellow onion
2 cloves garlic, minced
3 lbs ground beef (80/20)
1 cup cooked white rice
1 tsp paprika
2 tsp kosher salt
1 tsp black pepper
4 large eggs, beaten

HUNGARIAN SAUCE

2½ cups water
¼ cup canned tomato purée
¼ cup diced tomatoes
3 tsp paprika

ASSEMBLY

1–2 large heads green cabbage (yielding 12–15 large cabbage leaves)
Stuffed Cabbage Filling (see here)
Hungarian Sauce (see here)

Hungarian Stuffed Cabbage

SERVES 6 A cherished recipe that spans seven decades and three generations, these hearty cabbage rolls stuffed with a half-pound of filling carry on the tradition of Josh Garcia's grandfather, who learned from his parents. "They were Russian immigrants, but had some Hungarian roots as well," Garcia explains. "It's a legacy that we serve every single day."

Stuffed Cabbage Filling Heat oil in a skillet over medium heat. Add onions and cook for 5 minutes, or until onions are soft and translucent. Add garlic and cook for another minute. Remove from heat.

In a large mixing bowl, combine remaining ingredients with sautéed onions and garlic. Set aside.

Hungarian Sauce In a mixing bowl, whisk together all ingredients until smooth. Set aside.

Assembly Preheat oven to 350°F.

Fill a large pot with water and bring to a boil over high heat.

With a paring knife, remove the core from the cabbage heads. Add heads of cabbage, stem-end up, to boiling water. (Depending on size, you may have to cook one at a time.) Cook for approximately 8 minutes, or until largest leaves start to peel away. Using tongs, gently remove cabbage leaves one by one as they separate from the head. Set leaves on a cutting board or baking sheet to cool. Depending on the size of the cabbages, you will have 12–15 large leaves. Once cooled, pat leaves dry and set aside.

Lay out 1 large cabbage leaf (if the leaves are smaller, you may need 2–3 per roll to fully enclose the filling). Shape ½ pound (about 1 cup) of ground beef mixture into a log shape. Place in center of cabbage leaf. Tuck sides of cabbage leaf inwards and roll, placing stuffed cabbage roll seam-side down in a deep baking pan large enough to fit 6 rolls. Repeat with remaining meat and cabbage leaves.

Pour Hungarian sauce over cabbage rolls and cover with foil. Bake for approximately 75 minutes, or until meat is thoroughly cooked. Serve immediately.

1½ lbs ground beef (80/20)
Kosher salt and black pepper, to taste
1 lb sliced navel pastrami (see Note)
8 slices pepper Jack cheese
4 Signature Kaiser Rolls from Miracle Mile Deli, or your favorite hamburger buns
2–3 Tbsp butter (optional)

4 leaves green leaf lettuce
2 tomatoes, sliced
½ red onion, cut into rounds
½ cup of your favorite Thousand Island dressing
4 kosher dill pickle spears, to serve
French fries, to serve

The Mile Burger

SERVES 4 "We wanted to create a burger that featured one of our biggest staples that people can't find anywhere else," explains Josh Garcia. Topped with lettuce, tomato, onions, pepper Jack, and Thousand Island dressing, this mile-high mashup marries juicy ground beef with navel pastrami, a more luxurious cut than traditional brisket, for an only-in-Phoenix original.

Assembly Form ground beef into 4 patties. Season with salt and pepper.

Divide pastrami into 4 equal portions.

Heat a large skillet, flat-top griddle, or grill to medium-high. Cook burgers for approximately 3–4 minutes a side, depending on desired temperature. After the first flip, mound pastrami portions directly on the grilling surface. Top each of the burgers and the pastrami mounds with a slice of pepper Jack cheese.

If you would like the buns toasted, butter both sides and toast while cheese is melting. Prepare buns by topping each bottom bun with a lettuce leaf, followed by 2 tomato slices and slices of red onion.

When cheese melts, stack pastrami and cheese on top of burger.

Place burger with pastrami and cheese on top of the prepared bun, then spread 1–2 teaspoons of Thousand Island dressing on the top bun and set on top.

To garnish, skewer pickle spear onto the burger, or serve on the side.

NOTE Navel pastrami is made from the navel cut of beef located near the belly. Unlike traditional pastrami, which often uses brisket, navel pastrami is known for its rich marbling. Miracle Mile Deli exclusively serves navel pastrami, which is available for purchase by the pound for this recipe.

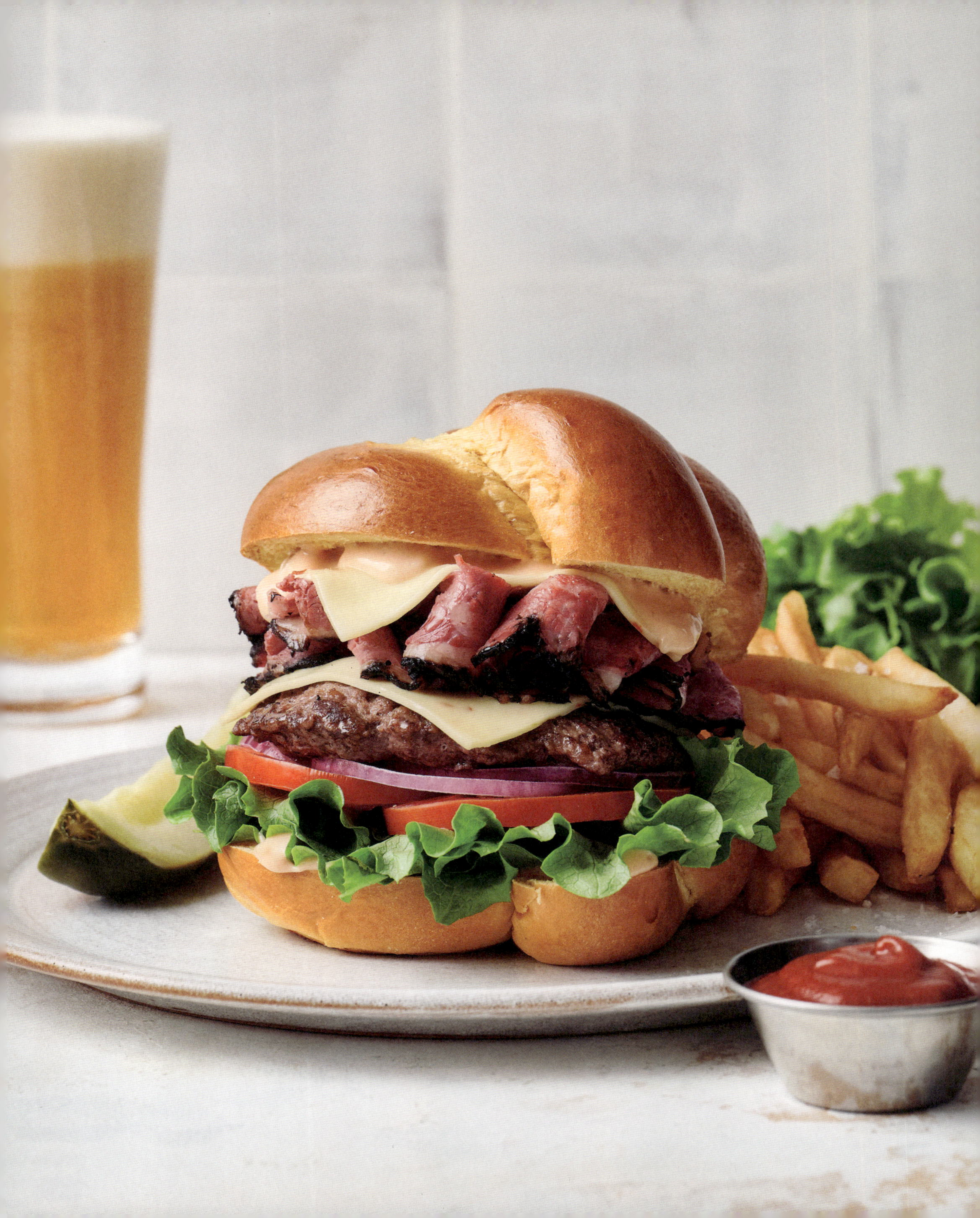

NELSON'S MEAT + FISH

Christopher Nelson

Behind the counter at Nelson's Meat + Fish, founder Christopher Nelson has assembled a team of former chefs who share their expertise with every customer. With locations in Arcadia and North Scottsdale and a thriving wholesale operation, Nelson emphasizes how "hospitality is super important to us. Food is a thread that connects us all and I want to hearken back to those days of personal connection and leave people feeling great about the investment they're making in our seafood, meat, and provisions."

Rather than offering the same seafood selection year-round, Nelson's follows nature's calendar, featuring delicacies like bay scallops, soft shell crabs, wild salmon, and Alaskan halibut at their peak freshness. Everything in the ready-to-go coolers is made in-house, from rémoulade to coleslaw. Shelves are stacked with premium tinned seafoods for purchase, which can also be enjoyed on the patio (along with rotating features like crab cake sandwiches, poke bowls, and award-winning lobster rolls). "Pick out your tins and we'll create a custom platter that comes with Nice Buns bread, European butter, and Barnacle Foods Kelp Chili Crisp out of Alaska," says Nelson.

He's just as proud of the meat and provision programs, which source "heritage pork from Salmon Creek Farms and 100% Japanese bloodline Wagyu from Terra Farm. We also carry small producers that have received Good Food Awards or are part of the Slow Food movement, like Italy's Ritrovo olive oils and legumes and Marsh Hen Mill's Carolina Gold rice, peas, and grits."

"I'm very proud of what we have," says Nelson. "I'm grateful every day for our guests and the team that my wife Danielle and I employ. I feel blessed."

3 lbs Nelson's hot smoked salmon
⅓ cup finely chopped chives
3 Tbsp finely chopped shallots
1 lemon, zested and juiced
2¼ cups sour cream
2¼ cups mayonnaise
1½ Tbsp Worcestershire sauce

2 tsp Tabasco, plus more to taste
1½ tsp kosher salt, plus more to taste
½ tsp cracked black pepper, plus more to taste
Crackers, toasted baguette slices, or vegetable crudités, to serve

Smoked Salmon Dip

SERVES 8–10 "This recipe is actually my mother's," Christopher Nelson shares, "though living in the Florida Keys, she made it with smoked mahi mahi." His rendition uses Faroe Island salmon belly, which he hot smokes for forty-five minutes to create a rich, creamy spread that's brightened with citrus and fresh herbs. "It's a bestseller," he adds with a smile.

Assembly Prepare the salmon by peeling off the skin and cutting away the bloodline (the dark, reddish-brown strip of flesh that runs along the center), if necessary. Break salmon into chunks.

Place all ingredients into a stand mixer fitted with the paddle attachment (or use a hand mixer). Whip on medium speed until the dip is smooth but still slightly chunky. Taste and adjust seasoning with Tabasco, salt, and pepper.

Serve with crackers, toasted baguette slices, or vegetable crudités.

Smoked salmon dip can be made up to 3 days ahead and stored in the refrigerator in an airtight container.

COOKED OCTOPUS
1 (4- to 5-lb) whole octopus
Kosher salt
1–2 large lemons

LEMON VINAIGRETTE
1 clove garlic, chopped
1 small shallot, chopped
1 lemon, juiced
1½ Tbsp red wine vinegar
1½ cups extra-virgin olive oil

Octopus Salad

SERVES 4–6 "I was in Boston for a seafood expo and fell in love with an octopus salad I had at Eataly," Christopher Nelson recalls. Inspired by that visit, his version delivers a parsley-flecked salad of tender octopus tossed with fennel, celery, and red onion in a vibrant lemon vinaigrette. For a time-saving alternative, Nelson offers a shortcut: "You can buy our cooked octopus in the case and make this salad in fifteen minutes."

Cooked Octopus Fill a large stockpot with enough water to fully submerge the octopus, ensuring the pot does not overflow due to displacement. For every gallon of water, add 2–3 tablespoons of salt and the peel of 1 lemon, cut into wide strips.

Over medium heat, bring to a very light simmer. Water should be barely moving, with tiny bubbles occasionally rising to the surface.

Hold the octopus by the head and carefully lower it tentacles-first into the pot, gently twisting the head so the tentacles splay outward under the water.

Reducing heat if necessary, maintain a gentle simmer for 2 hours, or until flesh is easily pierced with a knife.

Allow octopus to cool. Discard head and body and transfer tentacles to the refrigerator to chill.

Lemon Vinaigrette In a blender, combine garlic, shallots, lemon juice, and red wine vinegar. Purée at medium speed until garlic and shallots are broken down into a smooth consistency. With the blender still running, gradually pour in oil in a slow, steady stream. This process allows the oil to incorporate smoothly and fully with the lemon mixture, creating a thick, creamy emulsion. Continue blending until vinaigrette is fully emulsified. Transfer to an airtight container.

Vinaigrette is best used when made, but can be stored in the refrigerator for up to 3 days. Leftover vinaigrette can be used to dress salads, as a marinade, and to season roasted vegetables and seafood.

ASSEMBLY

2 lbs cooked octopus tentacles, sliced on the bias into thin medallions (see here)

2 large stalks celery, thinly sliced on the bias

1 medium red onion, thinly sliced

1 medium bulb fennel, thinly sliced on the bias

1 bunch flat-leaf parsley leaves, chopped fine

½ cup Lemon Vinaigrette (see here)

½ tsp Chimayó chile powder, or cayenne pepper (see Note)

Kosher salt, to taste

5 turns cracked black pepper (½ tsp)

Assembly (see Note) In a large mixing bowl, combine octopus, celery, onions, fennel, and parsley. Drizzle lemon vinaigrette over the salad. Be careful not to add too much vinaigrette at once; you want the salad to be well-coated but not overly wet. Gently toss to ensure all ingredients are evenly coated.

Season with Chimayó chile powder (or cayenne pepper), salt, and pepper. Taste and adjust seasoning. Serve immediately.

NOTE Octopus salad is best served when freshly made, but will keep for up to 3 days in the refrigerator. If prepared ahead, allow to come to room temperature and toss to re-emulsify the vinaigrette.

Chimayó chiles are grown only in the village of Chimayó in northern New Mexico from heirloom seeds passed down through generations. Sun-dried, they are ground into a bright red powder with a distinctive rich, sweet heat and earthy complexity. Look for Chimayó chile powder at retailers specializing in Southwest ingredients, specialty spice shops like Santa Cruz Chili & Spice Company, and online. If unavailable, substitute with cayenne pepper.

170 / Nelson's Meat + Fish

Octopus Salad

OSTERIA MIA

Mario Rana

"**I remember working** on the flat top cooking burgers in my parents' restaurant and thinking, one day I want to open my own place," reminisces Mario Rana. That wish came true, and he is now chef-owner of the Italian restaurant Osteria Mia, named for his daughter; the tropical-themed Tiki Star; and The Stetson Social, where global flavors meet comfort food.

But it all started with Osteria Mia, which emerged during the uncertain days of the COVID-19 shutdowns. While many restaurants were shuttering their doors, Rana took a bold gamble by launching with curbside service. The neighborhood was undeterred by the timing, however, and the response was overwhelming. "We were so busy, I had to apologize for how long orders were taking," he recalls, grateful for his customers' enthusiasm.

Today, that same community fills the light-filled space, where a wraparound patio and lively bar set the stage. Front and center is a Rosito Bisani pizza oven, imported from Italy, where wood-fired pizzas like the Funghi topped with Gorgonzola, cremini mushrooms, and a drizzle of truffle oil emerge with puffy blistered crusts. The from-scratch menu is showcased in plates of just-baked focaccia, crispy hand-pulled mozzarella triangles, and sandwiches made with warm puccia bread. Fresh pasta made in-house transforms into showstoppers like lupara (page 174), a Rana family favorite, and pasta fra diavolo with squid ink tagliatelle swimming in a white wine tomato sauce and an ocean's bounty of calamari, mussels, shrimp, and clams.

The community's support continues to be key to the restaurant's success. "Owning my own restaurant has always been my dream," says Rana, "and I'm grateful that the neighborhood supported us from the beginning."

RABBIT RAGU

1 (3–4 lb) rabbit, cut into 8 pieces (see Note)
2 Tbsp kosher salt
1 Tbsp black pepper
½ cup extra-virgin olive oil
2 medium carrots, finely diced
2 stalks celery, finely diced
1 yellow onion, finely diced
8 cloves garlic, minced
1 cup dry white wine
½ cup tomato paste
2 (28-oz) cans whole peeled San Marzano tomatoes
2 cups water
3 bay leaves
1 Tbsp fresh thyme leaves
1 tsp chili flakes

ASSEMBLY

1 lb pappardelle pasta
Rabbit Ragu (see here)
Shaved Pecorino Romano, for garnish
Chopped flat-leaf parsley, for garnish

Pappardelle with Rabbit Ragu

SERVES 4–6 "My parents are from Puglia, and this is a southern Italian dish that's one of our family favorites," says Mario Rana. A staple of the region's countryside, this rustic ragu involves slowly cooking rabbit with aromatic vegetables and wine to create a rich and hearty sauce. Though the braise takes two hours, the preparation is relatively simple, making it an ideal dish for gathering loved ones around the table.

Rabbit Ragu Pat rabbit pieces dry and season with salt and pepper. Heat oil in a large heavy-bottomed saucepan over medium-high heat. Add rabbit pieces and sear until browned on all sides. Remove seared rabbit and set aside.

To the same pan, add carrots, celery, onions, and garlic. Cook until vegetables are tender, 6–8 minutes. Return rabbit to pan and add white wine. Increase heat to a vigorous simmer and cook until reduced by half, 3–4 minutes.

Stir in remaining ingredients and bring to a boil. Reduce heat and simmer, covered, for 2 hours, stirring occasionally. Discard bay leaves.

Use tongs to remove rabbit from pan. Remove bones and shred meat. Return shredded rabbit to pan and keep warm.

Assembly Bring water to a boil in a large pot over high heat. Cook pasta according to package instructions until al dente.

Drain and add pasta to rabbit ragu. Toss with sauce to coat and cook for 1 minute.

To serve, divide among pasta bowls and garnish with Pecorino Romano and parsley.

NOTE Check with your favorite butcher shop for rabbit in stock or for special order. You can also find rabbit, typically frozen, at Asian markets. To portion rabbit (known as jointing), divide it into sections such as the hind legs, front legs, and back (cut in two). If you're buying from a butcher, they can do this for you.

MARINARA

- ½ cup extra-virgin olive oil
- ½ cup finely diced carrots
- ½ cup finely diced onions
- ½ cup finely diced celery
- 8 cloves garlic, minced
- 2 (28-oz) cans whole peeled San Marzano tomatoes
- 1 cup water
- 1 Tbsp kosher salt, or to taste
- 1 tsp black pepper, or to taste
- 8 basil leaves, cut into chiffonade

ASSEMBLY

- ¼ cup olive oil
- ½ lb ground Italian sausage
- 8 oz cremini mushrooms, sliced (3 cups)
- ½ cup dry red wine
- 1½ cups Marinara (see here)
- ½ cup heavy cream
- 1 Tbsp chopped Calabrian chiles, or to taste (see Note)
- ¾ lb rigatoni pasta
- Kosher salt and black pepper, to taste
- Freshly grated Pecorino Romano, for garnish
- Minced parsley, for garnish

NOTE Calabrian chiles, native to Italy's Calabria region, are moderately spicy small red peppers known for their fruity, slightly smoky flavor. Most commonly sold preserved in olive oil or as a crushed paste, they add flavor and heat to dishes like pasta, pizza, and antipasti. Look for jarred whole or chopped Calabrian chiles in oil at Italian markets, specialty grocers such as AJ's Fine Foods and Whole Foods, or online.

Lupara

SERVES 2–4 This dish is named after the lupara ("wolf-shot"), a sawed-off shotgun used by Sicilian farmers to protect their livestock. "The rigatoni is said to resemble the barrels of the shotgun," explains Mario Rana. "At Osteria Mia, we make it with ground fennel sausage, mushrooms, Calabrian chiles, a creamy marinara, and a splash of red wine, and it's one of our most popular dishes."

Marinara Heat oil in a stockpot over medium heat. Add carrots, onions, celery, and garlic. Cook, stirring occasionally, until vegetables are tender, 6–8 minutes. Add tomatoes, water, salt, and pepper. Bring to a boil, reduce heat, and simmer for 20 minutes, stirring occasionally. Using an immersion blender, purée sauce. (If using a stand blender, don't fill more than halfway and purée in batches to avoid steam buildup, then return sauce to pot.) Add basil and simmer for another 25 minutes, stirring occasionally. Adjust salt and pepper to taste.

Leftover marinara can be refrigerated for up to 5 days or frozen for up to 3 months.

Assembly Heat oil in a large heavy-bottomed sauté pan or pot over medium heat. Add sausage and brown, breaking it up with a wooden spoon or spatula, until cooked through, 7–10 minutes.

Remove sausage using a slotted spoon and set aside. Add mushrooms to same pan and sauté until tender. Return sausage to the pan and increase heat to high. Pour in wine to deglaze, scraping up any browned bits from the bottom of the pan. Bring to a boil, then reduce heat and simmer for 7–8 minutes, or until liquid is mostly evaporated. Stir in marinara, cream, and chiles, then bring back to a simmer and cook until thickened, 5–7 minutes.

Meanwhile, cook pasta to al dente according to package instructions. Drain pasta and add to the pan of sauce. Toss and cook for 1 minute. Season to taste with salt and pepper.

To serve, divide among 4 pasta bowls and sprinkle with Pecorino Romano and parsley.

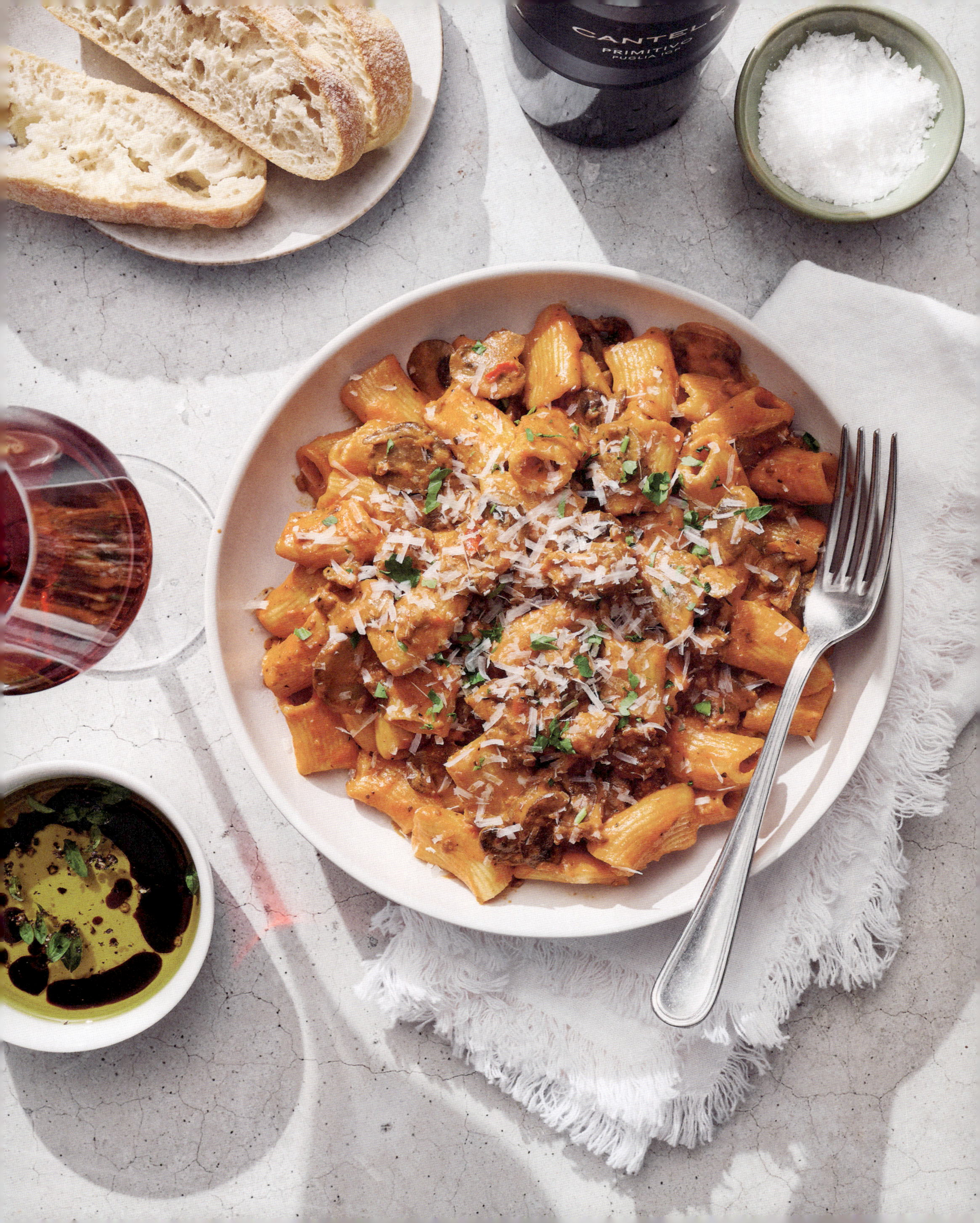
CANTELE
PRIMITIVO
PUGLIA IGP

PA'LA

Jason Alford

"**When you're walking** through the bustle of downtown and step into Pa'La, it's like entering a different world," says chef-owner Jason Alford. "It's sleek and dark, and if you want something more romantic, you can head upstairs for live jazz."

In 2021, Pa'La opened its doors downtown as an expansion of the original Pa'La, a beloved bungalow on Twenty-Fourth Street that gained a loyal following for its wood-fired simplicity and then-owner Claudio Urciuoli's Mediterranean dishes. The downtown location takes things up a notch, delivering the same thoughtful ethos but on a grander, urban stage.

At its heart beats a dual wood-fired system with an Italian oven and a robata grill reflecting Alford's Japanese fine-dining background. Before Pa'La, Alford spent ten years as executive chef at Roka Akor, leading the Japanese steakhouse from its Scottsdale origins to new locations in Chicago, Houston, and San Francisco. "Both cuisines have many similarities in highlighting ingredients," says Alford, whose "transparent sourcing" philosophy drives the daily-changing menu. Premium seafood is flown in by Wulf's Fish and Hook to Fork, prized A5 Takamori Wagyu makes its way from Japan, and local purveyors augment the menu, with contributions like Copper State's grass-fed beef and Steadfast Farm's locally harvested vegetables.

"If it's your first time, trust us with omakase, our tasting menu," Alford recommends. "That way you can experience all the aspects of Pa'La, from our sourcing of seafood and local beef, to vegetables that are a highlight instead of an afterthought. It's the best way to showcase all that we do."

POLENTA

4 cups water

2 cups polenta, such as McClendon's Select or Bob's Red Mill

Pinch of sea salt

2 Tbsp extra-virgin olive oil, plus more for oiling pan

ASSEMBLY

Polenta (see here)

1–2 Tbsp extra-virgin olive oil, plus more to garnish

4 links hot Italian sausages, such as The Meat Market

1 (28-oz) can crushed Bianco DiNapoli tomatoes (see Note)

Sea salt, to taste

Dried oregano, for garnish

NOTE Bianco DiNapoli tomatoes are a collaboration between Chris Bianco, a James Beard Award–winning local chef, and Rob DiNapoli. These organic tomatoes, seasoned with sea salt and fresh basil, are available at Bianco's restaurants, local grocery stores, Whole Foods, specialty markets like Sphinx Date Co. Palm & Pantry and Arcadia Meat Market, and online.

Seared Polenta with Tomatoes and Sausage

SERVES 4 Jason Alford offers this recipe as a homage to Pa'La's original founder, Claudio Urciuoli. "It's been a classic since the Twenty-Fourth Street location first opened," he explains. "Before I started working with Claudio, this was already one of my favorites, and it's a part of our roots."

Polenta In a pot over high heat, bring water to a boil. Add polenta, whisking to avoid lumps. Reduce heat to medium and cook, stirring frequently, until polenta is tender and thickened, about 10 minutes. Stir in salt and oil.

Using a spatula, spread cooked polenta into an 8- × 8-inch baking dish or pan brushed with oil. Allow to cool completely at room temperature, about 1 hour. Cover and chill in the refrigerator for at least 2 hours or overnight.

Assembly Cut polenta into 4 equal squares.

Heat oil in a large skillet over medium-high heat. Working in batches if necessary, sear polenta squares for 2 minutes on each side, or until golden brown. Remove and set aside.

Add sausages to the same skillet and cook, turning occasionally, until they reach an internal temperature of 150°F, 4–6 minutes. Remove and set aside. (They will continue to cook from residual heat.)

Reduce heat to medium-low and add crushed tomatoes to skillet, stirring occasionally until warmed through. Season to taste with salt.

For each serving, place 1 square of polenta on a plate. Slice 1 sausage diagonally and arrange on top of polenta. Spoon ½ cup of tomato sauce (or more to taste) over each serving of polenta and sausage. Drizzle with oil and garnish with oregano.

ALEPPO CHILI CRISP

½ cup extra-virgin olive oil
3 shallots, minced
6 cloves garlic, minced
¼ cup Aleppo chili flakes (see Note)
1 Tbsp white sesame seeds
1 Tbsp light brown sugar
½ cup tamari

ASSEMBLY

4 medium Japanese sweet potatoes
4 pinches sea salt, plus more to taste
Extra-virgin olive oil, for brushing
Aleppo Chili Crisp (see here)
Sesame seeds, for garnish
Cilantro leaves, for garnish
Nori (seaweed) powder, for garnish (optional)

NOTE The Aleppo pepper, named after the Syrian city of Aleppo, has a flavor profile that combines fruity and raisin-like notes with a moderate level of heat. Look for Aleppo chili flakes in the spice aisle of your local grocery store, at specialty spice shops, and online.

Japanese Sweet Potatoes with Aleppo Chili Crisp

SERVES 4 Jason Alford originally created this dish for a wine dinner at Roka Akor, and it quickly became a staple at his own Thanksgiving table. "I took it off the menu once, but people kept asking 'Where's the sweet potato?' so now it's here to stay," he says. "The chili crisp is delicious on anything where you want to add something crunchy-spicy-sweet, from a veggie rice bowl to grilled steak."

Aleppo Chili Crisp Heat a skillet over medium-low heat. Add oil, shallots, and garlic and bring to a simmer. Stirring frequently to prevent settling on the bottom and burning, sauté until shallots and garlic are almost crisp and starting to turn golden, 3–4 minutes.

Add chili flakes and sesame seeds and simmer for 2–3 more minutes, stirring frequently, until shallots and garlic are fully crisp. Immediately remove from heat, but keep stirring to prevent burning from residual heat.

Allow to cool for 20 minutes. Stir in brown sugar and tamari until combined.

This chili crisp can be stored in the refrigerator for up to 3 months and used to season meats, seafood, and vegetables, or drizzled over noodles, rice, and eggs.

Assembly Preheat oven to 400°F.

Scrub and rinse sweet potatoes, then pat dry. Wrap each sweet potato in foil with a pinch of salt. Place directly on rack and bake for 45 minutes to 1 hour, or until soft when pierced with a fork. Remove from foil and allow to cool to room temperature. Baked potatoes can be made the night before and stored in the refrigerator.

When ready to serve, slice each potato into ½-inch medallions, brush with oil on each side, and sprinkle with salt.

Heat skillet on medium-high heat (or turn on broiler or grill). Sear (or broil or grill) until lightly caramelized, 2–3 minutes per side.

For each serving, overlap potato slices on a plate and generously spoon Aleppo chili crisp over the top. Garnish with sesame seeds, cilantro, and nori powder (if using).

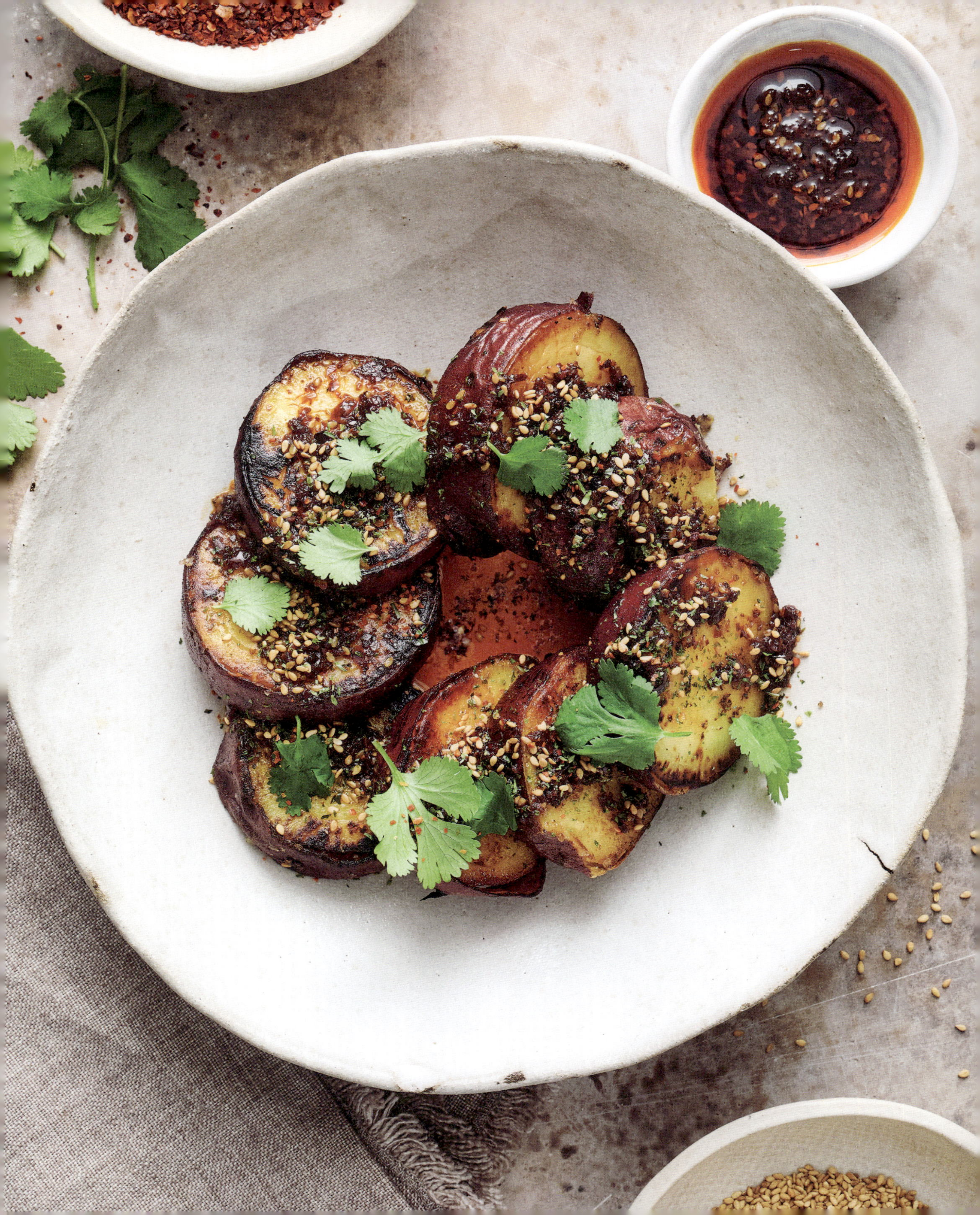

PARADISE VALLEY BURGER CO.

Bret Shapiro

With two locations in the Valley, Paradise Valley Burger Co. isn't your average burger joint. Sure, you order burgers, fries, and milkshakes at the counter, but here the classics get a serious upgrade, like their wildly popular Brûlée Burger. Yes, you read that right. It's topped with candied bacon, Havarti, a fried egg, and a bun glazed with a crispy caramelized sugar shell.

"I remember when I first opened and people would read the menu. They'd say, 'Dude, these things are crazy.' To me everything sounded normal," says owner Bret Shapiro with a chuckle. In addition to staples like the Brûlée Burger, specials rotate every two weeks. "People actually get a little pushy, asking when a burger is going to come back," he says. Such as the BBB with barbecued bacon and blueberry cream cheese, or the Thanksgiving burger topped with sweet potato gravy, green chili corn muffin stuffing, and cranberry-apple relish. "They've both become traditions," admits Shapiro.

But the creativity doesn't stop there. Milkshake flavors like bourbon pecan pie or fried ice cream (page 181) have become cult favorites, blending nostalgia and dessert into one sweet, crunchy sip. And if you think sides are just as important, you're in for a treat. A sixteen-spice blend elevates potato fries to must-try territory, while the jalapeño fries, paired with a brown sugar and truffle ketchup, might just steal the show.

"I've always liked pushing boundaries and stacking flavors," says Shapiro. "I'll eat something that's delicious and think, what if we add this?"

- 2½ quarts vanilla bean ice cream
- 3 cups half and half cream
- 2 cups frozen organic strawberries, stems removed
- ½ cup raw Arizona honey, plus more for garnish
- 1 Tbsp Pillsbury strawberry frosting
- 1½ tsp ground cinnamon, plus more for garnish
- 1 cup cornflakes, plus more for garnish
- Whipped cream, for garnish

Fried Ice Cream Shake

SERVES 4 "As a New York transplant in Arizona, I discovered the zen that is fried ice cream and it became one of my favorite things," says Bret Shapiro. "I took a strawberry shake and added all those elements—the cinnamon, honey, and crispiness of the cornflakes. It's perfect."

Assembly In a blender, blend ice cream, half and half, frozen strawberries, honey, frosting, and cinnamon on high for 1 minute until completely blended.

Add cornflakes and briefly pulse for 3 seconds to maintain some chunky texture.

Pour milkshake into 16-ounce glasses and garnish with whipped cream, honey, cinnamon, and cornflakes. Serve with a straw.

Paradise Valley Burger Co.

Fried Ice Cream Shake and Cinco Diablo Burgers

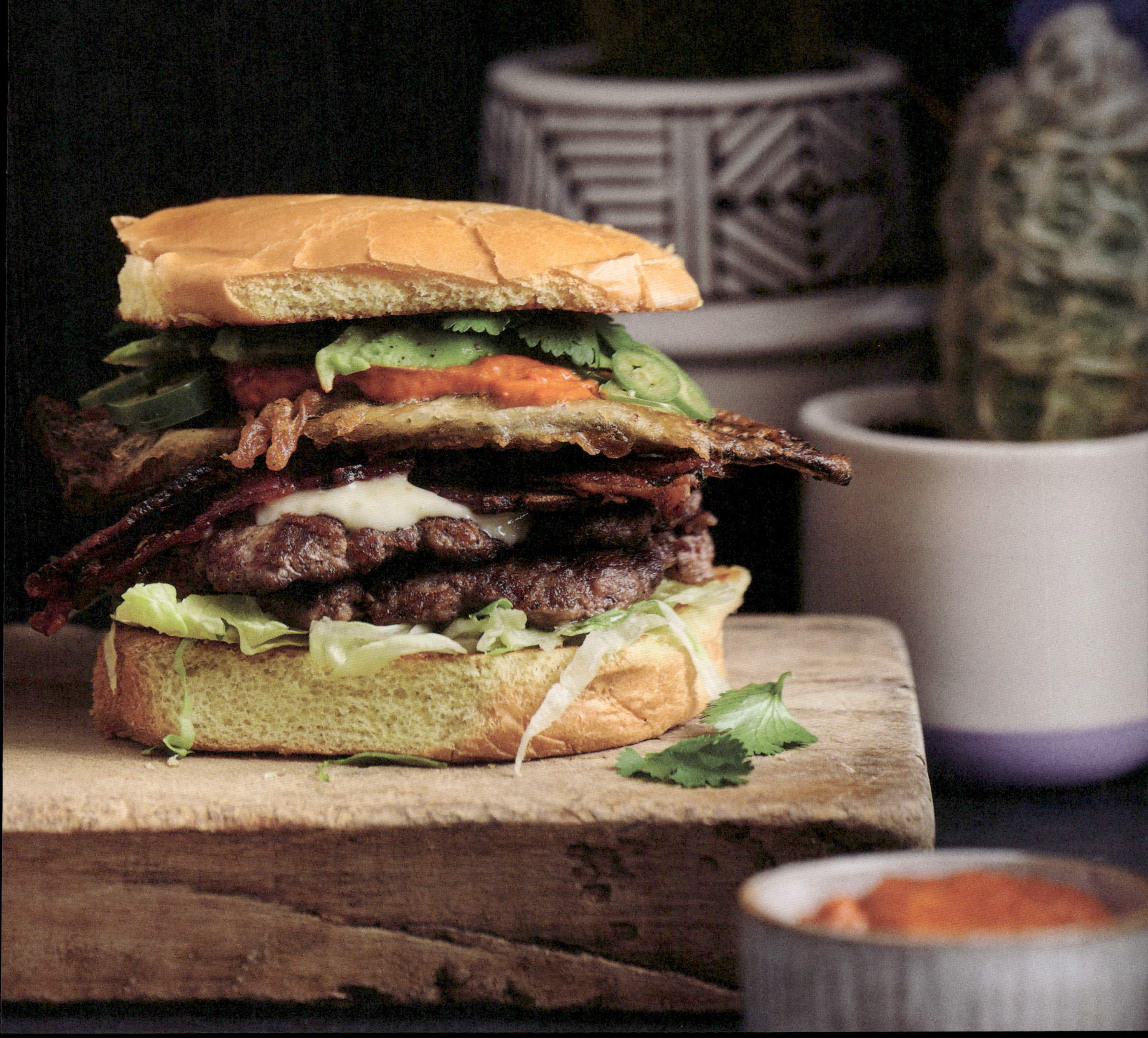

PICKLED SERRANOS
1 cup thinly sliced serrano chiles
⅓ cup blanco tequila
¼ cup granulated sugar
2 tsp kosher salt
1 lime, juiced

FRESNO CHILE PESTO
8 Fresno chiles, halved lengthwise, stemmed, and seeded
1 red bell pepper, halved lengthwise, stemmed, and seeded
½ cup extra-virgin olive oil
¼ cup chopped basil
2 Tbsp freshly grated Parmesan
Kosher salt and black pepper, to taste

JALAPEÑO RANCH DRESSING
6 jalapeños, halved lengthwise, stemmed and seeded
1 Tbsp olive oil
2 cups heavy cream
1 cup mayonnaise
1 Tbsp granulated garlic
1 Tbsp granulated onion
Kosher salt and black pepper, to taste

Cinco Diablo Burgers

SERVES 6 A favorite of Food Network star Guy Fieri's, this burger started out as a special but became so popular it earned a permanent spot. "It was originally for Cinco de Mayo," says Bret Shapiro. "I wanted to use five different chiles without making it too spicy." The result is a perfect blend of heat and savory, with ingredients like chipotle-glazed bacon, Fresno chile pesto, and creamy jalapeño ranch.

Pickled Serranos In a mixing bowl, combine all ingredients, stirring until sugar and salt are dissolved.

Transfer to an airtight container and refrigerate for at least 24 hours. Pickled serranos will keep for 10 days.

Fresno Chile Pesto Preheat oven to 450°F.

In a large bowl, toss chiles and bell peppers with oil to coat. Arrange in a single layer, skin-side up, on a sheet pan.

Roast for 10–15 minutes, or until skins are blistered. Allow to cool.

Transfer roasted chiles and peppers to a blender or food processor, add basil and Parmesan, and blend on medium speed until smooth. Season with salt and black pepper to taste.

Pesto can be made ahead and stored in the refrigerator for up to 5 days.

Jalapeño Ranch Dressing Preheat oven to 450°F.

In a large bowl, toss jalapeños with oil to coat. Arrange in a single layer, skin-side up, on a sheet pan.

Roast for 10–15 minutes, or until skins are blistered. Allow to cool.

Transfer to a blender or food processor. On low speed, blend with cream, mayonnaise, garlic, and onion. Increase speed to high and blend for an additional 3 seconds, being careful not to whip the cream. Season to taste with salt and pepper.

Dressing can be stored in the refrigerator for up to 1 week.

/ Paradise Valley Burger Co.

CHIPOTLE BACON

6 strips thick-cut bacon

½ cup canned chipotle peppers in adobo sauce, blended into a purée (see Note)

Cooking spray or neutral oil, for greasing

BEER-BATTERED POBLANO CHILES

3 large poblano chiles, halved lengthwise, stemmed and seeded

1 Tbsp olive oil

Kosher salt and black pepper, to taste

2–3 quarts vegetable oil, for frying

2 cups all-purpose flour, divided

1½ cups light beer

ASSEMBLY

1½ lbs ground beef (80/20)

Kosher salt and black pepper, to taste

6 brioche buns, trimmed into squares

½ cup (1 stick) butter, melted

½ head iceberg lettuce, thinly sliced

Jalapeño Ranch Dressing (see here)

Chipotle Bacon (see here)

Beer-Battered Poblano Chiles (see here)

Fresno Chile Pesto (see here)

1½ avocados, thinly sliced

Pickled Serranos (see here)

¼ cup cilantro leaves

NOTE Canned chipotle peppers in adobo sauce are dried, smoked jalapeños packed in a tomato-based sauce with garlic, vinegar, and spices. You'll find them in the international aisle or Mexican foods section of grocery stores, at Mexican markets, and online.

Chipotle Bacon Preheat oven to 450°F.

In a bowl, coat bacon with chipotle purée.

Place bacon on a greased baking sheet and bake for 10 minutes, or until bacon just begins to blacken. Remove from oven and allow to cool.

Cut each strip in half and set aside.

Beer-Battered Poblano Chiles Preheat oven to 450°F.

In a large bowl, toss chiles with olive oil and sprinkle with salt and pepper. Arrange in a single layer, skin-side up, on a sheet pan.

Roast for 10–15 minutes, or until skins are blistered. Place in a plastic bag or a bowl covered with plastic wrap, and set aside for 10 minutes for skin to loosen. Peel off blistered skin and allow to cool completely.

In a large cast-iron skillet, heat vegetable oil over medium-high heat to 350°F.

Measure 2 tablespoons of flour onto a plate. Place remaining flour in a mixing bowl, add beer, and whisk until batter is smooth.

Roll each half chile in flour and dip in batter, ensuring they are fully coated.

Fry until golden brown, 2–3 minutes per side. Remove and drain on a paper towel–lined plate.

Assembly Preheat grill to medium-high.

Form the ground beef into twelve 2-ounce patties. Press flat into a squarish shape roughly 4 inches across.

Place patties on grill and season tops with salt and pepper. Cook to medium-well, approximately 2 minutes per side.

While patties are cooking, brush buns with butter. Toast on grill until brown.

To assemble burgers, place a layer of lettuce on the bottom bun, followed by 2 patties, each spread with 1 tablespoon of jalapeño ranch. Top with 2 pieces of chipotle bacon and 1 battered poblano chile half. Spread 1 tablespoon of Fresno chile pesto over the poblano chile, followed by a quarter of a sliced avocado, 1 teaspoon of pickled serranos, a few cilantro leaves, and the top bun.

THE PHOENICIAN TAVERN

Ashley Traynor

Since its grand debut in 1988, The Phoenician, a AAA Five-Diamond resort, has been dazzling guests who visit the 250-acre property at the base of Camelback Mountain with its Italian marble finishes, luxe accommodations, and world-class amenities. But for those in the mood for a more laid-back vibe, head to The Phoenician Tavern on the second floor of the Golf Clubhouse. It's like having a favorite neighborhood pub that just happens to have a fancy degree.

With outdoor dining and views of the fairway, "we offer something for everyone," says Ashley Traynor, the assistant food and beverage operations manager. "If you want a cheeseburger, we have it, but if you want a fourteen-ounce split bone ribeye, we have that too."

Beyond the food, The Phoenician Tavern's beverage program is designed to educate and entertain. "The drinks are a huge focus and we've spent a lot of time curating the beverage menu," says Traynor of the signature selections that include exclusive bottlings of Private-Barrel Select Woodford Reserve bourbon and Gruet Blanc de Noirs Luxury Cuvée sparkling wine.

In addition to their popular happy hour is the weekly Journey on the Bourbon Trail, a nod to the bar's extensive collection, and Saturday Tavern Tap Tastings where "guests sample a flight of four local beers while our bartenders walk them through what makes them unique to Arizona," says Traynor.

"I joke with our regulars that we're an extension of their living room," laughs Traynor. "We have great drinks, food, and sports packages to catch all the games, but this living room comes with a golf course view."

2 oz Empress 1908 Gin
1 oz fresh lemon juice
½ oz Monin Lavender Syrup
1 oz Gruet Blanc de Noirs Luxury Cuvée sparkling wine
Edible flower, for garnish

Lavender Fairway

SERVES 1 "We don't think there's enough gin cocktails out there in the world," declares Ashley Traynor, and this effervescent refresher proves why we need more. While The Phoenician Tavern tops it with their exclusive label Gruet Blanc de Noirs Luxury Cuvée, feel free to use your favorite bubbly.

Assembly Pour gin, lemon juice, and lavender syrup into a cocktail shaker filled with ice. Shake vigorously for 15–20 seconds.

Strain into a coupe glass. Top with Gruet sparkling wine and garnish with the flower.

Kosher salt, for rimming glass
1 lime wedge
1½ oz Hornitos Reposado Tequila
½ oz Cointreau orange liqueur
½ oz blueberry purée
1 oz fresh lime juice
2 slices Fresno chile, divided
1 fresh or dehydrated lime wheel, for garnish

Fresno Blueberry Margarita

SERVES 1 "This is in the top two selling cocktails at The Phoenician Tavern," notes Ashley Traynor of this sophisticated margarita combining sweet blueberries with the warmth of Fresno chiles and the subtle oak of reposado tequila. Be sure to use a quality fruit purée, like Reàl brand, made from fresh blueberries and pure cane sugar syrup; look for it online or at Trevor's Liquor, Tops Liquors, and Total Wine & More.

Assembly Prepare a rocks glass by pouring a small amount of coarse salt onto a plate. Rub the lime wedge around the rim of half of the glass. Dip rim into salt.

Combine tequila, Cointreau, blueberry purée, lime juice, and one Fresno chile slice in a cocktail shaker filled with ice. Shake vigorously for 15–20 seconds.

Double strain (pour through shaker strainer and then through a fine-mesh strainer) into the prepared rocks glass over fresh ice.

Garnish with skewered Fresno chile slice and lime wheel.

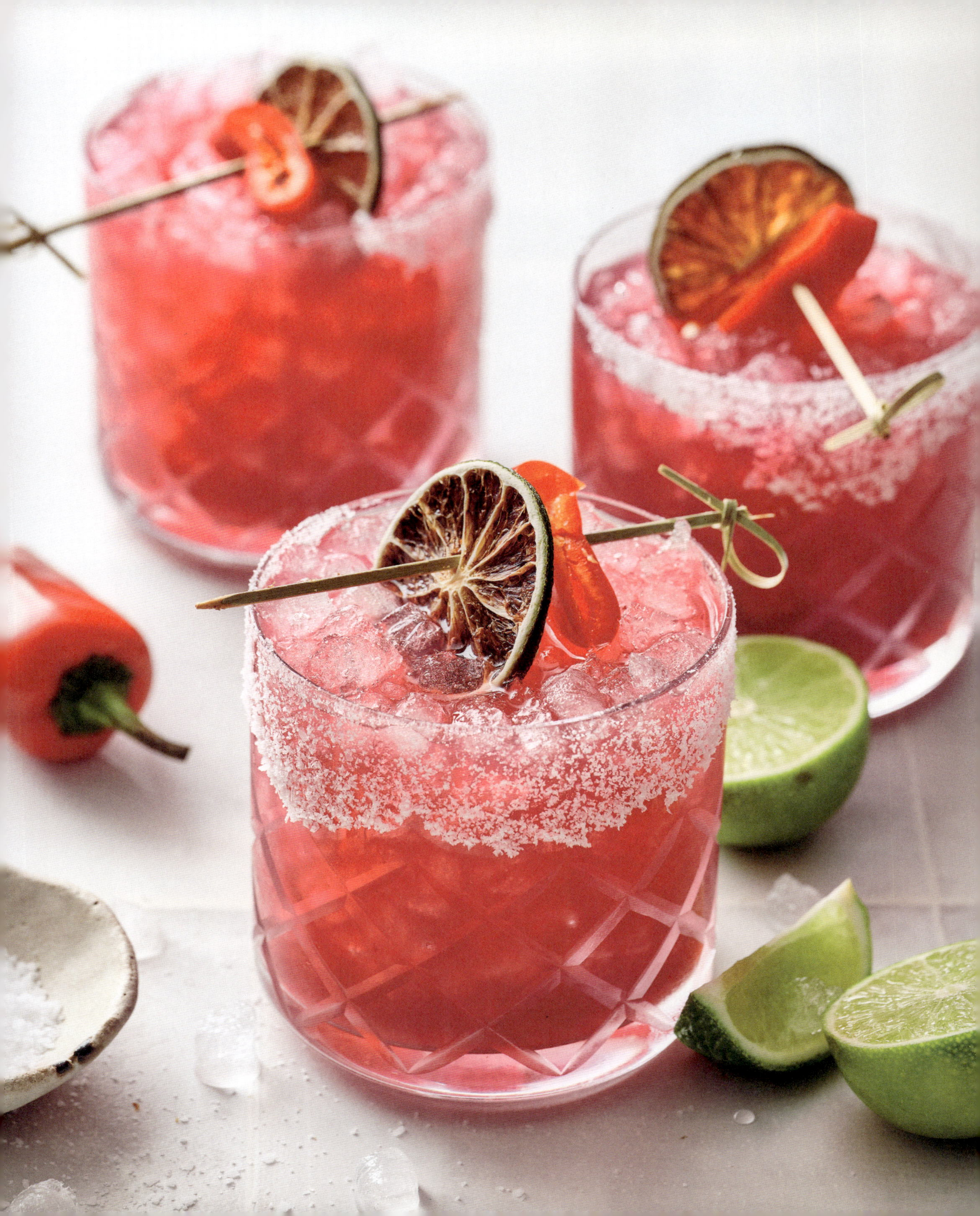

PHOENIX CITY GRILLE

Cory Asure, Uriel Telix

For twenty-eight years, Phoenix City Grille has balanced casual dining with cozy charm, creating an inviting atmosphere where locals gather from sunup to sundown. Whether it's the all-day menu, daily happy hour, or the Sunday brunch that draws crowds, the convivial tavern vibe has created a devoted following where 70% are neighborhood regulars.

And keeping those patrons well fed and happy is executive chef Uriel Telix, whose journey from dishwasher to the top began with an unexpected opportunity. "Somebody called out on Valentine's Day, and they put me on salads," he recalls with a smile. Soon he moved up the ranks and now, two decades later, he leads the kitchen alongside longtime colleague sous chef Cory Asure.

Drawing from his roots in Guerrero, Mexico, Telix informs the menu with Southwestern and Mexican influences, counting guajillo chiles and chiles d'árbol among his favorite ingredients. His commitment to local sourcing is also evident in cultivated partnerships with purveyors such as Rhiba Farms, Ramona Farms, McClendon's Select, and Crow's Dairy. "Not only is it a good thing to support the people, but their quality is so high," he notes.

Loyal fans return for crowd-pleasers like the steakhouse burger dressed with a black garlic steak sauce fermented in-house (a thirteen-day process), shrimp and grits with squash, corn, and chiltepin vinaigrette, and Uriel's Green Chile Pork, a tribute to Telix's childhood. "My mom used to make that so it reminds me of growing up in Mexico," he reminisces. It's a blend of elevated dining and genuine hospitality that continues to transform first-time visitors into lifetime regulars.

▶ Buttermilk Pie with Caramel Sauce and Fresh Berries

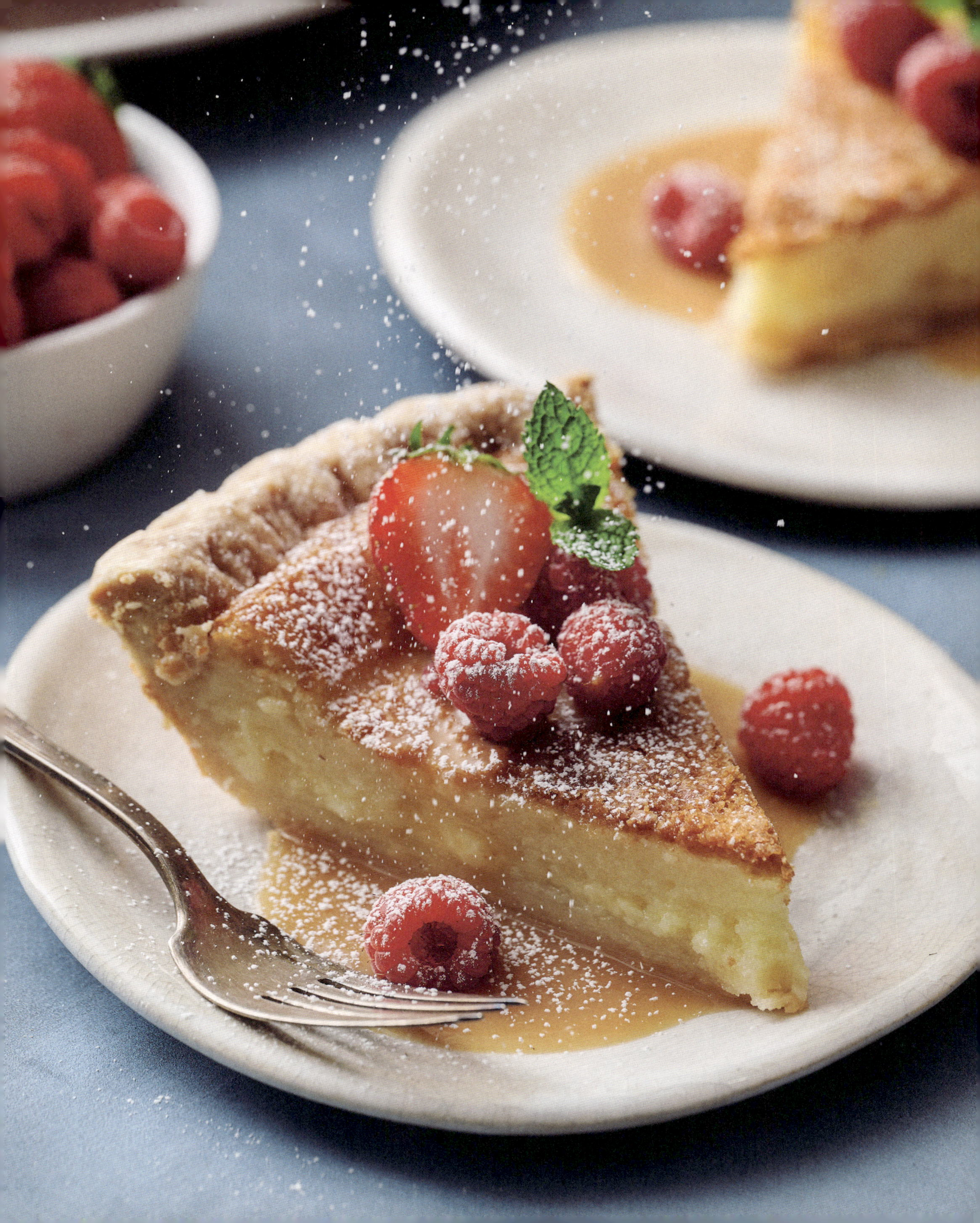

CHILI SALSA

- ¾ cup water
- 3 Roma tomatoes, quartered
- ½ cup diced yellow onions
- ½ tsp ground cumin
- 2 tsp kosher salt
- ½ tsp chopped garlic
- ½ tsp black pepper
- 2 Tbsp chopped cilantro
- 1 Tbsp adobo sauce from canned chipotle peppers in adobo sauce (see Note)

TEPARY BEAN CHILI

- 2 cups dried tepary beans, soaked overnight
- 4 strips bacon, diced
- 2 tsp achiote paste (see Note)
- Chili Salsa (see here)

PICO DE GALLO

- 2 Roma tomatoes, diced
- ¼ cup finely diced yellow onions
- 2 Tbsp minced cilantro
- ½ jalapeño, seeded and minced
- ½ tsp kosher salt
- 1 tsp lime juice

Ribeye Steaks with Tepary Bean Chili and Pico de Gallo

SERVES 4 This juicy ribeye gets a Southwestern flavor boost with chili, pico de gallo, avocado, and cilantro. The chili stars tepary beans, native to the American Southwest and cultivated for centuries by indigenous peoples like Ramona Button of Ramona Farms on the Gila River Indian Reservation. Source the beans online directly from Ramona Farms or find them at Whole Foods and local-centric markets like Sphinx Date Co. Palm & Pantry.

Chili Salsa Combine all ingredients in a saucepot and simmer over low heat for 45 minutes.

Purée using an immersion blender or countertop blender until smooth. Set aside.

Tepary Bean Chili Rinse soaked tepary beans well and place in a large pot. Add water to cover, and bring to a boil.

Reduce heat and simmer until tender, about 90 minutes, stirring occasionally and adding more water as necessary to keep the beans covered.

Meanwhile, in a sauté pan over medium heat, cook bacon until crispy.

Drain beans and return to the pot. Add achiote paste, chili salsa, and bacon, along with bacon fat, to the beans and return to medium heat. Simmer for 15 minutes, stirring occasionally.

Remove 1 cup of chili and purée in a blender until smooth. Add back to pot of chili and stir to combine. Simmer for an additional 15 minutes, stirring occasionally.

Chili can be made up to 3 days ahead and stored in the refrigerator.

PICKLED RED ONIONS

½ medium red onion, peeled and sliced thin
¼ jalapeño, sliced thin
½ cup white wine vinegar
4 Tbsp granulated sugar
1 Tbsp beet root powder
Pinch of dried Mexican oregano
Pinch of ground black pepper
½ tsp kosher salt
⅛ tsp ground cumin

ASSEMBLY

4 (12-oz) ribeye steaks, preferably Argentinian Devesa beef from WorldClass or other all-natural and grass-fed beef
4 Tbsp kosher salt
2 Tbsp cracked black pepper
Tepary Bean Chili, reheated if made in advance (see here)
Pico de Gallo (see here)
Pickled Red Onions (see here)
1 avocado, sliced
Cilantro leaves, for garnish

NOTE Canned chipotle peppers in adobo sauce are dried, smoked jalapeños packed in a tomato-based sauce with garlic, vinegar, and spices. You'll find them in the international aisle or Mexican foods section of grocery stores, at Mexican markets, and online. Unused peppers and sauce will keep in the refrigerator for 2–3 weeks, or purée the peppers and sauce together and freeze for later use.

Achiote paste is an earthy spice blend made from ground annatto seeds, garlic, vinegar, and spices such as cumin, oregano, and cloves. It originates from Mexico and is commonly used in Latin American and Caribbean cooking. Look for it packaged in jars or boxes in local grocery stores, Latin American markets, and online.

Pico de Gallo Combine all ingredients and refrigerate until needed. Pico de gallo can be made 1 day ahead, but for best flavor use on the same day.

Pickled Red Onions Bring onions and jalapeño slices to a boil in a pot of water over medium-high heat. Reduce heat and simmer for 2 minutes.

Drain, then transfer onions and jalapeños to a heatproof storage container.

Combine remaining ingredients in a separate pot and warm over medium heat, whisking often until the sugar dissolves, about 3 minutes.

Pour pickling mixture over blanched onions and jalapeños and allow to cool. Refrigerate for at least 6 hours and up to 1 week.

Assembly Season steaks on both sides with salt and pepper and set aside to rest for 30 minutes at room temperature.

While steaks are resting, preheat grill to medium-high heat.

Grill steaks to desired temperature. For medium-rare, aim for approximately 4 minutes per side or 130°F on an instant-read thermometer.

Remove from heat and rest at room temperature for 7–10 minutes. Slice steak.

To serve, divide chili among shallow bowls. Place sliced steak on top of chili. Top with pico de gallo, pickled onions, and avocado, and garnish with cilantro.

Phoenix City Grille

CARAMEL SAUCE

1 cup granulated sugar
¼ cup water
1 cup heavy cream

BUTTERMILK PIE CRUST

1¼ cups all-purpose flour, plus more for dusting
½ Tbsp granulated sugar
½ tsp iodized salt
½ cup (1 stick) cold unsalted butter, diced small
1⅓ cups cold buttermilk

Buttermilk Pie with Caramel Sauce and Fresh Berries

SERVES 6 Dating back to colonial times when resourceful cooks made the most of leftover buttermilk from butter churning, this pie is a beloved Southern classic. Featuring a silky custard filling in a flaky buttermilk crust, this version is gilded with homemade caramel sauce and fresh berries. Perfect for entertaining, the pie can be baked ahead of time and refrigerated.

Caramel Sauce Heat sugar and water in a saucepan over medium heat. Do not stir as that causes grainy sugar crystals. You can gently swirl the pan to help the sugar dissolve.

When sugar is fully dissolved, reduce heat. Simmer without stirring until syrup is a deep nutty brown and the consistency of a thin syrup, 7–10 minutes. Be patient and keep an eye on it to prevent burning. Remove from heat and allow to cool for 5 minutes.

Slowly stir in cream. The mixture will bubble up, so add cream gradually while stirring continuously.

Return pot to low heat and simmer for 2 more minutes, stirring occasionally.

Prepare an ice bath (a larger bowl filled with ice and water). Strain caramel through a fine-mesh strainer into a heatproof bowl and place bowl in ice bath to cool quickly. Transfer cooled caramel sauce to a container.

Caramel sauce can be refrigerated for up to 2 weeks. Before using, allow to come to room temperature.

Buttermilk Pie Crust Combine flour, sugar, and salt in a food processor and pulse to blend. Add butter and pulse until crumbly with butter in pea-sized pieces.

Add buttermilk and pulse until just incorporated. Do not overmix.

Turn dough out onto a lightly floured surface and knead until it just comes together. Form into a round disk and wrap in plastic wrap.

Refrigerate for at least 2 hours and up to 7 days (or freeze for up to 6 months, thawing before use).

Roll dough to a ⅛-inch thickness with a floured rolling pin.

ASSEMBLY

4 Tbsp all-purpose flour

Pinch of iodized salt

¾ cup (1½ sticks) softened unsalted butter

2 cups granulated sugar

4 large eggs, beaten

1 tsp vanilla extract

1⅓ cups cold buttermilk

¾ cup warm Caramel Sauce (see here)

1½ cups (1 pint) mixed berries, such as raspberries and strawberries, for garnish

Fresh mint, for garnish

Confectioners' sugar, for garnish

Transfer dough to a 9-inch pie plate. Trim dough so it overhangs the plate by 1 inch. Fold the overhang under the dough edge to create a thick rim. Using two fingers, pinch the dough at regular intervals to form a scalloped edge. Cover with plastic wrap and refrigerate until use.

Assembly Preheat oven to 300°F.

Combine flour and salt in a small bowl and set aside.

Place butter and sugar in the bowl of a stand mixer fitted with a whisk attachment. Cream together, starting at low speed until incorporated and increasing to medium-high until light and smooth.

Slowly add eggs and beat until incorporated. Add vanilla and beat until combined. Reduce speed to low and add flour mixture. Slowly add buttermilk and beat until smooth.

Pour filling into the prepared pie shell and bake until golden brown and a toothpick inserted in center comes out clean, about 60 minutes.

Remove from oven and allow to fully cool. Refrigerate pie for at least 3 hours (and up to 4 days) before serving.

To serve, slice pie into 6 pieces.

Spread 2 tablespoons of caramel sauce on each serving plate and top with a slice of pie. Garnish each slice with ¼ cup of berries and mint leaves and dust with confectioners' sugar.

PIZZERIA VIRTÙ

Gio Osso

It was a twist of fate that would take more than twenty years to come full circle. Back when Gio Osso and his buddy walked into Grazie in Old Town Scottsdale, they were just looking for Roman pizza. Instead, they found what would become a life-changing connection. "Maurizio, the owner, said, 'Hey, if you're looking for extra work, you can come sling some pizzas,' and I ended up working there for about a year and a half," Osso recalls.

Fast forward to 2019, and Maurizio, the Rome-born pizzaiolo, was dreaming of returning to his beloved Italy. Meanwhile, Osso was now a James Beard Award–nominated chef at Virtù Honest Craft, located just a few blocks away. "Maurizio said, 'You know what, if you bought it, it would bring it back full circle,'" explains Osso. "So I said 'Let's do it,' and that was that."

Before launching Pizzeria Virtù, Osso earned the prestigious VPN (Vera Pizza Napoletana) Americas certification, a benchmark of Neapolitan pizza-making. "While I do abide by VPN rules for things like the pizza dough and marinara, I love to use different ingredients that they might not see in Italy," he explains, describing his unique approach as "a combination of old-school Italian, traditional Italian, and a sprinkle of New York Italian."

Among the standout dishes are sausage meatballs ("everyone raves about them") and the Milano pizza, a bold creation topped with stracchino, peppered pancetta, caramelized onions, and chestnut honey drizzle ("people go crazy for it").

In 2025, Gambero Rosso, Italy's prestigious food and wine publishing group, recognized Pizzeria Virtù as the top pizzeria in Arizona. "Like Virtù Honest Craft, we're creating another memorable dining experience," says Osso, "but this time we're doing it through pizza."

Pizzeria Virtù

INSALATA DI POMODORO

4 ripe red tomatoes, cut into wedges
½ cup thinly sliced red onion
½ tsp dried Italian oregano
3 Tbsp extra-virgin olive oil
Flaky or fine sea salt and black pepper, to taste

ASSEMBLY

1 (55-oz) porterhouse steak, prime grade
2 cloves garlic
Olive oil
Sprigs of fresh herbs, such as rosemary, thyme, oregano, and sage
1½ Tbsp flaky sea salt
1½ Tbsp cracked black pepper
Insalata di Pomodoro, to serve (see here)

Bistecca alla Fiorentina

SERVES 2–4 Tracing its roots to Florence, Italy, bistecca alla Fiorentina is a hefty, thick-cut porterhouse steak prepared simply and grilled to perfection. "When I make this, I cook the steak directly on wood coals," says Gio Osso, "but for the home cook, you can use a charcoal or gas grill, getting it as hot as possible." Consider sourcing your steak from local butchers such as The Meat Market, Nelson's Meat + Fish (page 166), or Arcadia Meat Market, as you may need to place a special order for a porterhouse of this size.

Insalata di Pomodoro In a medium bowl, combine tomatoes with onions, oregano, and oil. Toss gently to coat.

Season with salt and pepper to taste.

Assembly Approximately 45 minutes before cooking, remove steak from the refrigerator and allow to come to room temperature to ensure even cooking.

Prepare your charcoal or gas grill, making sure the side you are cooking on is as hot as possible.

Smash garlic cloves and transfer to a small bowl. Cover with oil.

Make a basting bouquet by gathering sprigs of herbs such as rosemary, thyme, oregano, and/or sage. Align stems to form a brush-like shape. Using butcher's twine, wrap the stems several times, knotting firmly to make a bouquet.

Dip the herb bouquet in oil and brush both sides of steak. Sprinkle with salt and pepper.

Grill steak for 4–5 minutes. Baste again and turn a quarter turn. Baste again and grill for another 4–5 minutes. Baste once again and flip. Repeat process, cooking to your desired temperature (though bistecca alla Fiorentina is traditionally served rare).

To plate, slice the steak off the bone, then carve the meat into thick slices. Arrange the sliced meat around the bone on a platter for an impressive presentation, and drizzle with any resting juices.

Serve with insalata di pomodoro.

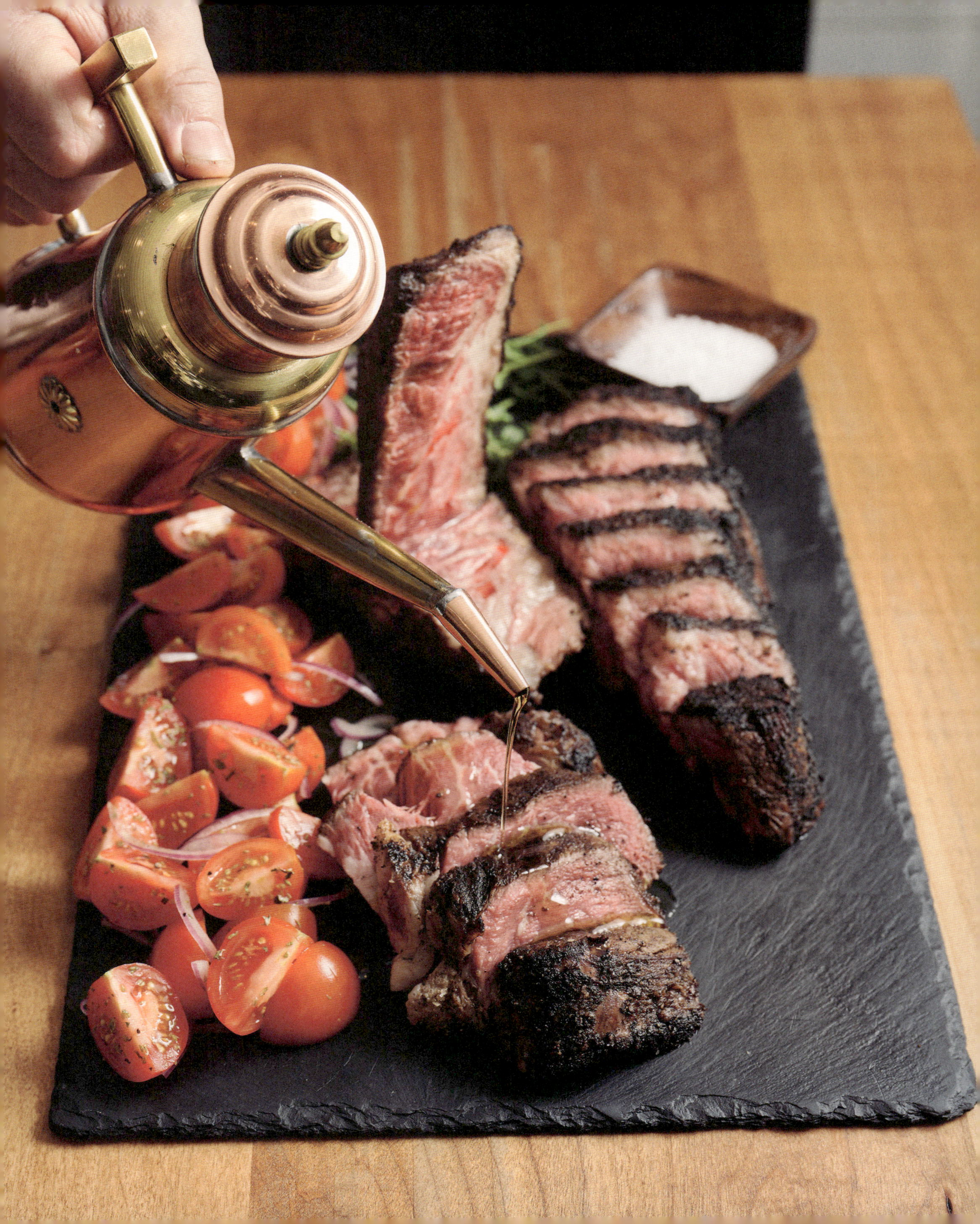

CREPES

1 cup whole milk
1 large egg
1 tsp granulated sugar
½ tsp fine sea salt
1 Tbsp unsalted butter, melted
½ cup all-purpose flour
Butter, oil, or cooking spray, for greasing pan

RAGU

1 lb ground pork
1 lb ground beef
½ lb pancetta, chopped
½ lb prosciutto di Parma, chopped
1 large carrot, finely diced
2 stalks celery, finely diced
1 large red onion, finely diced
1 sprig rosemary
1 Tbsp tomato paste
1 cup dry red wine
2 cups tomato passata (see Note)
½ cup beef stock, or water, plus more if needed

Virtù Timballo

SERVES 4 Chef Gio Osso brings back a bestseller from more than twenty years ago that landed on the front page of *The Arizona Republic*'s food section. "The food critic, Howard Seftel, went crazy for it," he recalls with a chuckle. Inspired by the timpano—a massive baked pasta pie showcased in the movie *Big Night*—Osso re-created it as individual servings. "It's basically a lasagna wrapped in a crepe so it looks like a little package. People love it."

Crepes Add milk, egg, sugar, salt, melted butter, and flour to a blender and blend until smooth and well combined. Chill crepe batter for at least 1 hour in the refrigerator before use.

Place a clean kitchen towel on a large plate.

For each crepe, lightly oil, butter, or spray an 8-inch nonstick skillet or crepe pan and place over medium-low heat. Pour in enough batter to thinly coat bottom of pan, swirling to spread batter thinly and evenly.

Cook for 1–2 minutes or until edges start to lift and bottom is lightly browned. Flip and cook for another 1–2 minutes, then transfer to the towel-lined plate. Repeat with remaining batter, greasing pan as needed and stacking crepes as they are cooked.

Crepes can be stored until needed wrapped in a towel at room temperature.

If preparing ahead, let crepes cool completely, placing squares of waxed paper or parchment between them to prevent sticking. Store in an airtight container or sealed plastic bag for up to 3 days in the refrigerator or freeze for up to 2 months and defrost before use.

Ragu To a large saucepot over medium-high heat, add ground pork and beef. Cook, stirring occasionally, until meat is evenly browned and liquid has evaporated, 10–12 minutes. Use a slotted spoon to transfer meat to a bowl, reserving fat in the pan, and add pancetta and prosciutto to the pan.

GARLIC BUTTER

¼ cup (½ stick) unsalted butter, softened

1 Tbsp grated garlic

2 tsp finely chopped flat-leaf parsley

BÉCHAMEL

1½ cups whole milk

2 Tbsp unsalted butter

2 Tbsp all-purpose flour

2½ tsp ground nutmeg

Fine sea salt and white pepper, to taste

Sauté pancetta and prosciutto over medium-high heat, stirring occasionally, for 5–7 minutes, until they begin to brown.

Add carrots, celery, onions, and rosemary sprig. Cook until vegetables begin to caramelize, 10–15 minutes. Stir in tomato paste and cook for 2–3 minutes, until tomato paste begins to darken and caramelize. Add wine to deglaze, scraping up any browned bits from the bottom, and cook for 2–3 minutes until slightly reduced. Add ground meat, stirring to combine.

Add tomato passata. Use stock (or water) to rinse out the passata jar or carton and pour it into the pot. Reduce heat to a simmer and cover pot, leaving it slightly ajar. Simmer for at least 1 hour for flavors to develop, adding more stock (or water) if needed.

Ragu can be stored in the refrigerator for up to 5 days or frozen for up to 3 months.

Garlic Butter In a bowl, mix butter, garlic, and parsley together until smooth and well combined.

Béchamel Heat milk in a small saucepot over medium-low heat until hot, but not boiling.

In a separate pot over medium heat, melt butter. Whisk in flour to form a roux and cook, whisking constantly, 2–3 minutes, or until it develops a fragrant, nutty aroma. Do not allow to color.

Gradually (to avoid lumps) add hot milk, whisking constantly, and cook for 3–5 minutes, until sauce thickens to a little thicker than a heavy cream consistency.

Remove from heat and stir in nutmeg. Season with salt and pepper to taste.

ASSEMBLY

½ lb cooked and drained pasta of your choice, such as pappardelle

Ragu, warmed (see here)

Béchamel, warmed (see here)

4 slices prosciutto cotto, diced (see Note)

4 slices white American cheese, diced

1 cup grated Parmigiano-Reggiano, divided

Garlic Butter (see here)

4 Crepes (see here)

4 large basil leaves

Assembly Preheat oven to 400°F.

In a large bowl, toss cooked pasta with 1½ cups of ragu and ½ cup of béchamel, adding more if needed to coat the pasta.

Stir in prosciutto cotto, American cheese, and 2 tablespoons of Parmigiano-Reggiano until well combined.

Liberally brush the inside of four 10-ounce soufflé ramekins with garlic butter.

Place a crepe in each ramekin, carefully pressing it against the sides while leaving enough overhang to create a package.

Add a portion of pasta and top with dollops of ragu and béchamel.

To enclose the filling, carefully fold the overhanging crepe edges over the top, creating a sealed package. Secure the closure with a dollop of garlic butter and sprinkle generously with Parmigiano-Reggiano.

Bake the timballi until you see the centers are bubbling (indicating the filling is hot and cheeses have melted).

Remove from oven and allow to set for 3–5 minutes.

To unmold, place a small plate over each ramekin. Carefully invert and lift off ramekin.

To plate, spread a thick bed of ragu in the center of each serving dish. Carefully place a timballo on top, and garnish with a basil leaf.

NOTE Unlike tomato sauce, tomato passata is uncooked tomato purée with no added ingredients and is preferred for its bright tomato flavor and smooth consistency. Look for passata in glass bottles at Italian specialty markets, well-stocked grocery stores, and online.

Prosciutto cotto is cooked Italian ham rather than cured, like traditional prosciutto. Look for it in the deli case of specialty grocers like AJ's Fine Foods and Whole Foods, or Italian markets such as DeFalco's Italian Deli & Grocery, Romanelli's Italian Deli, and Andreoli Italian Grocer. If you can't find prosciutto cotto, high-quality cooked ham can be substituted, though it will have a different flavor and texture.

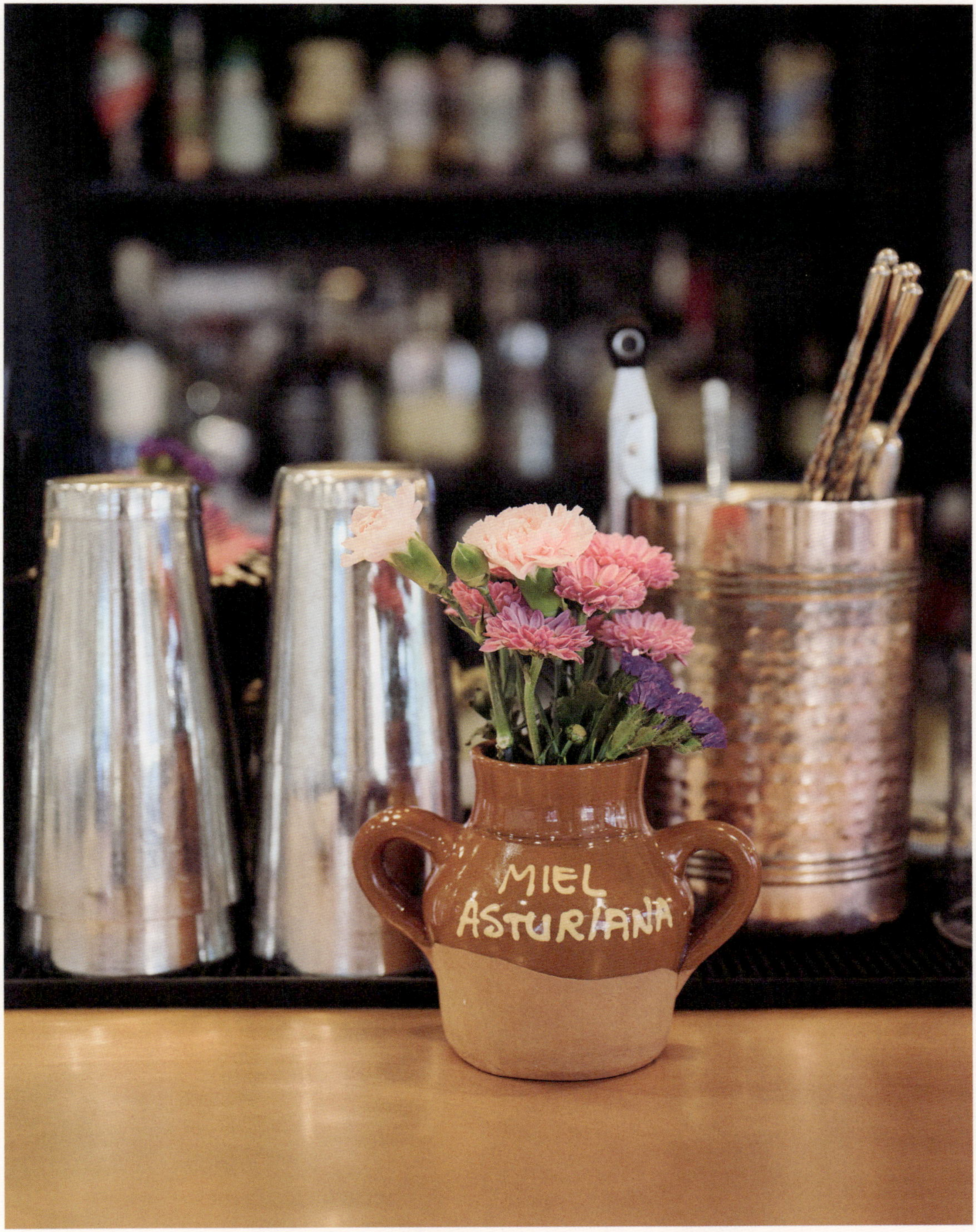
MIEL
ASTURIANA

POPPY'S OFFICE

Adam Downey, Matt Keeler

Hidden away in North Scottsdale, Poppy's Office is a heartfelt homage to a man who helped shape the Valley's dining scene. As founder of Keeler Hospitality Group, behind restaurants like Liberty Station, Market Street Kitchen, and Keeler's Neighborhood Steakhouse, Paul Keeler—affectionately known by his grandchildren as Poppy—left behind a legacy of hospitality.

After Paul's passing, his son Matt Keeler found inspiration in an unexpected place. "It came to me in a dream," Matt shares, describing the moment he envisioned transforming a storage space—one he and his father had often discussed repurposing—into a speakeasy-style lounge.

Entered through a swinging bookcase, the hidden space features tufted leather booths beneath the warm glow of sconces and whimsical chandeliers crafted from stacked books. A sleek marble bar gleams under classic desk lamps, while walls and shelves display family photos and memorabilia, from vintage business cards chronicling Paul's career to prized sports collectibles that once graced his office.

Under beverage director Adam Downey's guidance, the cocktail program is worthy of Poppy's memory. "I look at cocktailing like music," says Downey, who introduces a new spring, summer, and fall/winter change-up three times a year. "I love when an artist comes up with an album where every single song is enjoyable, so our goal is to only create cocktails that will wow you."

"The cocktails are just phenomenal and I'm amazed at the talent of the team," says Keeler. "My dad was a big part of my life, but also a big part of the restaurant community. I'm proud to be able to take this dream, show everybody who he was, and have him continue to live on through this legacy."

RICH DEMERARA SIMPLE SYRUP

2 cups (16 oz) turbinado cane sugar (see Note)
1 cup (8 oz) water

GRILLED PINEAPPLE–INFUSED TEQUILA

1 whole pineapple, preferably organic
1 liter Angelisco Reposado Tequila

ASSEMBLY

1½ oz Grilled Pineapple–Infused Tequila (see here)
½ oz Rich Demerara Simple Syrup (see here)
½ oz Alma Tepec Chile Liqueur
½ oz Liquid Alchemist Mango Syrup (see Note)
½ oz fresh lime juice
½ oz fresh lemon juice
Mint sprig, for garnish
Grilled pineapple cubes, for garnish (see here)

NOTE Turbinado sugar is a minimally processed sugar made from sugar cane juice, retaining some of its natural molasses. It has large, golden-brown crystals and caramel notes, which adds extra richness to simple syrups. You can find turbinado sugar in the baking aisle of local grocery stores or online.

Liquid Alchemist specializes in premium cocktail syrups made with natural ingredients, known for their rich texture and true-to-fruit flavor. Find their products at local liquor stores like Total Wine & More and Paradise Liquor, online retailers, or purchase directly from their website at liquidalchemist.com.

100 Grand

SERVES 1 Bar manager Tait Ludwick's love for tequila and margaritas inspired this cocktail creation. "The addition of Alma Tepec, a small-batch artisanal smoked chile pepper liqueur, complements the grilled pineapple extremely well, and the tropical mango rounds everything out," says Adam Downey. "It's now the number-two bestselling cocktail on the menu, and for good reason."

Rich Demerara Simple Syrup In a saucepan over medium heat, combine sugar and water. Whisk continuously until sugar dissolves completely. Do not allow water to boil.

Allow to cool and transfer syrup to an airtight container to chill in the refrigerator. Syrup can be stored in the refrigerator for up to 2 weeks.

Grilled Pineapple–Infused Tequila Preheat grill to medium-high.

Trim the pineapple by cutting off the top and bottom. (Leaves can be rinsed, dried, and frozen in a freezer bag to use as cocktail garnishes.)

Using a sharp knife, carefully shave the peel off the pineapple.

Cut the pineapple flesh into 1-inch cubes.

Grill cubes on an open flame grill until all sides have dark grill marks. If you don't have a grill, broil cubes on a baking sheet, turning occasionally, until all sides have darkened and caramelized. Remove and allow to cool.

Place pineapple cubes into a container and add tequila. Allow tequila to infuse for 24 hours in the refrigerator.

Strain the tequila into the Angelisco tequila bottle or an airtight container, reserving pineapple cubes for garnish.

Infused tequila can be stored in the refrigerator indefinitely and used in cocktails, salsas, and marinades.

Assembly Combine all liquid ingredients in a shaker and fill with ice. Shake vigorously for 15 seconds until cocktail is chilled. Strain over ice (pebble ice is preferred) in a Collins glass.

Garnish with mint and skewered grilled pineapple cubes.

SALTED ESPRESSO SIMPLE SYRUP
1 cup (8 oz) freshly brewed espresso
1 cup (8 oz) granulated sugar
½ tsp kosher salt

ASSEMBLY
2 oz Buffalo Trace Bourbon
½ oz Salted Espresso Simple Syrup (see here)
4 dashes Fee Brothers Black Walnut Bitters
1 orange peel, cut into a 1-inch-wide strip with minimal white pith, for garnish

Silver Fox

SERVES 1 "As part of the interview process for beverage director of the Keeler Group, I created eight different original recipes, one being this salted espresso old-fashioned riff," says Adam Downey. "At the end of the tasting, Paul Keeler said it was his favorite and the best old-fashioned he had ever had," words that make this sophisticated sipper, now the #1 seller, even more special.

Salted Espresso Simple Syrup In a small heatproof bowl, whisk together hot espresso, sugar, and salt until the sugar and salt are fully dissolved. Allow to cool.

Transfer the mixture to an airtight container and place in the refrigerator to chill.

Syrup can be stored in the refrigerator for up to 2 weeks.

Assembly Pour all liquid ingredients into a mixing glass. Fill to three-quarters full with ice cubes.

Stir until chilled, 12–15 seconds, and strain over a large ice cube in a rocks glass.

Garnish with an expressed orange peel and drop it into the glass. (To express, hold peel over the glass with outer side facing down and give it a gentle squeeze to release the oils onto the surface of the drink).

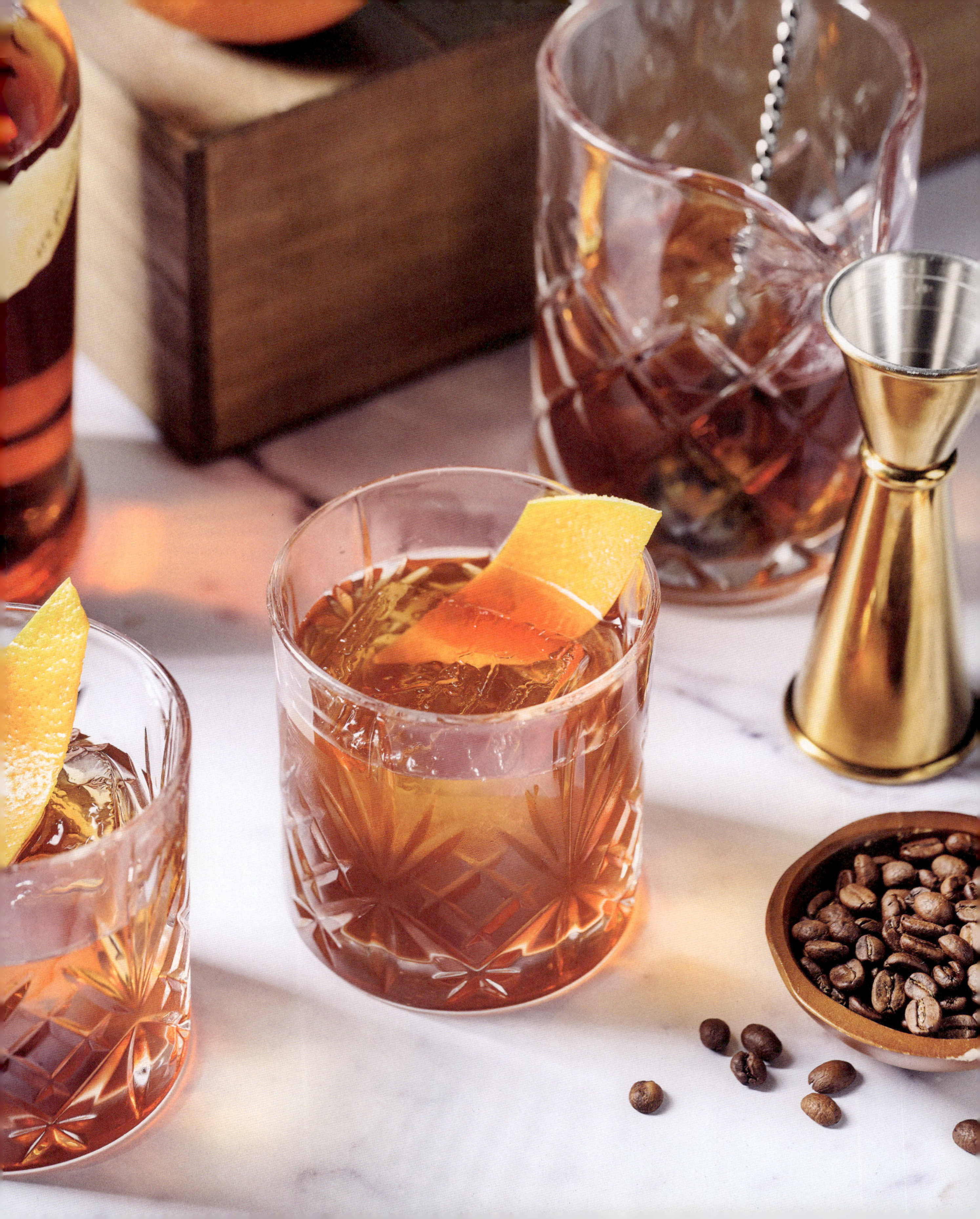

RENATA'S HEARTH

Daniel Weber

The Arizona Biltmore, often referred to as the "Jewel of the Desert," has a rich history dating back to its Hollywood celebrity–attended debut in 1929. Designed by architect Albert Chase McArthur, a draftsman of Frank Lloyd Wright, who consulted on the project, it's a stunning blend of Spanish Colonial Revival and Art Deco architecture.

When this grande dame emerged from her $170-million metamorphosis in 2021, she had a new culinary gem in her crown: Renata's Hearth. Here, chef de cuisine Daniel Weber brings his passion for fire and Latin American flavors to every dish. While Mexico's rich culinary history frames the menu, Weber's vision extends beyond its borders. As he explains, "Though we focus on Mexico, flavors of Central and South America are sprinkled throughout. I've worked with people from all over the Latin world—Puerto Rico, Cuba, Dominican Republic, Brazil, and Peru—and have learned a lot."

It's a culinary wanderlust that shows up in dishes like Brazilian coxinha (smoked chicken croquettes), Mexican tetelas (stuffed masa pockets), sea bass and blue crab ceviche nestled in a Peruvian leche de tigre (page 210), and shareable platters of pollo pibil (page 212) and lamb barbacoa thanks to a custom smoker.

"I tell my sous chefs to focus on an ingredient or certain flavor and build around that," says Weber when describing his food philosophy. "Using that in multiple ways in the same dish keeps it simple but amplifies the flavor profile in a more creative and complex way. The most important thing for me is to create a memorable experience that people want to return to."

▶ Sea Bass and Blue Crab Ceviche with Passion Fruit Leche de Tigre

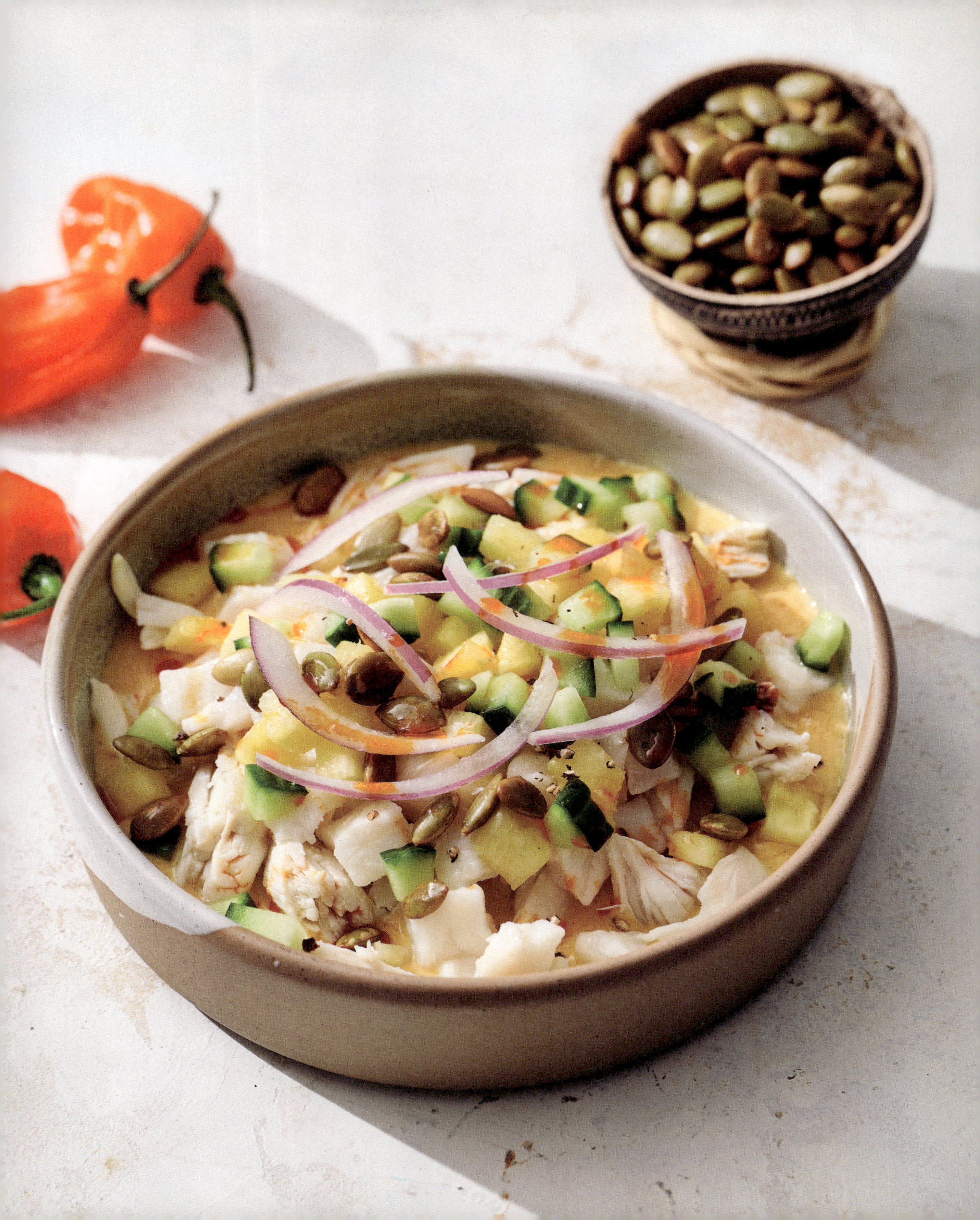

FISH STOCK

1 lb fish bones/trimmings, rinsed
1 cup chopped yellow onion
2 stalks celery, chopped
1 cup tomato juice

PASSION FRUIT LECHE DE TIGRE

2 cups passion fruit juice, such as Kudo or Twisted Alchemy brand
⅓ cup chopped red onion
1 medium stalk celery, chopped
½ cup Fish Stock (see here)
1 habanero chile
1 heaping Tbsp dark brown sugar
¼ cup sea bass trimmings (reserved from cubing sea bass, see here)
¾ cup coconut milk (preferably Chaokoh brand)
1 Tbsp kosher salt, plus more to taste

Sea Bass and Blue Crab Ceviche with Passion Fruit Leche de Tigre

SERVES 6 This Peruvian-style ceviche features *leche de tigre,* a tangy marinade whose name means "tiger's milk." The addition of passion fruit adds tropical sweetness to the traditional blend, while Spanish smoked paprika (pimentón) brings subtle smokiness. To save steps, fish stock can be purchased from local fishmongers like Nelson's Meat + Fish (page 166) and Chula Seafood.

Fish Stock Place all ingredients in a stockpot over medium heat and add enough water to just cover. Simmer for 20 minutes (do not allow to boil). Strain through a fine-mesh strainer into a heatproof container and allow to cool. Refrigerate to chill.

Passion Fruit Leche de Tigre Place all ingredients in a blender and blend until smooth. Taste and adjust salt if needed.

Strain through a fine-mesh strainer or cheesecloth-lined colander and refrigerate until ready to use.

Pimentón Oil Heat oil and dried chipotle in a saucepot over medium heat to 250°F. Remove from heat and stir in smoked paprika. Allow to steep at room temperature for 30 minutes. Stir well and strain through a coffee filter into a glass jar. Store in the refrigerator for up to 1 month.

Leftover oil can be drizzled on rice, eggs, and roasted vegetables, and used in dips and marinades.

PIMENTÓN OIL

1 cup extra-virgin olive oil

1 dried chipotle chile (see Note)

1 Tbsp smoked paprika (preferably La Chinata brand)

ASSEMBLY

1 lb sea bass fillets, cut into ¼-inch cubes

2–3 cups fresh lime juice

1 to 1½ cups Passion Fruit Leche de Tigre (see here)

1 lb colossal lump blue crab, shredded

Kosher salt, to taste

¾ cup diced pineapple

¾ cup diced English cucumber

½ cup roasted and salted pepitas (pumpkin seeds)

½ medium red onion, thinly sliced

Pimentón Oil, for garnish (see here)

Assembly Place sea bass in a bowl and add enough lime juice to completely submerge fish (do not use pasteurized lime juice as it lacks flavor and acidity). Allow to marinate for approximately 1 hour until opaque, and strain.

To serve, pour leche de tigre into a large shallow serving bowl, arrange sea bass and crab on top, and sprinkle with salt. Scatter pineapple and cucumber on top and sprinkle with another pinch of salt.

Top with pepitas and red onions, and garnish with a drizzle of pimentón oil.

NOTE Whole dried chipotle peppers are smoked, dried jalapeños, and known for their deep, smoky flavor and medium heat. Find dried chipotle peppers at well-stocked grocery stores, Mexican markets, spice shops, and online retailers.

ACHIOTE MARINADE
⅓ cup annatto seeds (see Note)
10 cloves garlic
1 habanero chile
1 lime, peeled
1 orange, juiced
2 Tbsp dark brown sugar
¼ cup + 2 Tbsp white vinegar

BRINED AND MARINATED CHICKENS
6 cups water
¼ cup kosher salt
2 Tbsp granulated sugar
4 cups pickling spice
2 (3- to 4-lb) chickens
Achiote Marinade (see here)

PICKLED RED ONIONS
2 red onions, thinly sliced
4 cups red wine vinegar
1 cup granulated sugar
2 Tbsp + 1½ tsp pickling spice
2 Tbsp + 1½ tsp kosher salt

Pollo Pibil with Guasacaca and Pickled Red Onions

SERVES 6 "This recipe combines flavors from Mexico and Venezuela," explains Daniel Weber. "The achiote rub, which originated in the Yucatán Peninsula, is made from ground annatto seeds, chiles, and citrus, creating a savory and acidic marinade that pairs perfectly with guasacaca, a smooth Venezuelan guacamole. For best results, grill the chicken over charcoal or hardwood fire, though it will still be delicious using a gas grill."

Achiote Marinade Using a spice grinder or molcajete, grind annatto seeds into a fine powder.

Place annatto powder and remaining ingredients in a food processor. Blend into a fairly smooth paste.

Brined and Marinated Chickens In a medium saucepot, bring water, salt, sugar, and pickling spice to a simmer over medium heat. Stir occasionally until sugar and salt are completely dissolved. Strain into a large container and discard pickling spice. Add ice to hot liquid to make 6 cups in volume. Set aside to cool completely.

Rinse chickens and pat dry. To spatchcock, place chicken on a cutting board breast-side down. Using kitchen shears, cut along both sides of the backbone from neck to tail and discard it.

Flip chicken over to breast-side up. Using a sharp boning knife, trim off the tip and flat portion of the wings, leaving the drum wings attached to the breast. Repeat with second chicken.

Submerge chickens in cold brine and refrigerate for 24 hours.

Remove chickens from brine and allow to thoroughly drain. Pat dry and rub generously with achiote marinade. Cover and allow to marinate overnight in the refrigerator.

Pickled Red Onions Place onions in a large heatproof container.

In a saucepan over medium heat, bring remaining ingredients to a simmer. Stir until salt and sugar are completely dissolved. Remove from heat.

GUASACACA

- 4 ripe avocados
- 1 large poblano chile, stemmed, seeded, and chopped
- 1 serrano chile, stemmed, seeded, and chopped
- ¼ cup chopped onion
- ¼ cup chopped flat-leaf parsley
- ½ cup chopped cilantro
- ¼ cup + 2 Tbsp fresh orange juice
- 3 Tbsp fresh lime juice
- Kosher salt, to taste

ASSEMBLY

- Brined and Marinated Chickens (see here)
- Guasacaca (see here)
- Pickled Red Onions, for garnish (see here)
- Roasted and salted pepitas (pumpkin seeds), for garnish

Strain liquid into the container over the onions and discard pickling spice. Place a small plate or weight on the onions to keep them submerged.

Allow to cool, then chill in the refrigerator for at least 24 hours.

Guasacaca Place all ingredients in a blender with a generous pinch of salt. Blend until smooth (a food processor can be used, though the purée will be less smooth). Season with more salt if needed.

Assembly Prepare grill for high heat, setting up for two-zone cooking with direct heat on one side and no flames on the other (direct heat and indirect heat are needed for best results). Coals should be hot enough that you can only hold your hand over them for 2 seconds.

Place spatchcocked chickens on grill over direct heat and let marinade char, turning chickens every 1–2 minutes to evenly char without burning.

Once charred, move chickens to indirect heat side, close grill cover, and cook until internal temperature reaches 165°F in thickest part of the chicken, 15–20 minutes.

Remove from grill and set on a rack for 5–10 minutes to allow internal juices to redistribute.

Using a sharp, heavy knife, separate breasts from leg quarters. Cut breasts in half and separate thighs from legs.

To serve, spread guasacaca evenly over a serving platter. Arrange chicken pieces on top and garnish with pickled onions and pepitas.

NOTE Annatto seeds are used in Latin American and Caribbean cuisines for their vibrant reddish-orange color and earthy, peppery flavor. You can find them in Latin American markets such as Los Altos Ranch Market and Food City, specialty spice shops, or online.

ROUGH RIDER

Kyla Hein, Ian Herschberg

You're on a mission to find Rough Rider, the speakeasy-style gem hiding in downtown Phoenix. Armed with an address, you circle the nondescript Ten-O-One building on Roosevelt Row like a lost desert explorer. Once inside, you find yourself in a white tiled office lobby, still questioning if your GPS has led you astray. That is, until you spot the lone wood-paneled elevator. "That's part of the charm," says operating owner and beverage director Kyla Hein, "the element of surprise that awaits you."

Whisked down to the basement, you're suddenly transported to the Victorian era. The restaurant is bathed in a warm amber glow, with custom woodwork, tufted leather furniture, vintage memorabilia, and an elegant marble bar. "It turned out more beautiful than I could have ever imagined," says Hein of the space designed to evoke the spirit of Teddy Roosevelt and his legendary Rough Riders regiment.

Bar manager Salvatore Scibona isn't just mixing drinks; he's concocting liquid history with cobblers and punches. Meanwhile, executive chef Ian Herschberg is dishing up oysters with apple mignonette and chicory-rubbed duck that would have even Teddy leading a charge to the table. "Everything is built and designed around the 1800s," says Hein. "Cocktails are inspired by Jerry Thomas's *Bartenders Guide* and the food is based on an old cookbook from that period that Ian found. It's very cohesive."

"I hope guests feel like they had more than just a meal and drinks—that they had an experience," says Hein. "I want them to feel like they were transported to another time where they felt fulfilled because everyone took such great care of them."

▶ Fried Cauliflower with Pickled Onions and Malt Aioli and The Sea Queen Punch

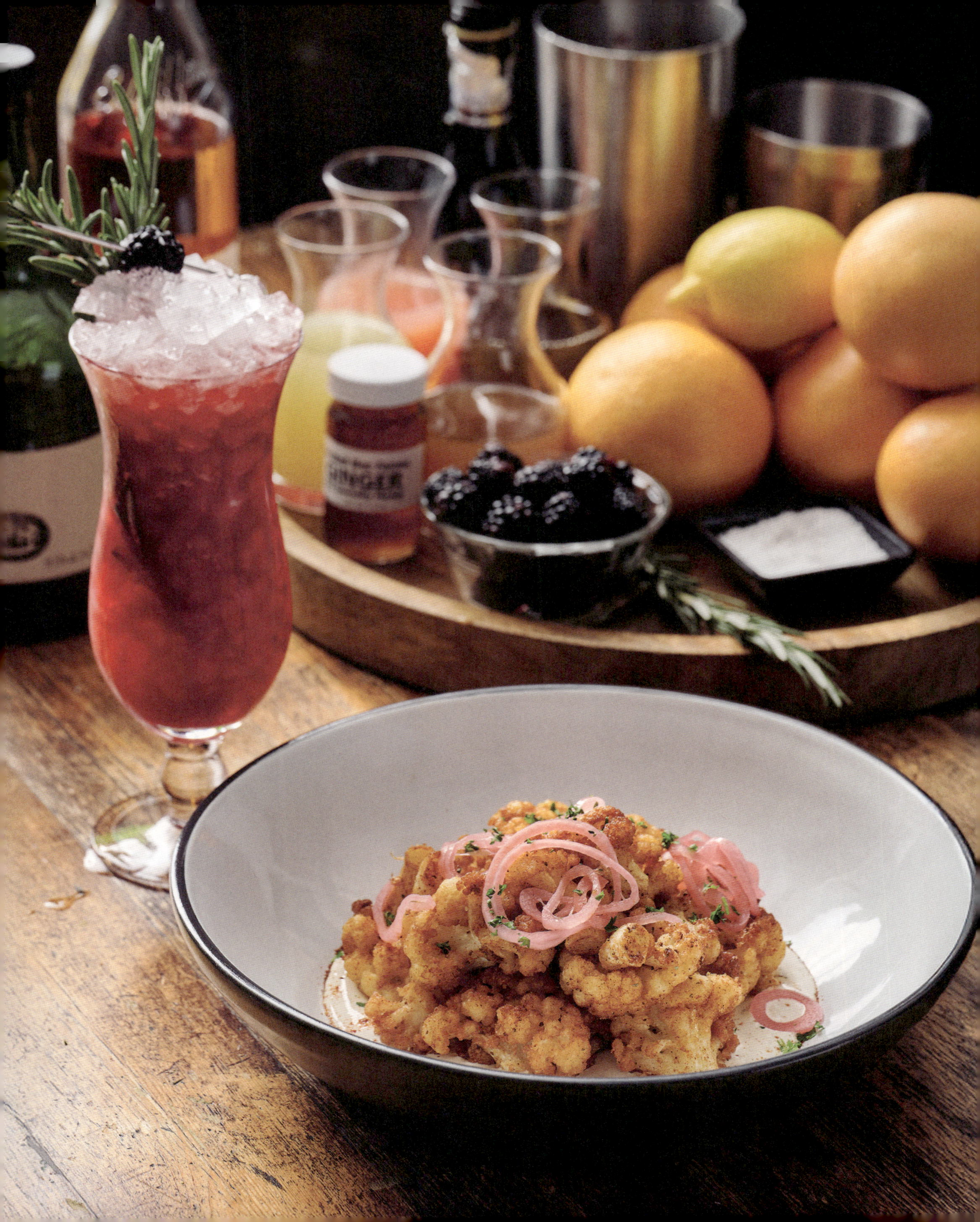

MALT AIOLI

½ cup mayonnaise
½ cup sour cream
2 Tbsp malt vinegar
½ tsp dried thyme
2 cloves garlic, minced
Kosher salt and black pepper, to taste

PICKLED ONIONS

1 large red onion
1 cup apple cider vinegar
¼ cup granulated sugar
1 tsp pickling spice

ASSEMBLY

2 Tbsp kosher salt, plus more to taste
1 large head cauliflower, cut into bite-sized florets
6 cups vegetable oil
2 Tbsp cornstarch
1 Tbsp Old Bay Seasoning, plus more for garnish
Malt Aioli (see here)
¼ cup Pickled Onions (see here)
1–2 tsp finely chopped flat-leaf parsley, for garnish

Fried Cauliflower with Pickled Onions and Malt Aioli

SERVES 2–4 Chef Ian Herschberg's shareable plates are just as popular as his raw bar offerings and hearty entrées, and this is a crowd favorite. Here, golden nuggets of cauliflower are dusted with Old Bay and enhanced with a creamy aioli made with malt vinegar.

Malt Aioli Place all ingredients in a bowl and combine well. Season with salt and pepper to taste.

Malt aioli can be made up to 7 days ahead and stored in the refrigerator.

Pickled Onions Peel and cut red onion into thin whole slices. Place onions in a large heatproof container.

In a pot over medium-high heat, bring vinegar, sugar, and pickling spice to a simmer, stirring to dissolve sugar. Remove from heat and pour over onions. Allow to sit for 4–6 hours at room temperature, then refrigerate until use.

Pickled onions can be stored in the refrigerator for up to 1 week.

Assembly In a pot over high heat, bring water and salt to a boil. Once boiling, add cauliflower and cook until tender, 3–5 minutes.

Drain cauliflower and transfer to a bowl. Cool completely in the refrigerator.

In a large heavy-bottomed pot or deep fryer, heat oil over medium-high heat to 350°F.

Place cornstarch in a large mixing bowl. Add cauliflower florets and toss until evenly coated.

Working in batches, carefully lower cauliflower into hot oil using a slotted spoon or frying basket. Fry for 4–5 minutes, stirring occasionally, until cauliflower is golden brown, crispy, and tender but not soft.

Remove cauliflower and place in a bowl lined with paper towels to drain. While cauliflower is still hot, toss with Old Bay. Add salt to taste.

To serve, spread ½ cup aioli (or more to taste) across the bottom of a shallow serving bowl. Mound the fried cauliflower in the center of the dish. Top with pickled onions and sprinkle with Old Bay and parsley.

BLACKBERRY-INFUSED RHUM J.M 100

2 cups fresh blackberries
1 (750-mL) bottle of Rhum J.M 100

SAGE-INFUSED GREEN TEA

1 packet organic green tea
3 fresh sage leaves
1 cup hot water

ASSEMBLY

1½ oz Blackberry-Infused Rhum J.M 100 (see here)
1 oz Twisted Bee ginger honey
1 oz Sage-Infused Green Tea (see here)
¼ oz Giffard Vanille de Madagascar liqueur
¾ oz fresh grapefruit juice
½ oz fresh lemon juice
Brut Champagne
1 Luxardo cherry, for garnish (see Note)
Fresh rosemary sprig, for garnish
Sea salt, for garnish

The Sea Queen Punch

SERVES 1 (SEE NOTE) "Punches are my favorite style of drink to both make and enjoy," says Kyla Hein, and this creation is a blend of some of her most loved flavors. She even shares tips for batching the cocktail, making it perfect for entertaining. "I always incorporate that into my cocktail classes," she explains, "because people love hosting pool parties and gatherings."

Blackberry-Infused Rhum J.M 100 Place ingredients in a blender and blend on high for 1 minute. Strain through a fine-mesh strainer into a container. Pour into a glass jar or the original Rhum J.M 100 bottle.

Blackberry-infused Rhum J.M 100 can be stored in a cool, dark place indefinitely, although the flavor may change over time.

Sage-Infused Green Tea Steep tea bag and sage leaves in hot water for 15 minutes.

Strain, and allow to cool.

Assembly Add infused rum, ginger honey, green tea, vanilla liqueur, and both juices to a shaker with ice and shake vigorously for 10 seconds.

Pour contents of the shaker into a tall glass, leaving space at the top.

Top with Champagne and garnish with the Luxardo cherry, rosemary sprig, and a sprinkle of sea salt.

NOTE To make a punch bowl or large batch serving approximately 15 drinks, combine 1 (750-mL) bottle of Blackberry-infused Rhum J.M 100, 1 (16-oz) jar of Twisted Bee ginger honey, 2 cups sage-infused green tea, ½ cup Giffard vanilla liqueur, 1½ cups grapefruit juice, and 1 cup lemon juice. Top with Champagne.

Originally created by the Luxardo family in Croatia, these marasca cherries are candied in a rich syrup made from the fruit's own juices. Darker and denser than standard maraschino cherries, they have notes of almond and chocolate and are used in cocktails and desserts. Find jarred Luxardo cherries at specialty grocers such as AJ's Fine Foods and Whole Foods, liquor stores like Total Wine & More and BevMo, or online.

T. COOK'S

Mireya Ryan

In the shadow of Camelback Mountain, T. Cook's at Royal Palms Resort captures the beauty of Arizona's Spanish Colonial past. The property's story began in 1929, when it was built as a winter estate for New York financier Delos W. Cooke and his wife, Florence, as a respite from the East Coast's cold weather. They commissioned the construction of a grand mansion, modeling it after properties they had admired in Europe and decorating it with treasures from their travels—colorful tiles, elegant antiques, and the namesake palm trees that would later line the estate's distinguished drive.

By 1948, their private retreat had transformed into the Royal Palms Resort, drawing Hollywood stars like Eva Gabor, Groucho Marx, and Buster Keaton to its sunny courtyards. However, it wasn't until an ambitious renovation that T. Cook's emerged in 1997 as a culinary destination, quickly gaining recognition and collecting awards and accolades.

Today, executive sous chef Mireya Ryan delights guests with "our style, which is very homey, approachable, and honest," she explains, showcasing local bounty in delicious dishes like Hitchcock Farms iceberg hearts dressed in blue cheese and bacon, beets paired with candied walnuts and Crow's Dairy goat cheese, and a juicy K4 Copper State Reserve ribeye partnered with potato pavé.

The enduring charm of the luxurious property continues to draw not only guests but also culinary talent back through its doors. For Ryan, who first joined in 2012 and returned in 2019 after time in San Diego, there's an ineffable quality that defines the resort. "There's something familiar here; it's like a calling," she muses. "It's a magical place."

T. Cook's / **219**

VEGAN RICOTTA

1½ cups whole raw cashews
½ cup plant-based non-dairy heavy cream
½ cup (4 oz) firm tofu
1 tsp nutritional yeast (optional; see Note)
2 Tbsp chopped flat-leaf parsley
1 Tbsp chopped chives
Lemon juice, to taste
Salt, to taste

VEGAN BOLOGNESE

2 cups button or cremini mushrooms
2 red bell peppers, stemmed, seeded, and minced
2 large yellow onions, minced
2 large carrots, minced
4 stalks celery, minced
6 cloves garlic, minced
3 Tbsp extra-virgin olive oil
Kosher salt, to taste
½ cup minced firm tofu
1 cup tomato paste
¼ cup Bragg Liquid Aminos, or plant-based soy sauce (see Note)
2 cups plant-based non-dairy heavy cream
1 Tbsp paprika
1 tsp chili powder
2 Tbsp chopped flat-leaf parsley
1 Tbsp chopped chives
Red wine vinegar, to taste

Vegan Spaghetti Bolognese with Vegan Ricotta

SERVES 4–6 "I like to use nutritional yeast and amino acids in vegan dishes to add umami and depth of flavor," Mireya Ryan explains. Her delicious plant-based bolognese proves the point, with mushrooms and minced vegetables creating a savory sauce. The crowning touch is a dollop of "ricotta" made from cashews that have been soaked and blended with herbs, to add creamy richness to every bite.

Vegan Ricotta In a large pot, bring water to a boil over medium-high heat. Add cashews and boil until soft, 15–20 minutes. Strain, reserving liquid.

Place cashews and vegan cream in a blender. Blend until smooth, 2–3 minutes, adding reserved cashew liquid as needed. Mixture should be smooth, but not loose. Transfer to a mixing bowl.

Blend tofu in a blender until smooth. Add nutritional yeast, if using. Add to cashew cream along with herbs and stir to combine.

Season with lemon juice and salt to taste, adding in small increments until seasoned to preference. Vegan ricotta can be stored in the refrigerator for up to 1 week.

Vegan Bolognese Mince mushrooms by hand or in a food processor, leaving no pieces larger than a dime.

In a mixing bowl, combine minced peppers, onions, carrots, celery, and garlic.

Heat oil in a large pot over medium-high heat until small whisps of smoke appear. Add mushrooms and a pinch of salt to help release their natural liquid. Cook, stirring occasionally, until mushrooms are golden brown and most of the liquid has evaporated, 6–7 minutes.

Add minced vegetables. Cook for 3–5 minutes until vegetables are softened, stirring and scraping bottom of pot with a rubber spatula to prevent burning.

Lower heat to medium-low and add remaining ingredients, except herbs and vinegar. Stir to combine and simmer for 45–60 minutes,

ASSEMBLY

1 lb spaghetti

1–2 tsp extra-virgin olive oil

Vegan Bolognese (see here)

Kosher salt, to taste

Vegan Ricotta, for garnish (see here)

Vegan grated Parmesan or mozzarella, for garnish

scraping the bottom of the pot every 15–20 minutes, until bolognese is reduced to desired thickness. Turn off heat and stir in herbs. Add salt and vinegar in small increments, tasting after each addition, until seasoned to preference.

Assembly Cook spaghetti according to package instructions. Drain, reserving 2 cups of pasta water. Add a drizzle of oil to the pasta in the strainer and toss to coat.

Meanwhile, warm bolognese in a pot over medium heat.

In the pasta pot, heat enough reserved pasta liquid to prevent pasta from sticking. Add spaghetti and stir until hot. Add bolognese and stir to combine. Season with salt to taste.

To serve, divide among serving bowls. Garnish each bowl with a generous spoonful of vegan ricotta and a sprinkle of vegan cheese.

NOTE Nutritional yeast is a deactivated yeast sold as yellow flakes or powder with a distinctive cheesy, nutty flavor, making it a popular ingredient in plant-based cooking. It's readily available at local grocers in the baking or spice aisle, as well as health food stores and online retailers.

Liquid aminos are savory, soy sauce–like seasonings made from soybeans but without added salt or fermentation. They are often used to add savory umami depth to tomato-based sauces, mushroom preparations, and vegetable pasta dishes. You can find Bragg Liquid Aminos at most supermarkets, natural food stores, and online retailers.

CORN SOUBISE

½ cup (1 stick) unsalted butter

1 large yellow onion, sliced

Pinch of kosher salt, plus more to taste

4 ears yellow corn, shucked and kernels cut off the cob

2½ cups heavy cream

ASSEMBLY

4 ears yellow corn, shucked and silks removed

1 lb dried rigatoni

1–2 tsp extra-virgin olive oil

Corn Soubise (see here)

2 Tbsp unsalted butter

1 medium shallot, minced

6 cloves garlic, minced

1 lemon, juiced, to taste

Kosher salt, to taste

Mexican crema, or crème fraîche, for garnish

Chili crisp, such as Mr. Bing brand, for garnish

Crumbled cotija cheese, for garnish

Chopped cilantro or micro cilantro, for garnish

Elote Rigatoni

SERVES 2–4 "This reflects my Mexican culture," Mireya Ryan explains, "though it's also a collaboration between my fellow Latino sous chefs." Here, street-food elote gets dressed up for dinner with a silky soubise sauce and traditional garnishes of crema and cilantro mingling with a modern drizzle of chili crisp. For the full restaurant experience, purchase the same handmade pasta T. Cook's uses, which is available at the front desk.

Corn Soubise Melt butter in a medium pot over medium-low heat.

Add onions and sauté until translucent, 3–4 minutes. While cooking, sprinkle with salt to help release the onions' natural juices.

Add corn kernels and stir to combine. Add cream and stir, then cover with a lid. Simmer for 20–25 minutes or until soft and mushy, stirring every 10 minutes.

Transfer to a blender. Be careful when blending hot liquids. Remove cap on blender lid and cover with a folded dish towel to allow steam pressure to escape and catch any splashes. Purée the corn mixture in batches if needed, being careful not to fill the blender more than halfway. Starting on low speed and gradually increasing to high, blend until velvety smooth.

Season with salt to taste.

Assembly Preheat oven to 350°F. Place corn on a baking sheet and roast for 40 minutes. Allow to cool to room temperature and cut kernels off cobs. Set aside.

Cook rigatoni according to package instructions. Strain, reserving ½ cup of pasta water. Add a drizzle of oil to the pasta in the strainer and toss to coat.

Heat reserved pasta water in same pot over medium-high heat and stir in corn soubise. Add pasta and stir to combine.

Melt butter in a large sauté pan over medium-high heat. Add shallots and garlic and allow to sweat for 20–30 seconds to soften. Stir in corn kernels and season with lemon juice and salt to taste.

To serve, divide pasta among serving dishes and top with sautéed corn mix. Garnish with crema (or crème fraîche), chili crisp, cotija, and cilantro.

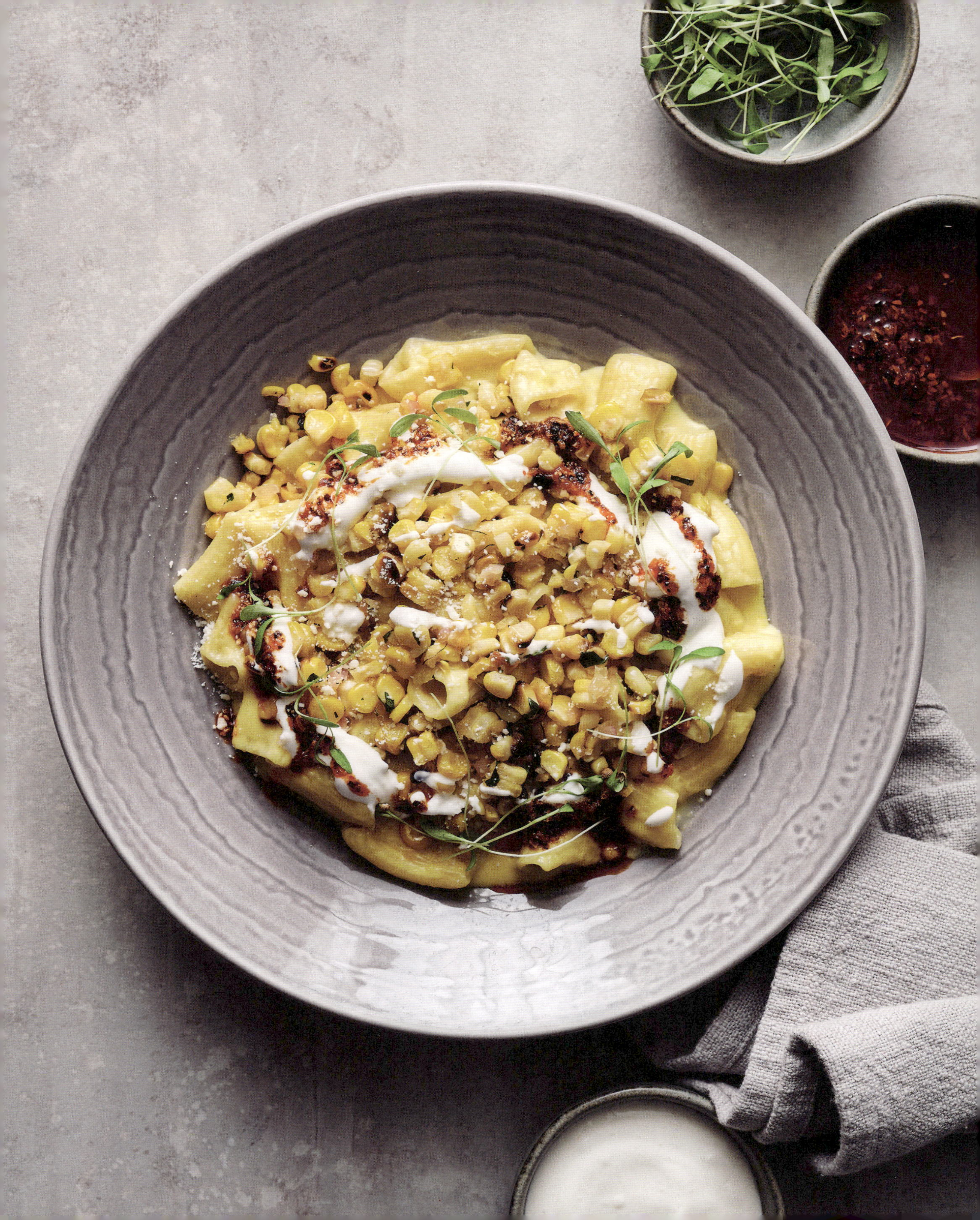

Charismatic restaurateur, author, and Bravo *Top Chef* alum Angelo Sosa possesses a special gift for drawing diners into an experience that resonates far beyond the plate. At Tía Carmen, within the JW Marriott Desert Ridge, the talented chef-owner has created a "love letter to the flavors of the Southwest." Named for his beloved *tía* (aunt) Carmen, the restaurant embodies her nurturing spirit while celebrating Arizona's riches. Together with his right-hand man, destination chef Dejan Djukic, Sosa elevates regional ingredients in dishes like tuna-studded coconut-corn broth perfumed with smoked chile oil, and a spice-crusted ribeye accompanied by the aged mole of ancient traditions. "The valley just continues to surprise me with its beauteous products," Sosa says. "It's an amazing time to embrace the incredible agriculture of Arizona."

But Sosa's storytelling doesn't end there. Enter Kembara, his latest venture, a transportive exploration of Asian flavors under the same roof. The name means "journey" in Malay, fitting for a menu that meanders through the aromatic spice markets, bustling street stalls, and ancestral kitchens of Southeast Asia. "The epitome of the concept is discovery and seeking out the fusion of cultures. Whether it's Malaysia, Singapore, Thailand, Vietnam, or India, it's all so beautiful," Sosa enthuses. It's a passion that materializes in dishes like lamb spring rolls fragrant with coriander and cumin (page 228) and Wagyu beef rendang gently braised in coconut milk and lemongrass.

Together, Sosa and his business partner, restaurateur Mark Stone, have introduced two distinct, unforgettable dining experiences that honor tradition while deliciously redefining it. Each bite at Tía Carmen and Kembara share a narrative, and with Sosa as the storyteller, it's one you'll want to hear again and again.

TÍA CARMEN/ KEMBARA

Dejan Djukic, Angelo Sosa

▶ Tía Carmen's Southwest Tri-Tip Kebabs

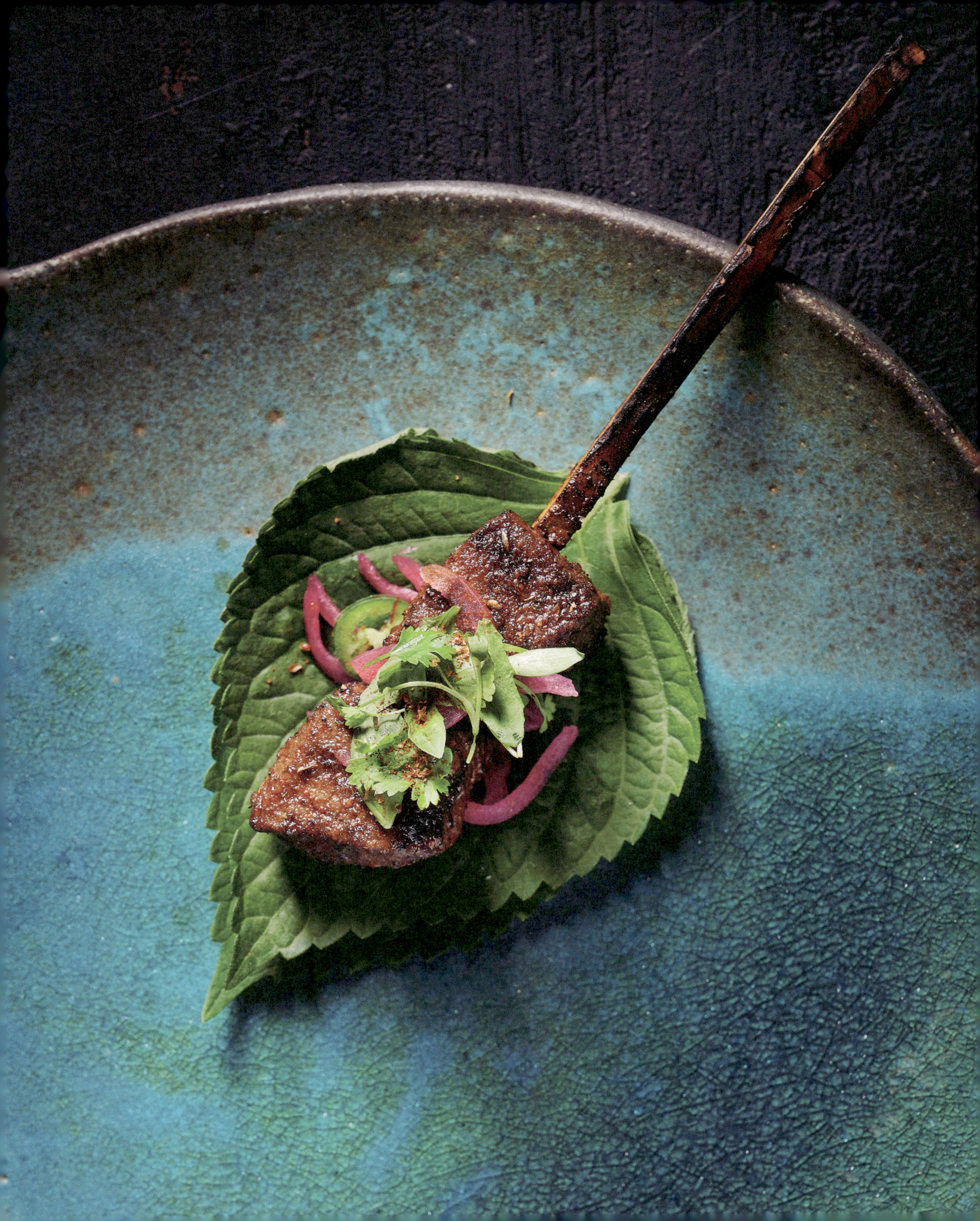

PICKLED ONIONS

1 large red onion, thinly sliced
1 Tbsp pickling spice
1 (2-inch) cinnamon stick
4 Tbsp granulated sugar
1 tsp Diamond Crystal kosher salt
1¼ cups white vinegar
½ cup water

SOUTHWEST SPICE

3½ Tbsp Diamond Crystal kosher salt
1 Tbsp white sesame seeds
4 Tbsp Chimayó chile powder (see Note)
5½ Tbsp sumac
3 Tbsp ground cumin
½ tsp ground turmeric
2 Tbsp dried oregano

MARINATED TRI-TIP

½ lb tri-tip, cut into 1- × 2-inch pieces
2 tsp Southwest Spice (see here)
1 Tbsp grapeseed or other neutral oil
1½ tsp low-sodium soy sauce

Tía Carmen's Southwest Tri-Tip Kebabs

SERVES 2 "When I was creating the menu for Tía Carmen, I realized kebabs would be a perfect canvas for introducing Southwestern flavors, like Chimayó chiles," says Angelo Sosa. "We serve them with perilla leaves for a lighter version of a taco. And the spice blend is so delicious. Try it with Mexican-style rice, fish, or even grits; it's very versatile."

Pickled Onions Place onions into a heatproof container.

Add remaining ingredients to a pot. Bring to a boil over medium-high heat, stirring occasionally to ensure sugar dissolves completely.

Strain hot pickling liquid over onions and allow to cool at room temperature for at least 2 hours. Pickled onions can be stored in the refrigerator for up to 1 month.

Southwest Spice In a spice grinder, blend salt and sesame seeds into a powder. Be careful not to over-blend into a paste. Transfer to a bowl. Add remaining ingredients and stir to combine.

Spice blend can be stored in an airtight container for up to 6 months.

Marinated Tri-Tip In a bowl, mix beef with the remaining ingredients. Allow to marinate in the refrigerator for at least 20 minutes and up to 1 hour.

ASSEMBLY

½ lb Marinated Tri-Tip (see here)
4 fresh perilla leaves (see Note)
½ serrano chile, sliced
1 sprig epazote, leaves only (see Note)
1 sprig Thai basil, leaves only
Pickled Onions, for garnish (see here)
Southwest Spice, for garnish (see here)
Micro cilantro or cilantro leaves, tossed with olive oil and salt, for garnish

Assembly Preheat grill to medium-high heat.

Skewer 1–2 pieces of cubed tri-tip on 4- to 6-inch skewers and place on grill. (To avoid burning skewers, leave ends hanging over edge of grill.)

Grill for 6–10 minutes (depending on desired temperature), rotating to allow even charring.

Remove kebabs from grill and let rest for 2 minutes to let internal juices settle.

Meanwhile, arrange 2 perilla leaves on a plate pointing in alternating directions for each serving. Top each leaf with 1 slice of serrano, a leaf each of epazote and Thai basil, and slices of pickled onion.

To serve, arrange kebabs on prepared perilla leaves. Garnish with a sprinkle of Southwest spice and cilantro.

NOTE Chimayó chiles are grown only in the village of Chimayó in northern New Mexico from heirloom seeds passed down through generations. Sun-dried, they are ground into a bright red powder with a distinctive rich, sweet heat and earthy complexity. Look for Chimayó chile powder at retailers specializing in Southwest ingredients, specialty spice shops like Santa Cruz Chili & Spice Company, and online.

Perilla leaves (called *shiso* in Japanese and *kkaennip* in Korean) are broad, serrated leaves with flavors of mint, basil, and anise. Find perilla at Asian markets like Asiana, H Mart, and Lee Lee International Supermarket, or online through specialty produce suppliers.

Epazote is a Mexican herb with earthy, citrusy, and slightly bitter notes. Look for fresh bundles at Mexican grocers like El Super, Food City, or Los Altos Ranch Market.

CILANTRO YOGURT

1¾ cups plain Greek yogurt
1 cup packed, roughly chopped cilantro
1 tsp chopped green Thai chile
¼ cup lime juice
1 tsp Diamond Crystal kosher salt
⅓ cup grated palm sugar (see Note)

LAMB FILLING

½ cup avocado oil
1½ cups diced white onion
2 Tbsp minced ginger
2 Tbsp minced garlic
1 Tbsp ground coriander
½ tsp ground turmeric
¼ tsp ground cayenne pepper
½ tsp ground toasted cumin seeds
2 tsp Diamond Crystal kosher salt
1 lb ground lamb (80/20)
2½ Tbsp grated palm sugar
2 Tbsp tamarind water (see Note)
⅔ cup diced Roma tomatoes
1 minced green Thai chile
½ cup chopped cilantro

Kembara's Lamb Spring Rolls with Cilantro Yogurt

SERVES 2–4 "This is my version of a samosa in a spring roll," says Angelo Sosa. "We use robust spices and beautiful Colorado lamb that is really clean in flavor, and serve the crispy spring rolls with a cooling cilantro yogurt." Look for ingredients like tamarind pulp (commonly sold in blocks), fresh curry leaves, palm sugar, and spring roll sheets (Sosa recommends Spring Home TYJ brand) in Asian markets.

Cilantro Yogurt At least 48 hours before planning to serve the spring rolls, strain yogurt by lining a strainer with a piece of cheesecloth and setting it over a bowl. Spoon yogurt into center of cheesecloth. Gather edges of cheesecloth together and tie with kitchen twine or a rubber band to form a bundle. Position strainer so that the yogurt is suspended well above the bottom of the bowl, allowing whey to drain. Refrigerate for 48 hours. The strained yogurt should be just over half its original weight.

Prepare an ice bath by filling a large bowl with ice and water. Blanch cilantro by placing it in boiling water for 15–20 seconds, then shock it in the ice bath for 1–2 minutes. Strain and wring out until very dry.

Transfer strained yogurt to a bowl. Add cilantro, chile, lime juice, salt, and palm sugar. Combine until smooth and chill immediately.

Cilantro yogurt can be made 2 days ahead and stored in the refrigerator.

Lamb Filling Heat oil in a sauté pan over medium heat and cook onions, ginger, and garlic until soft and translucent, about 5 minutes. Add coriander, turmeric, cayenne, cumin, and salt. Bloom spices by stirring for 1–2 minutes until they become fragrant.

Add lamb and break it up into the onion and spice mixture, stirring until lamb is well-crumbled and almost fully cooked.

Add palm sugar, tamarind water, and tomatoes. Cook until tomatoes soften and palm sugar is fully dissolved. Do not brown the mixture or over-reduce the sauce; the filling should be soft and moist.

CURRY SALT

½ cup loosely packed
fresh curry leaves

2 Tbsp Diamond Crystal kosher salt

ASSEMBLY

3 large egg yolks

1 package of 8- or 10-inch spring roll wrappers, thawed if frozen

Lamb Filling, chilled (see here)

1–2 quarts olive or avocado oil, for frying

Curry Salt, for garnish (see here)

Cilantro Yogurt, to serve (see here)

Remove from heat and fold in Thai chile and cilantro.

Refrigerate to chill completely before assembling the spring rolls. Lamb filling can be made up to 2 days ahead.

Curry Salt Place curry leaves in a microwave-safe dish and microwave in 20-second increments until completely dry and brittle. This method helps lock in the green color and preserve essential oils.

Combine leaves and salt in a blender or food processor. Blend on high into a fine powder.

Transfer salt to an airtight container and store in a cool, dry place for up to 6 months.

Assembly Make an egg wash by whisking yolks with a few drops of water.

Brush edges of a wrapper with a thin layer of egg wash.

Position wrapper with a corner pointing toward you to form a diamond. Spoon ⅓ cup of the lamb filling in a cylinder shape along the lower third of the wrapper, leaving a 1-inch border on each side. Fold the bottom corner up and over the filling, tucking it snugly. Fold in the sides to enclose the filling, then roll tightly toward the top point. Repeat with the remaining filling and wrappers, covering the finished rolls with a dry towel as you work. You should have about a dozen rolls. Spring rolls can be prepared up to 3 hours ahead, covered, and refrigerated.

In a deep, heavy-bottomed pot, heat oil to 350°F. Fry rolls until golden brown, 4–5 minutes. Remove and drain on a paper towel–lined plate.

To serve, garnish each roll with a dusting of curry salt and serve with cilantro yogurt on the side for dipping.

NOTE Palm sugar is made from the sap of certain varieties of palm tree flowers, which is boiled until it crystallizes and hardens. Typically sold in discs or blocks, it has a rich, caramel-like flavor with butterscotch notes. Grate or finely chop before use for easier measuring.

Tamarind pulp is preferred over paste for its unprocessed flavor. To make tamarind water, soak 1 tablespoon of tamarind pulp in 3 tablespoons of hot water for 30 minutes to 1 hour. Mash pulp to release its flavor, then strain to remove seeds and fibers.

VALENTINE

Crystal Kass, Donald Hawk

At Valentine in downtown Phoenix, a talented team that includes the dynamic duo of executive chef Donald Hawk and executive pastry chef Crystal Kass has propelled Valentine into the national spotlight, earning accolades and James Beard Award nominations along the way.

Hawk, a 2025 James Beard Foundation semifinalist for Best Chef: Southwest, captures the region with bold creativity in dishes like bison tartare tostadas with carne seca XO sauce, tomatillos, and beef chicharrones, and a grass-fed tomahawk steak with Ramona Farms tepary beans seasoned with pork belly, accompanied by tortillas slathered with huitlacoche butter. "Arizona has always been home to me, and I love to show what Arizona has," he explains.

On the sweeter side, Kass, a 2025 James Beard Foundation finalist for Best Pastry Chef, likewise celebrates the region in her signature desserts. "I'm not from Arizona, so it's really exciting to work with native ingredients I've never come across before. I love discovering something new and incorporating it into our desserts and pastry case," she says.

And there's more. The beverage program, overseen by co-owner Blaise Faber, is showcased in both the restaurant and as a deep dive into desert biomes in tucked-away Bar 1912, which earned the cocktail lounge a spot as one of the Regional Top 10 Honorees for Best U.S. Restaurant Bars of the 2025 Spirited Awards.

It's this synergy that makes every visit an experience. "It's all of us," acknowledges Hawk. "It's what my kitchen team does with the food, what Blaise does in the front of house with service and the beverage program, and what Crystal does with pastry. We all work in unison, and I think that's really special."

▶ Sarsaparilla-Glazed Lamb Ribs with Chayote Salad and Burnt Desert Blossom Honey Flan

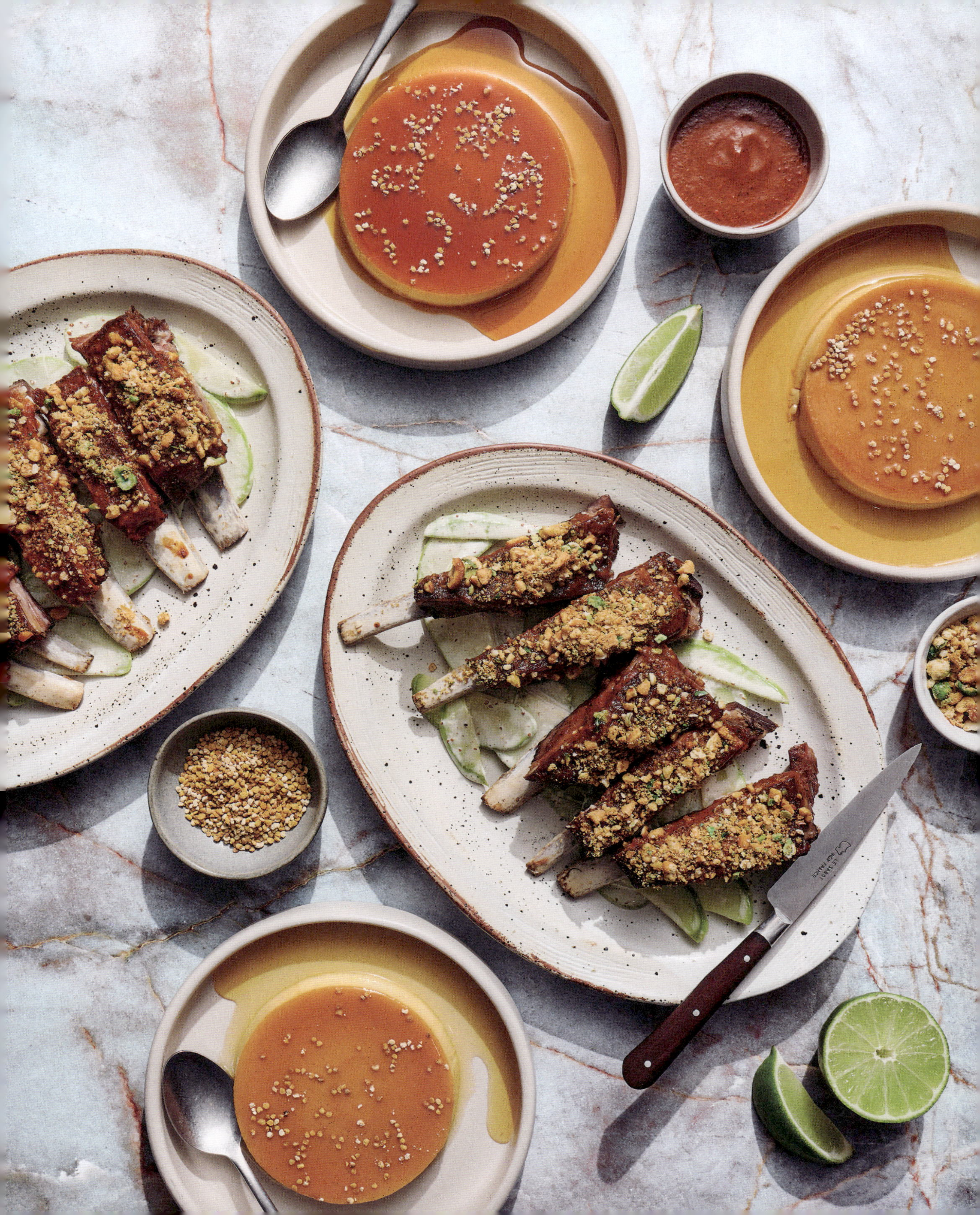

RIB RUB

1 cup kosher salt

1 cup grated piloncillo sugar (or dark brown sugar)

1 Tbsp paprika

1 Tbsp black pepper

1 tsp ground fennel seeds

1 tsp ground coriander seeds

1 Tbsp mesquite flour (see Note)

SARSAPARILLA GLAZE

½ cup toasted sesame oil

2 large yellow onions, diced

6 Fresno chiles, seeds removed and halved

½ cup grated piloncillo sugar (or dark brown sugar)

¼ cup soy sauce

½ cup unseasoned rice wine vinegar

3 (12-oz) bottles of your favorite sarsaparilla (or root beer)

Sarsaparilla-Glazed Lamb Ribs with Chayote Salad

SERVES 4 For this dish, Donald Hawk sources Arizona lamb, a collaboration between Rovey Family Farms and Heartquist Hollow Farm. "It's one of our most popular dishes," he notes, "though we also make it with pork ribs." Chayote squash, native to Mexico, is also known as mirliton and is pear-shaped with wrinkly light green skin. Piloncillo is an unrefined Mexican cane sugar with a rich, caramel-like flavor traditionally sold in cone-shaped pieces. Look for both at local grocers and Latin American markets like Food City and Los Altos Ranch Market.

Rib Rub Combine all ingredients in a bowl and mix until well blended.

Store leftover rub in an airtight container in a cool, dry place for up to 6 months. Rub can be used for smoked meats or to season beef, chicken, and fish.

Sarsaparilla Glaze Heat a large saucepot over high heat and add oil.

Once oil is smoking, add onions and Fresno chiles and lower heat to medium-high. Sauté onions and chiles, stirring occasionally, until golden brown, 10–12 minutes.

Add sugar and stir until dissolved. Add soy sauce, vinegar, and sarsaparilla.

Bring to a simmer and cook, stirring occasionally, until sauce is reduced by half, 15–20 minutes. Allow to cool slightly to prevent steam buildup.

Transfer to a blender. Be careful when blending hot liquids: Remove cap on blender lid and cover with a folded dish towel to allow steam pressure to escape and catch any splashes. Purée the mixture in batches if needed, being careful not to fill the blender more than halfway. Starting on low speed and gradually increasing to high, blend until smooth, then allow to cool completely. Refrigerate until use.

RIBS

2 racks (7-8 lbs) lamb ribs, chine bone removed
1 cup Rib Rub (see here)
1 cup yellow mustard

CHAYOTE SALAD

½ cup Japanese Kewpie mayonnaise (see Note)
2 Tbsp cider vinegar
1 large chayote
Flaky sea salt and black pepper, to taste

ASSEMBLY

Ribs (see here)
Sarsaparilla Glaze (see here)
Chayote Salad (see here)
Sea salt, to taste
2 limes, halved
Mount Hope Spicy Sonoran Snack Mix (optional)

NOTE Mesquite flour, made from the ground pods of the mesquite tree, has a naturally sweet and nutty flavor. It can be sourced from specialty food stores, farmers' markets, or online retailers. If unavailable, omit (do not substitute with all-purpose flour).

Kewpie mayonnaise is a Japanese condiment made with egg yolks and seasoned with rice vinegar that's richer and slightly sweeter than standard American mayonnaise. It's available at grocery stores like Safeway, Albertson's, and AJ's Fine Foods, at Asian markets, or online.

Ribs Up to a day before you plan to serve, coat each rib rack evenly on both sides with ½ cup of rib rub, then apply ½ cup of mustard to each rib rack and spread to evenly coat.

Tightly wrap each rib rack twice in aluminum foil (to protect ribs during roasting).

Allow to marinate in the refrigerator for a minimum of 4 hours and a maximum of 24 hours.

Preheat oven to 300°F.

Place ribs in a single layer on a baking sheet on the lowest rack. Cook for about 3 hours, or until ribs are easily pierced with a knife.

Leaving ribs in foil, allow to cool, then transfer to the refrigerator to chill at least 3 hours or overnight.

Chayote Salad In a mixing bowl, whisk mayonnaise and vinegar together until well combined.

Cut chayote in half lengthwise, then shave or thinly slice chayote crosswise.

In a large bowl, toss chayote with ¼ cup of the mayonnaise dressing, or more to taste. Season with salt and pepper. Refrigerate until needed.

Assembly Turn on broiler or heat grill to medium-high heat.

Remove ribs from foil, reserving liquid to thin glaze if necessary.

Grill or broil ribs for 7–10 minutes, or until just warmed through. Remove and brush ribs generously with sarsaparilla glaze.

Return to grill and cook until ribs are hot and glaze thickens, approximately 5 minutes, watching carefully to prevent burning. Cut racks into individual ribs.

Divide chayote salad among individual serving plates. Divide ribs into portions and place on top. Season with salt and a squeeze of fresh lime juice. Sprinkle with Spicy Sonoran Snack Mix, if using.

BURNT DESERT BLOSSOM HONEY

¾ cup (200 mL) desert blossom or other mild honey

2 Tbsp (30 mL) water, plus more as needed

ASSEMBLY

¼ cup (57 g) water

¾ cup (150 g) granulated sugar

4 large eggs

1 (14-oz) can sweetened condensed milk

1 (12-oz) can evaporated milk

1 tsp (5 g) vanilla paste

½ tsp (3 g) kosher salt

1 Tbsp (25 g) Burnt Desert Blossom Honey (see here)

Bee pollen, for garnish (see Note)

Burnt Desert Blossom Honey Flan

SERVES 6 "This recipe isn't my grandma's, but it's an homage to her," says Crystal Kass. "Anytime there was a birthday, holiday, or special occasion she made flan and it was everybody's favorite. This is my version, with a Southwestern twist using McClendon's desert blossom honey."

Burnt Desert Blossom Honey In a high-sided saucepan over medium heat, bring honey to a simmer. Cook, stirring frequently with a heatproof spatula, until honey develops a rich brown color or measures 300°F using a candy thermometer. This process should take 5–6 minutes.

Remove saucepan from heat. Stand back and slowly add water, as honey will bubble vigorously and release steam. Once honey has stopped bubbling, stir to combine and pour it into a heatproof liquid measuring cup. Add enough water to measure 200 mL of burnt honey.

Allow to cool to room temperature before transferring to a clean jar or airtight container. Leftover honey can be stored in a cool, dark place for up to 6 months and used to sweeten beverages, batters, and marinades, and drizzled over yogurt, pancakes, cheese, and roasted vegetables.

Assembly Preheat oven to 325°F. Arrange six 4-ounce ramekins in a 13- × 9-inch baking dish, ensuring they don't touch each other or the sides of the pan.

Heat water and sugar in a small saucepan over medium heat until sugar caramelizes and reaches a dark amber color, 10–15 minutes.

Working quickly (caramel will harden as it cools), spoon just enough into each ramekin to coat the bottom. If needed, tilt the ramekins in a circular motion to help the caramel spread evenly.

In a mixing bowl, whisk eggs together. Add sweetened condensed milk, evaporated milk, vanilla, salt, and burnt honey and whisk until combined.

Strain twice through a fine-mesh sieve into a clean bowl to ensure a smooth custard. Divide strained custard evenly among the ramekins, leaving about ¼ inch of space at the top.

Create a water bath by carefully pouring hot water into the baking dish halfway up the sides of the ramekins. (Avoid splashing water into the custards as it will ruin the flan.) Cover baking dish tightly with aluminum foil to create a seal that will trap steam. Carefully place in the oven, taking care not to slosh water.

Bake for 40–50 minutes, or until flan jiggles in the center when ramekins are tapped.

Using pot holders, remove hot ramekins from water bath and transfer to a baking sheet or cooling rack. Allow to cool to room temperature, then cover and refrigerate overnight.

To unmold, run a thin knife around the outside of a flan. Place the serving plate on top of the flan and quickly flip the plate and ramekin over. Gently tap bottom of ramekin to help release the flan. Repeat for remaining flans.

To serve, sprinkle each flan with bee pollen.

NOTE Collected by bees from flower blossoms, bee pollen comes in granular form and adds a subtly sweet floral and earthy flavor. Find jarred bee pollen in the health food aisles of grocery stores, at specialty markets, or online.

VECINA

James Fox

In Spanish, *vecina* means neighbor, and at his Phoenix gathering spot, chef-owner James Fox is busy defining what it means to be part of the culinary neighborhood. Here, traditional boundaries between Latin American cuisine and global flavors don't just blur; they throw block parties together.

"I love Mexican and Latin food," says Fox, who lived in Mexico for a year as a personal chef. "I joke with my guys in the kitchen and say in Spanish that though I'm a large white man, my soul, *mi alma, es Mexicano*. It always gets a pretty good chuckle, but they know it to be true."

Under the tagline "Modern American, Latin-Inspired," Vecina deliberately avoids traditional constraints. "We didn't want to pigeon-hole it with people thinking 'These tacos should be coming with rice and beans,' or 'Why don't you have a fried-fish taco on the menu?'" Instead, Fox focuses on "trying to flip things on their head and make the menu as different and exciting for people as we can."

This approach extends throughout his cuisine with an innovative flair that weaves in Asian, Middle Eastern, and Southwestern influences. There's smoked chicken with tomatillo nam prik and peanut mole, brisket confit suadero tacos with chile jam, and fish tacos garnished with Thai basil, mint, and cilantro (page 240), the latter being "the most popular item on the menu by far," notes Fox.

"The menu is fun and unique," Fox explains. "I want to share how much love and appreciation I have for Mexican food and culture and honor that in my own way."

▶ Papas Verde with Green Chorizo

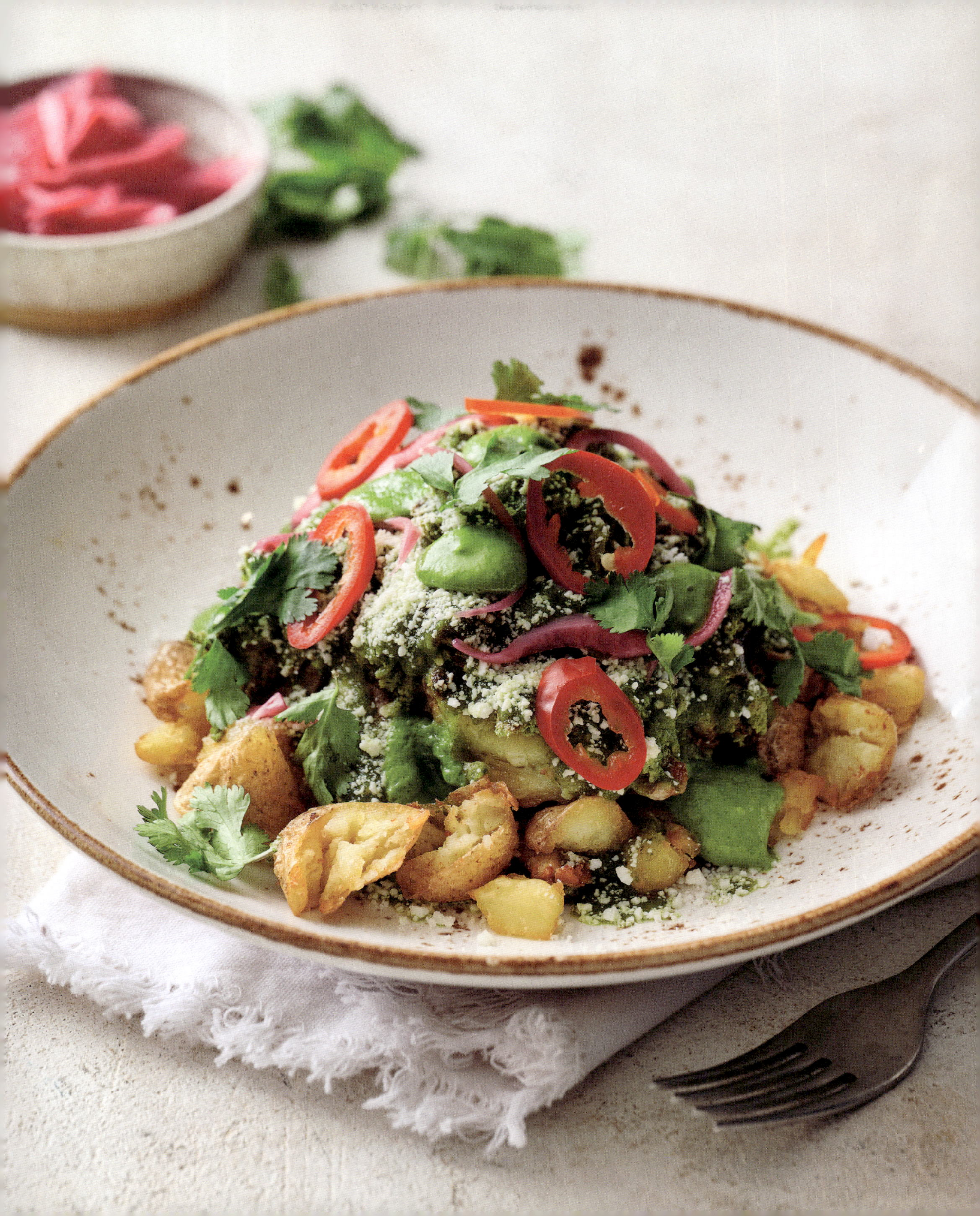

GREEN CHORIZO
1 poblano chile
2 serrano chiles, stemmed
1½ cups flat-leaf parsley
1½ cups cilantro
3 cloves garlic
2 Tbsp + 2 tsp apple cider vinegar
1 tsp jalapeño powder
2 tsp kosher salt
½ tsp black pepper
1 tsp white vinegar powder
⅛ tsp ground cumin
⅛ tsp ground coriander
1 lb ground pork

SMASHED FINGERLING POTATOES
½ lb fingerling potatoes
1 Tbsp light olive oil
½ tsp kosher salt

TOMATILLO SALSA
½ lb tomatillos, husked and rinsed
½ serrano chile
1 clove garlic
¼ cup diced yellow onion
½ cup tightly packed cilantro
½ tsp kosher salt

Papas Verde with Green Chorizo

SERVES 2 For his sophisticated take on Mexican drive-thru comfort food, James Fox reimagined "the loaded fries I'd order at Filiberto's-type places when I was younger." To do that, he loads up crispy fingerling potatoes with herb-packed chorizo, cheese, tomatillo salsa, and charred jalapeño crema. "These make a fantastic snack anytime," Fox adds, "or put a couple eggs on top for a delicious breakfast."

Green Chorizo Roast poblano chile over an open flame or under a broiler, turning until all sides begin to blister and char. Place in a plastic bag or a small bowl covered with plastic wrap. Set aside for 10 minutes to steam and loosen skin. Peel off skin and remove stem and seeds.

Add roasted poblano and the remaining ingredients, except pork, to a blender and blend into a smooth paste.

In the bowl of a stand mixer fitted with the paddle attachment (or by hand), combine ground pork and seasoning paste until well combined. Chorizo is best when freshly made but can be stored in the refrigerator for up to 4 days. Leftover chorizo can be stuffed into tacos, burritos, and quesadillas and added to queso dip, nachos, and scrambled eggs.

Smashed Fingerling Potatoes Preheat oven to 400°F.

In a bowl, toss potatoes with oil and salt. Arrange on a sheet pan and roast for 30 minutes or until pierced easily with a knife. Allow to cool, then refrigerate.

Once potatoes are chilled, press down on them with your hand or a spatula until potatoes are flattened but still intact.

Tomatillo Salsa In a medium pot over high heat, combine tomatillos, serrano, garlic, and onions and add enough water to just cover.

Bring to a boil and boil for 2 minutes, until all vegetables have softened. Refrigerate until chilled, 10–15 minutes.

Transfer to a blender, add cilantro and salt, and blend until smooth.

JALAPEÑO CREMA

2 Tbsp finely chopped, roasted jalapeño (see Note)
¼ cup roasted garlic paste (homemade or store-bought)
2 whole bunches cilantro
½ tsp kosher salt
½ cup jocoque, or crème fraîche or sour cream

PICKLED RED ONIONS

2 red onions, sliced thin
1 cup red wine vinegar
1½ tsp granulated sugar
1 tsp kosher salt

ASSEMBLY

2 quarts + 1 Tbsp light olive oil, divided
½ cup Green Chorizo (see here)
2 cups Smashed Fingerling Potatoes (see here)
1 tsp kosher salt
¼ cup shredded queso menonita, divided (see Note)
¼ cup Tomatillo Salsa (see here)
1 Tbsp crumbled cotija cheese
7–9 jarred pickled peppers
7–9 slices Pickled Red Onions (see here)
2 Tbsp Jalapeño Crema (see here)
1 Fresno chile, sliced, for garnish
Cilantro leaves, for garnish

Jalapeño Crema Add roasted jalapeño, garlic paste, cilantro, and salt to a blender and purée until smooth. Mix with jocoque (or crème fraîche or sour cream) until well combined.

Pickled Red Onions Place onions in a container.

Stir vinegar, sugar, and salt together in a bowl until sugar and salt are dissolved.

Pour over onions and allow to pickle at room temperature for at least 1 hour. Pickled onions will keep in the refrigerator for up to 1 month.

Assembly Turn oven on to broil.

Heat 2 quarts of oil in a pot over medium-high heat to 350°F.

On another burner, heat the remaining 1 tablespoon of oil in an oven-safe pan over medium-high heat. Add green chorizo and brown, breaking it up with a spatula, until it is fully cooked.

Meanwhile, deep-fry smashed potatoes for 3–4 minutes, or until they are crispy and golden brown. Use a slotted spoon or frying basket to remove potatoes and transfer to a bowl. Toss with salt.

Add potatoes and half of the menonita cheese to the pan of green chorizo and stir until evenly combined.

Sprinkle remaining menonita on top and place pan under the broiler for 30 seconds to 1 minute, just until cheese has melted.

Transfer hot chorizo and potato mixture to a serving bowl or platter. Garnish with tomatillo salsa, cotija, pickled peppers, pickled red onions, jalapeño crema, Fresno chiles, and cilantro.

NOTE To roast, place jalapeño over an open flame or under a broiler, turning occasionally, until skins are charred and blistered. Place in bag to steam for 10 minutes. Peel off skin and remove stems and seeds.

Queso menonita is a semi-soft, mild cheese that originated with Mennonite settlers in northern Mexico and has a creamy texture that melts easily. Look for it at Mexican markets like Food City, Pro's Ranch Market, and Los Altos Ranch Market, or online. If unavailable, substitute with Monterey Jack.

CHORIZO SEASONING BLEND
1 cup chili powder
1 Tbsp chili flakes
2 Tbsp kosher salt
3 Tbsp granulated sugar
2½ tsp garlic powder
2 tsp black pepper
2 tsp ground coriander
4 tsp ground oregano
2 tsp ground cinnamon
1 tsp ground cloves
1 tsp white vinegar powder (see Note)

YUZU KOSHO AIOLI
1 cup mayonnaise
¼ tsp yuzu kosho
3 Tbsp aji amarillo paste

ASSEMBLY
⅛ cup cilantro leaves
8 mint leaves
8 Thai basil leaves
Extra-virgin olive oil, to dress herbs
4 (2-oz) salmon fillets, cut to fit tortillas
¼ tsp kosher salt
3 Tbsp Chorizo Seasoning Blend (see here)
2 Tbsp light olive oil
4 (6-inch) flour tortillas
¼ cup Yuzu Kosho Aioli (see here)
¼ cup peeled and diced ruby red grapefruit segments
¼ cup peeled and diced orange segments
½ tsp pink peppercorns, crushed in a mortar and pestle
Lime wedges, to serve

Faroe Island Salmon Tacos with Yuzu Kosho Aioli

SERVES 2 "I love working with citrus," says James Fox, who pairs spice-crusted salmon with fresh orange and grapefruit segments in these tacos. "The aioli adds more of it with yuzu kosho and aji amarillo peppers, which also have a citrusy note." Look for jars of yuzu kosho (a Japanese citrus-chile condiment) at Asian grocers and aji amarillo paste (made with Peruvian chiles) at Latin markets, or source both online.

Chorizo Seasoning Blend Mix all ingredients until well combined.

Seasoning can be stored in an airtight container for up to 3 months and can also be used for making pork chorizo, as a BBQ rub, or as a seasoning for chicken and beef.

Yuzu Kosho Aioli Place all ingredients in a bowl and whisk together until well combined.

Leftover aioli will keep in the refrigerator for 2 weeks and can be used as a dipping sauce or spread for sandwiches and burgers.

Assembly In a small bowl, toss herbs with a drizzle of extra-virgin olive oil and set aside.

Season salmon fillets with salt on one side and chorizo seasoning on both sides.

Heat light olive oil in a nonstick pan over medium heat and add salmon. For medium-rare, sear fillets for 30 seconds to 1 minute depending on thickness, then flip and cook for an additional 10 seconds. Cook longer if you prefer your salmon more well done.

Meanwhile, warm tortillas in a skillet or comal over medium heat, about 5 seconds per side.

To serve, divide salmon between the tortillas. For each taco, place 3 dollops of aioli around the salmon and garnish with 1 tablespoon each of grapefruit and orange segments. Divide herb salad between the tacos and sprinkle with crushed pink peppercorns. Serve with lime wedges.

NOTE White vinegar powder is a dehydrated form of white vinegar that adds a tangy flavor without adding liquid. You can find it in specialty spice shops or online.

Vecina / **241**

WEFT & WARP ART BAR + KITCHEN

Sam DeMarco, Ethan Blanset

In 2023, Andaz Scottsdale Resort & Bungalows welcomed the arrival of gregarious executive chef Sam DeMarco, affectionately known as "Sammy D." "At this point in my career, I'm ready to concentrate on the Mediterranean side of things at Weft & Warp," says the seasoned chef, whose experience spans continents, cuisines, and even television screens.

Born and raised in Brooklyn, DeMarco earned his stripes in some of New York City's most prestigious kitchens, including The River Café and Regine's, before launching his first restaurant, aptly named First, which earned him the moniker "The King of Comfort Food." Stints in Australia, Dubai, and Amsterdam followed, before he returned stateside to Las Vegas landmarks like The Venetian and the Bellagio, and, most recently, the Comus Inn in Maryland. TV audiences may also recognize him from *Chow Masters*, a Travel Channel series where he and his best friend, Hollywood director Frank Coraci, crisscrossed the country in search of creative comfort food.

At Weft & Warp, expect to find a menu with a vibrant Mediterranean flair that still makes room for DeMarco's Italian roots; that Lebanese chicken paillard with fattoush salad is as much a knockout as the handmade gemelli pasta with rabbit ragu. Inspired by the nearby Cattle Track Arts Compound, the restaurant features custom art pieces along with floor-to-ceiling windows that frame breathtaking views of Camelback Mountain—a setting where DeMarco feels right at home. "The weaving of the restaurant's beauty, food, and art represents so much of who I am," says DeMarco. "It resonates with me conceptually and I feel very fortunate to be part of it."

▸ Porcini Lasagna

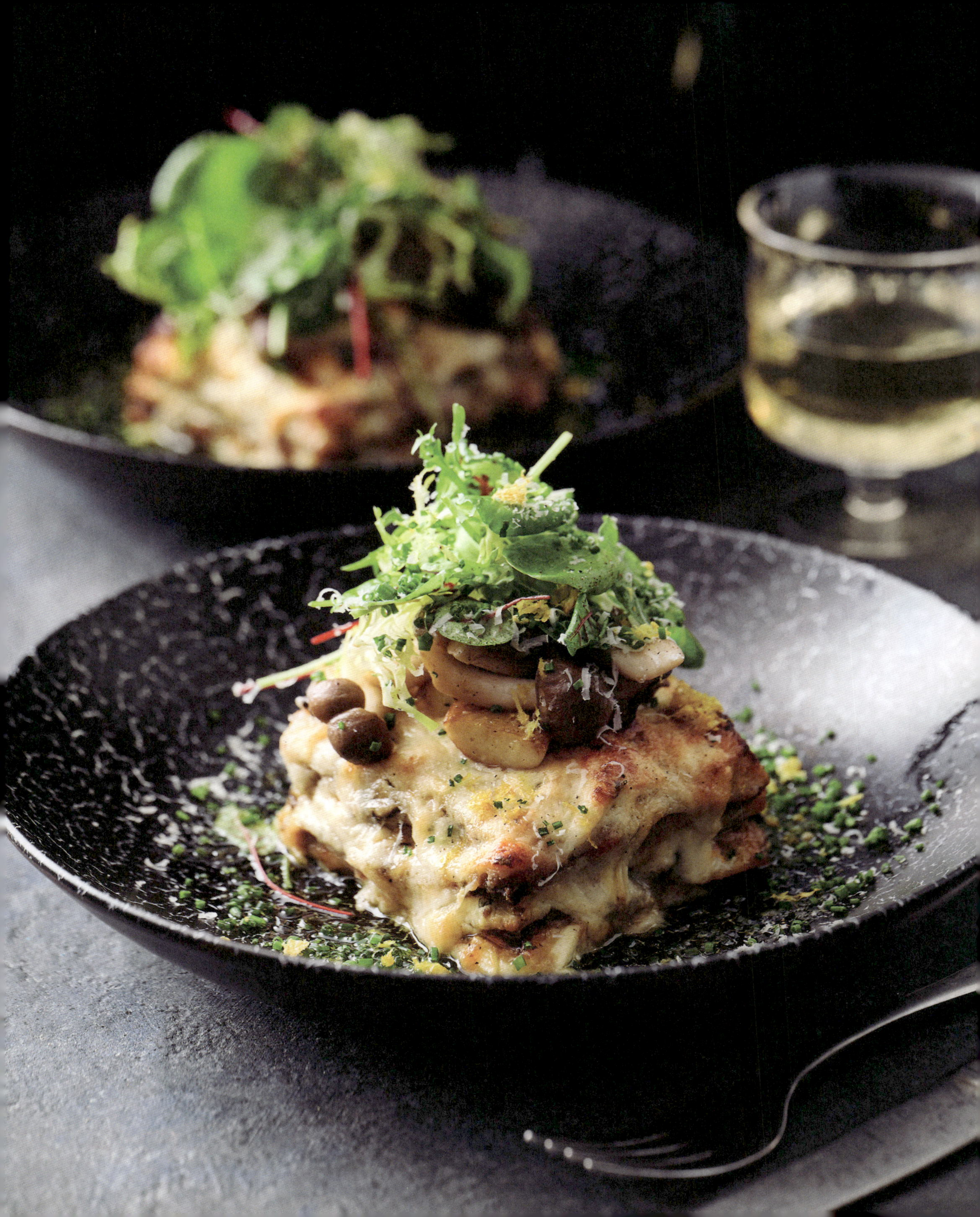

RICOTTA FILLING

3 lbs ricotta cheese
1 Tbsp finely chopped basil
1 tsp chili flakes
1 anchovy fillet, minced
1 Tbsp kosher salt
1½ tsp black pepper
3 Tbsp extra-virgin olive oil

BÉCHAMEL

½ cup (1 stick) butter, cut into 1 Tbsp chunks
1 bay leaf
½ tsp ground nutmeg
1 tsp kosher salt
½ tsp black pepper
½ cup all-purpose flour
8 cups (½ gallon) whole milk

PORCINI MUSHROOM RAGU

½ cup canola oil, divided
2 lbs cremini mushrooms, sliced
1 (2-lb) bag frozen porcini mushrooms, defrosted in refrigerator and sliced
10 Tbsp (1¼ sticks) butter, divided
2 tsp minced thyme leaves, divided
2 cups finely diced celery
2 cups finely diced onion
2 cups finely diced carrot
1 cup black truffle peelings (see Note)
2 cups sweet Marsala wine
2 tsp truffle salt
1 tsp black pepper

Porcini Lasagna

SERVES 8–10 "I grew up with Sicilian Italian great-grandparents," says Sam DeMarco. "We always had lasagna, and I like to make things that are nostalgic to me. While this isn't grandma's lasagna, it's based on my memories of old-school Italian."

Ricotta Filling Mix all ingredients in a bowl until smooth and well combined. Refrigerate until ready to use.

Béchamel Melt butter in a large pot over medium heat with bay leaf, nutmeg, salt, and pepper.

Sprinkle flour over the melted butter. Using a wooden spoon, mix flour into butter, creating a roux, or thick paste. Cook roux, stirring frequently, for 30 seconds to 1 minute. Be careful not to brown the roux; it should remain a light color.

Remove pot from heat and gradually add milk, whisking continuously to break up any lumps.

Return pot to heat and reduce to medium-low. Cook sauce, whisking often, until it thickens to the consistency of runny sour cream, 8–10 minutes. Lower heat as needed to prevent it from boiling.

Cook until béchamel is smooth and coats the back of the spoon without running back when you draw your finger across it, another 3–5 minutes. Keep warm.

Porcini Mushroom Ragu Heat a large sauté pan over medium-high heat and add enough oil to coat the bottom. Combine cremini and porcini mushrooms in a bowl.

In 4 batches, sauté mushrooms until they release their moisture and start to brown. For each batch, when the mushrooms are almost golden brown, add 2 tablespoons of butter and a pinch of thyme. Stir to coat mushrooms. Transfer to a bowl.

Repeat process with remaining mushrooms, adding more oil, butter, and thyme as needed for each batch. Set aside.

In a medium pot over medium heat, melt 2 tablespoons of butter and add 2 tablespoons of oil. Add celery, onions, and carrots and sauté

RED WINE VINAIGRETTE

⅓ cup red wine vinegar
1 Tbsp Dijon mustard
1 tsp honey
½ cup extra-virgin olive oil
½ tsp black pepper
½ tsp kosher salt

PORCINI LASAGNA

Butter, for greasing
5 (13- × 9-inch) cooked homemade or store-bought pasta sheets (or two 1-lb boxes of lasagna noodles, cooked according to package instructions)
Béchamel (see here)
Ricotta Filling, divided into 3 equal portions (see here)
3 cups grated Parmesan
3 cups grated smoked mozzarella
Porcini Mushroom Ragu, divided into 2 equal portions (see here)

until softened, stirring occasionally. Add cooked mushrooms and truffle peelings to the pot and stir to combine.

Add wine and deglaze by scraping up any browned bits from the bottom of the pot. Simmer until liquid has reduced significantly, 10–15 minutes. Ragu should be moist but not soupy. Add truffle salt and pepper.

Red Wine Vinaigrette Combine all ingredients in a mason jar and shake vigorously to emulsify.

Red wine vinaigrette will keep in the refrigerator for up to 2 weeks. Vinaigrette is also delicious as a marinade for meat, fish, and chicken, drizzled over roasted vegetables, or tossed with pasta salad.

Porcini Lasagna Preheat oven to 325°F.

Butter a lasagna pan or 9- × 13-inch baking dish.

Place one layer of pasta in the bottom of the pan. Spread 2 cups of béchamel over pasta, then one-third of the ricotta filling. Sprinkle with ½ cup of Parmesan and ½ cup of mozzarella.

Add another pasta layer. Spread 2 cups of béchamel over pasta, then half of the mushroom ragu. Sprinkle with ½ cup of Parmesan and ½ cup of mozzarella.

Add another pasta layer. Spread 2 cups of béchamel, then one-third of the ricotta filling. Sprinkle with ½ cup of Parmesan and ½ cup of mozzarella.

Add another pasta layer. Spread 2 cups of béchamel, then the remaining mushroom ragu. Sprinkle with ½ cup of Parmesan and ½ cup of mozzarella.

Cover with final pasta sheet(s). Spread 2 cups of béchamel, then the remaining ricotta filling. Sprinkle with the remaining cheeses.

Wrap lasagna with food-grade plastic wrap, cover with foil, and bake for 45 minutes.

Remove plastic wrap and foil and increase oven temperature to 425°F. Bake until top is golden brown, 15–20 minutes.

Allow lasagna to set for 15–20 minutes before serving.

ASSEMBLY

2 to 2½ cups frisée lettuce

2 to 2½ cups watercress

¼ cup Red Wine Vinaigrette (see here)

Kosher salt and black pepper, to taste

Baked Porcini Lasagna (see here)

2–3 cups cooked mushrooms, for garnish (optional)

Grated Parmigiano-Reggiano, for garnish

1 large lemon, zested, for garnish

Minced chives, for garnish

Assembly In a large bowl, combine frisée and watercress, toss with red wine vinaigrette, and season with salt and pepper.

Cut lasagna into 8–10 pieces. For each serving, place a piece of lasagna in the center of a plate. Top with a few cooked mushrooms, if using, and then approximately ½ cup of salad mix. Garnish with Parmigiano-Reggiano, lemon zest, and chives.

NOTE Black truffle peelings are thinly sliced black truffles preserved in brine or oil. Look for them at specialty grocers, or from online gourmet retailers such as D'Artagnan Foods and Urbani Truffles.

LAMB DEMI-GLACE

4 lbs lamb bones
2 Tbsp tomato paste
1 cup red wine
1 onion, chopped
1 large carrot, peeled and chopped
2 large stalks celery, chopped
6 cups (1½ quarts) water
2 sprigs thyme
1 bay leaf
10 black peppercorns

BRAISED LAMB SHANKS

4 (12- to 14-oz) volcano lamb shanks (see Note)
1 Tbsp kosher salt
1 Tbsp black pepper
1 cup canola oil
6 large stalks celery, chopped
2 large onions, chopped
3 large carrots, chopped
1½ cups white wine

2 cups plain Greek yogurt
3 preserved lemons, pulp removed (see Note)
3 lemons, halved
1 sprig Greek oregano
1 bunch fresh thyme
1 Calabrian chile
2 heads garlic, cut in half crosswise

Shawarma Spiced Lamb Shank with Garlic Sauce, Herb Salad, and Saffron Couscous

SERVES 4 "This is a play on lamb shawarma but on a whole different level," says Sam DeMarco. "Instead of cooking it the traditional way, we braise a lamb shank for an elevated restaurant setting but still with those familiar flavors. It's so tender you can shred it with your fork to create your own lamb pitas with the herb salad and creamy garlic sauce."

Lamb Demi-Glace Preheat oven to 350°F.

Place lamb bones in a roasting pan and roast until golden brown, rotating bones for even browning, 30–45 minutes. Add tomato paste, stir to coat bones, and continue roasting until tomato paste darkens, about 15–20 minutes. Add onions, carrots, and celery to the pan. Roast until vegetables are golden brown, 20–30 minutes.

Transfer bones and vegetables to a stockpot over low heat. Deglaze the roasting pan with wine, scraping up any browned bits, and add to the pot. Add water, thyme, bay leaf, and peppercorns. Simmer for 8–10 hours.

Strain stock through a fine-mesh sieve or cone strainer and return to pot, discarding bones and solids. Continue to simmer, stirring occasionally for 8–10 hours, or until reduced to 2 cups and thick and glossy.

Allow demi-glace to cool and store in the refrigerator, where it will keep for 1 week. Demi-glace can also be frozen for up to 3 months.

Braised Lamb Shanks Preheat oven to 325°F.

Season lamb shanks with salt and pepper.

Heat oil in a large skillet on high heat. Sear lamb shanks until golden brown on all sides. Place shanks in a roasting pan, reserving oil in skillet.

To the same skillet over medium heat, add celery, onions, and carrots. Cook until softened, about 8 minutes. Deglaze with wine, scraping up any browned bits from the bottom of the skillet.

Pour sautéed vegetables and wine over shanks in the roasting pan. Stir in yogurt and preserved lemons. Squeeze the juice from the fresh lemons over the meat and discard peels. Add oregano, thyme, chile, and garlic to the pan. Pour enough

CREAMY GARLIC SAUCE
½ cup plain Greek yogurt
½ cup mayonnaise
¼ cup tahini
2 tsp lemon juice
2 cloves garlic, grated
Kosher salt and black pepper, to taste

PICKLED RED ONIONS
1 medium red onion, thinly sliced
2 tsp sugar
2 tsp kosher salt
¾ cup red wine vinegar

SAFFRON COUSCOUS
2½ cups chicken bone broth
1 Tbsp butter
Pinch of saffron
1 lemon, juiced
1 (16-oz) package couscous
½ cup Craisins, or dried cranberries
½ cup dried apricots, chopped
½ cup Marcona almonds, chopped
1 tsp kosher salt
½ tsp black pepper

water into the roasting pan to just cover the shanks.

Cover pan with food-grade plastic wrap and then with aluminum foil. Cook for 3 hours, until fork tender, and set aside, reserving braising liquid.

Braised shanks can be refrigerated in their braising liquid for up to 1 week. To reheat, allow to come to room temperature, cover, and place in a 325°F oven, and braise until internal temperature reaches 130°F, 30–45 minutes.

Creamy Garlic Sauce Combine all ingredients in a bowl and whisk together until smooth. Season to taste with salt and pepper and store in the refrigerator for up to 1 week.

Pickled Red Onions Layer onions in a mason jar or other heatproof glass container. Simmer sugar, salt, and vinegar in a pot over medium heat, stirring until salt and sugar dissolve. Pour pickling liquid over onions and allow to cool. Pickled onions can be stored in the refrigerator for up to 2 weeks.

Saffron Couscous In a pot over medium-high heat, bring broth, butter, saffron, and lemon juice to a boil. Add couscous and stir well to combine.

Reduce heat to low and stir in Craisins (or dried cranberries), apricots, almonds, salt, and pepper. Cover, remove from heat, and let sit for 15 minutes. Remove lid and fluff couscous with a fork. Keep warm.

HERB SALAD

¾ cup dill fronds
¾ cup mint leaves
¾ cup flat-leaf parsley leaves
2 tsp lemon oil
1 tsp lemon juice

PISTACHIO PITA

4 (6-inch) pita breads
Extra-virgin olive oil
1 Tbsp za'atar spice (see Note)
1 Tbsp toasted pistachios, finely chopped

ASSEMBLY

4 Braised Lamb Shanks (see here)
1 cup of lamb shank braising liquid (see here)
2 cups Lamb Demi-Glace (see here)
6 Tbsp (¾ stick) unsalted butter
Saffron Couscous (see here)
Creamy Garlic Sauce (see here)
Herb Salad, for garnish (see here)
Pickled Red Onions, for garnish (see here)
Pistachio Pita, to serve (see here)

Herb Salad Combine herbs in a bowl and toss with lemon oil and lemon juice.

Pistachio Pita Heat a skillet or grill pan to medium-high heat. Warm pita and drizzle top with oil. Sprinkle with za'atar and pistachios and cut into wedges.

Assembly In a saucepan, combine lamb shanks, braising liquid, demi-glace, and butter. Simmer over low heat. Baste lamb shanks, allowing liquid to reduce and thicken, until shanks are coated and sticky.

To serve, place 1 cup of couscous in center of each plate. Nestle lamb shank into couscous and drizzle with pan sauce. Top with a dollop of garlic sauce and garnish with herb salad and pickled onions. Serve each plate with pistachio pita wedges.

NOTE Volcano lamb shanks are traditional shanks with the bone cleaned or "frenched" and can be sourced from online retailers such as Case Custom Meats, D'Artagnan Foods, and Allen Brothers. Regular lamb shanks are available at Arizona farms such as Heartquist Hollow, local butchers like Arcadia Meat Market, specialty grocery stores, and Middle Eastern markets.

Preserved lemons, a staple in North African and Middle Eastern cooking, are citrus cured in salt and their own juices. Before cooking, rinse off excess salt. Typically the pulp is discarded and only the softened peel used.

Za'atar is a Middle Eastern spice blend typically made with dried thyme, oregano, sumac, and toasted sesame seeds. Look for it in the spice aisle of most grocery stores, specialty markets like Baiz Market and Caspian Food Market, or online.

WREN & WOLF

Jackson "Jax" Donahue, Ivan Gonzalez

From Mexican hotspot Chico Malo and retro plane-themed Carry On lounge to Creampuff Donuts and Wren & Wolf—with its hidden Trophy Room—co-owners Thor Nguyen and Teddy and Katie Myers of Pretty Decent Concepts have built a portfolio that defies convention. By the end of 2025, they will have added five more concepts, but Wren & Wolf may be their most dramatic: a 10,000-square-foot downtown space that's both daring and refined.

Located on the ground floor of Renaissance Square, the restaurant, which serves breakfast, lunch, and dinner, blends modern luxury with a wild, untamed aesthetic. "It's a surprise to find a beautiful restaurant like this downtown," says culinary director Ivan Gonzalez. "It's like a museum." Caramel leather booths curve around marble-topped tables against a backdrop of striking wildlife murals. Overhead, cascading greenery intertwines with suspended birds, while fur-draped chairs lend an unexpected opulence.

The menus mirror the dramatic decor, with Gonzalez's bold dishes spanning the globe—from cheese-stuffed za'atar man'ouche, a Middle Eastern flatbread, to a showstopping beef Wellington for two. As beverage director, James Beard Award nominee Jackson "Jax" Donahue oversees the group's innovative beverage program that, as he notes, "is designed to appeal to both the casual drinker and the cocktail geek." For a more clandestine experience, duck behind a drape to discover the Trophy Room, where a vintage storage cabinet equipped with phone chargers ensures the cocktail sanctum's mysteries remain untold—no devices allowed.

Pretty Decent Concepts has solidified a reputation for trendsetting projects, and with talents like Gonzalez and Donahue leading the charge, the menus are as memorable as the spaces themselves.

10 Anaheim chiles

7 poblano chiles

7 green bell peppers

2 (1½-lb) Niman Ranch pork shanks

3 Tbsp salt, divided

1 Tbsp ground black pepper, divided

2 Tbsp canola oil

2 yellow onions, peeled and quartered

1 head garlic, cloves separated and peeled

4 cups amber beer

6 cups chicken stock

Mexican crema, for garnish

Warm flour or corn tortillas, to serve

Braised Pork Shank Chili Verde

SERVES 2 "Being from Sonora, we didn't make a lot of moles, but we did have a lot of chiles," says Ivan Gonzalez. "This was a dish my grandmother made that I've re-created. There were thirteen kids in our house, so we didn't eat pork often. But when we did, it was a fiesta with my aunts and uncles there and my grandparents making tortillas and roasting chiles."

Assembly Preheat oven to 350°F.

Roast the chiles and bell peppers over an open flame or under a broiler, turning until all sides begin to blister and char. Place in a plastic bag or a large bowl covered with plastic wrap. Set aside for 10 minutes to steam and loosen skins. Peel off skins and remove stems and seeds.

Season pork shanks with 1 tablespoon of salt and 1½ teaspoons of black pepper.

Heat oil in a large sauté pan over medium-high heat. Once the oil is hot, add pork shanks and sear, turning with tongs to ensure they are evenly browned on all sides. Remove and set in a large roasting pan with a lid.

Add onions, garlic, roasted chiles and peppers, beer, chicken stock, and the remaining salt and pepper to the roasting pan.

Cover and roast for approximately 2½ hours, or until pork shanks are fork tender. Remove pork shanks and set aside.

Carefully transfer braising liquid and vegetables from the roasting pan to a blender. To avoid steam and pressure buildup, you may need to do this in batches, filling the blender no more than halfway. Remove cap on blender lid to allow steam to escape (cover with a folded towel when blending to catch any splashes). Begin blending on the lowest speed, gradually increasing to a higher speed until the sauce is smooth.

To serve, place pork shanks in shallow bowls, pour sauce over each shank, and garnish with crema. Serve with warm tortillas.

RED BELL PEPPER SYRUP
4–6 red bell peppers
1 cup granulated sugar

CHILTEPIN COINTREAU
6 oz (¾ cup) Cointreau orange liqueur
1 tsp chiltepin chiles

ASSEMBLY
3 basil leaves
1 oz lime juice
½ oz tangerine juice
¾ oz Red Bell Pepper Syrup (see here)
½ tsp Chiltepin Cointreau (see here)
¼ oz Liquore Strega
1½ oz Ketel One Vodka
1 orange peel, cut into a 1-inch-wide strip with minimal white pith, for garnish
1 basil leaf, for garnish

Chil-te-bell

SERVES 1 For a sipper that captures the spirit of the Southwest, Jax Donahue wanted to create an approachable vegetal and citrus-forward daisy-style cocktail with a kick. Highlighting Arizona's treasures, he incorporates Cointreau infused with chiltepin, the only chile native to the state. Find these fiery red peppercorn-sized chiles at Mexican markets (sometimes labeled as chile tepin), specialty spice shops like Santa Cruz Chili & Spice Company, or online.

Red Bell Pepper Syrup Slice peppers in half and remove stems and seeds.

Put peppers through a juicer and strain through a fine-mesh strainer into a measuring cup to measure 8 ounces, adding more peppers if necessary. (If you don't have a juicer, purée in a blender and strain through a cheesecloth, pressing to extract as much juice as possible.)

Transfer juice to a blender, add sugar, and blend until sugar is dissolved and syrup is smooth. Refrigerate until use.

Chiltepin Cointreau To sous-vide, fill container with water, attach immersion circulator, and heat water to 140°F.

Pour Cointreau into a zip-top or vacuum seal bag. Add chiles, ensuring they are submerged in the Cointreau. Place in the sous-vide bath and infuse for 1 hour.

After timer has elapsed, remove bag from water. Using a fine-mesh strainer, strain infused Cointreau into a container and discard solids. (If you don't have a sous-vide circulator, pour ingredients into a container and infuse at room temperature for 24 hours, shaking every few hours, then strain.)

Assembly Add ingredients in order, except garnishes, to a cocktail shaker and fill with ice.

Shake vigorously for 8–12 seconds (depending on size of ice) to chill and dilute. Strain through a fine-mesh sieve over a large ice cube in a rocks glass.

Express orange peel by holding it over the glass with the outer side facing down and give it a gentle squeeze to release oils onto the surface of the drink. Discard peel.

Smack basil leaf between your hands to release oil and aroma, and place on top of ice cube.

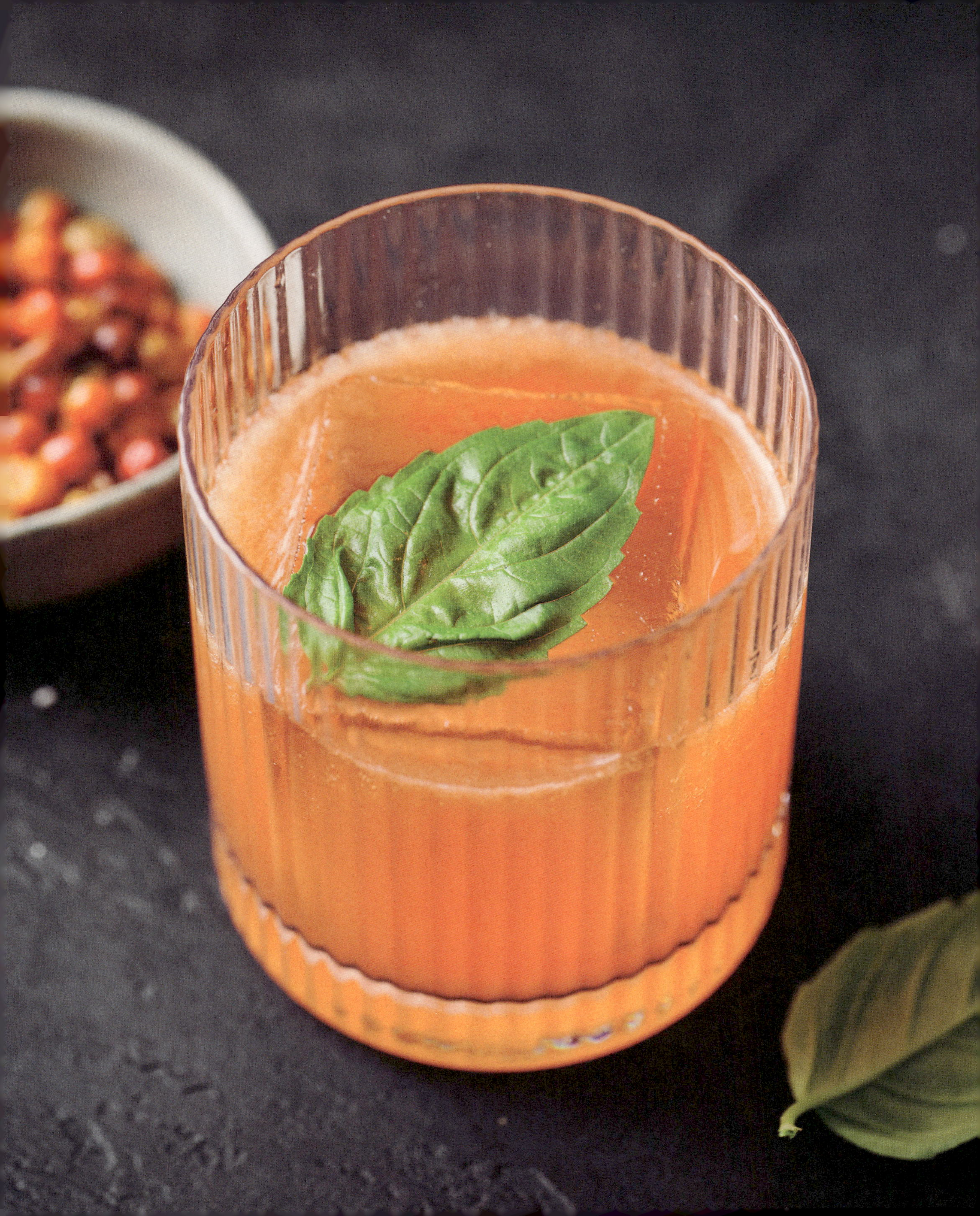

ZINC BISTRO

Aaron Gonzalez, Matt Carter

Chef-owner Matt Carter's homage to the City of Light welcomes diners with a patio dotted with marble tables and rattan chairs reminiscent of the cafés lining Boulevard Saint-Germain. Inside Zinc Bistro, an oyster bar tempts with the freshest selections and a glass replica of the Eiffel Tower twinkles in the dining room. But the pièce de résistance? A twenty-five-foot zinc bar hammered into shape by a local artisan. "Even in France, this bar would be special," Carter says. "It's molded, not poured, which is very unique."

Though Carter's culinary stable spans bold Latin flavors at The Mission and refined Italian at Fat Ox, it all began with France. A Scottsdale Culinary Institute graduate, he found his calling in a French bistro where "it just clicked—the food, the environment, the discipline," he recalls. That epiphany sparked two years in France, a formative time spent working for Christopher Gross (page 48), and stints at other renowned kitchens, including Napa's The French Laundry.

At Zinc Bistro, where executive chef Aaron Gonzalez leads the kitchen, Carter puts his own stamp on tradition. Take his moules marinières, inspired by Brittany's éclade technique of mussels cooked with smoldering pine needles. "We can't do that here," Carter says, "so we char rosemary on the grill and blend it into the butter."

Carter's trophy shelf got a little heavier in 2024 with a Foodist Food Pioneer Award. But it's more than the many accolades—it's about bringing a slice of the world he loves to the Valley of the Sun. "There's something about that soft lighting, the zinc, the red banquettes, and the black and white floors," Carter muses. "It's so inviting, so warm, and so classic."

▶ Endive Salad with Foie Gras, Mimolette Cheese, and Hazelnut Mustard Vinaigrette

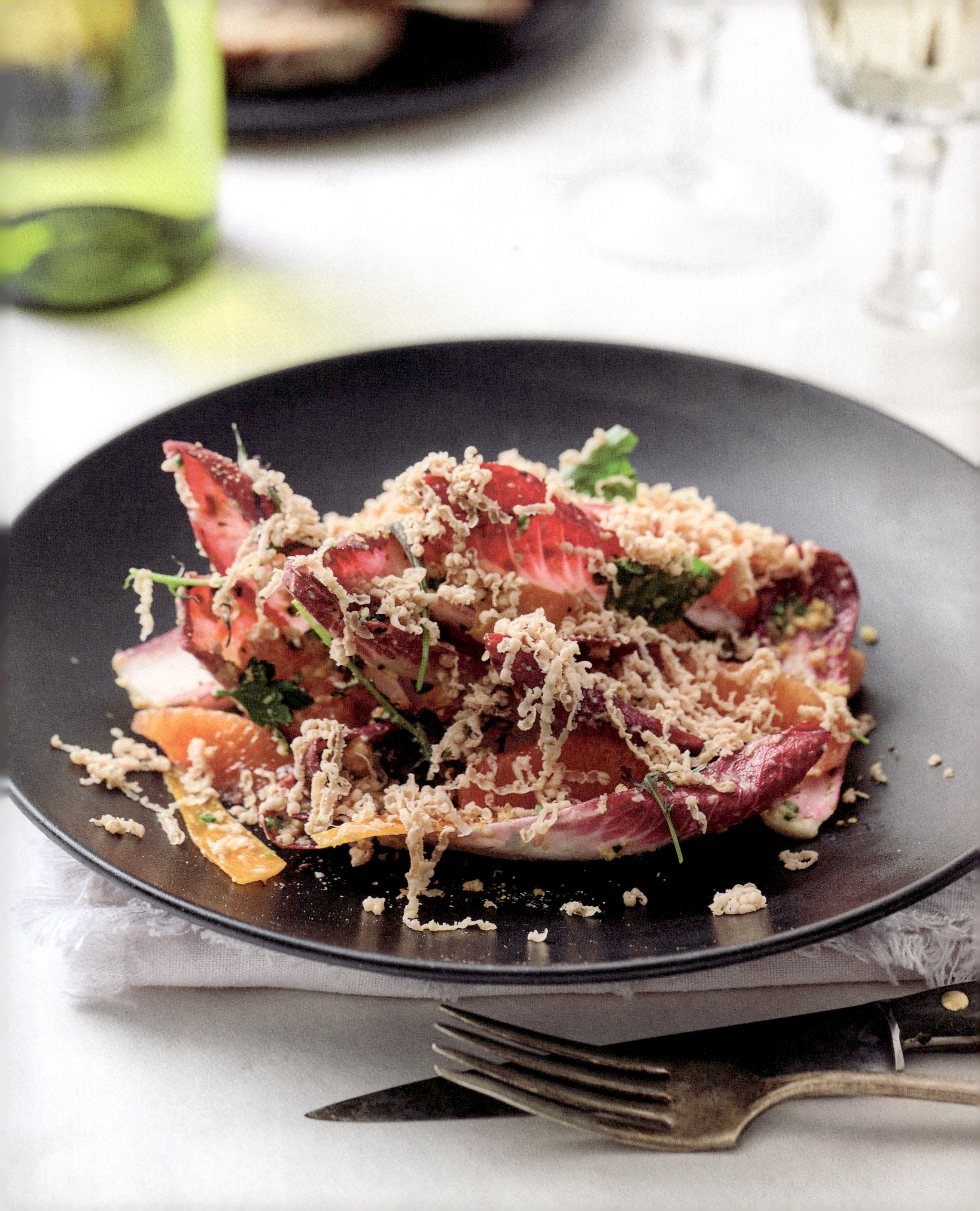

HAZELNUT MUSTARD VINAIGRETTE

1 large egg
1 Tbsp Dijon mustard
1 clove garlic, grated
1 Tbsp crème fraîche
1 Tbsp hazelnut oil
2 Tbsp extra-virgin olive oil
½ Tbsp Chinese black vinegar (Matt Carter recommends Kon Yeng brand; see Note)
1 Tbsp Banyuls vinegar, or sherry vinegar (see Note)
1 Tbsp orange juice
Pinch of orange zest
1 large shallot, sliced and caramelized over low heat, then minced
2 Tbsp thinly sliced flat-leaf parsley
Kosher salt and black pepper, to taste

HAZELNUT CRUMBLE

½ cup fine breadcrumbs
1 Tbsp extra-virgin olive oil, plus more if needed
1 tsp minced garlic
1 Tbsp grated Parmesan
Pinch of Espelette pepper
Pinch of toasted cracked black pepper
1–2 Tbsp toasted crushed hazelnuts
Pinch of orange zest
Pinch of lemon zest
Kosher salt, to taste

Endive Salad with Foie Gras, Mimolette Cheese, and Hazelnut Mustard Vinaigrette

SERVES 4 This elegant salad combines the bitter crunch of endive with luxurious foie gras and aged Mimolette, a hard Dutch-French cheese known for its distinctive orange color and a caramel-like flavor that develops during its aging process. Look for it in markets with well-stocked cheese sections and at gourmet grocers like AJ's Fine Foods and Whole Foods.

Hazelnut Mustard Vinaigrette In a blender or food processor (or in a bowl using a whisk), combine egg, mustard, garlic, and crème fraîche. Slowly drizzle in hazelnut oil, olive oil, black vinegar, Banyuls vinegar (or sherry vinegar), and orange juice, until fully emulsified. Once mixture is smooth, stir in orange zest, caramelized shallots, and parsley. Taste and adjust vinegar or citrus for acidity, and season with salt and pepper to taste. Set aside.

Hazelnut Crumble Preheat oven to 350°F.
In a bowl, mix breadcrumbs with oil, garlic, Parmesan, and Espelette pepper. Spread out on a parchment-lined baking sheet and toast in oven until golden brown, 8–10 minutes, watching carefully to prevent burning. Transfer to a bowl and stir in black pepper, hazelnuts, orange zest, and lemon zest. The mixture should resemble loose, slightly moist sand. Add a little more olive oil if needed, and season with salt to taste.

Assembly Cut off top and bottom of oranges to create flat surfaces. Using a sharp knife, cut away peel and white pith, following the curve of the fruit. Cut along membranes to release segments (supremes). Set aside.
Trim bases of endives and separate leaves. Rinse, pat dry, and toss with desired amount of dressing in a bowl. Add orange supremes, zest, and basil.

ASSEMBLY

2 oranges, 1 zested

2 heads red endive (radicchio)

2 heads speckled Castelfranco endive

Hazelnut Mustard Vinaigrette (see here)

4–6 torn basil leaves

Hazelnut Crumble (see here)

1 (2-oz) wedge Mimolette cheese, microplaned or finely grated

2 pinches fennel pollen

8 sprigs chervil

2 Tbsp extra-virgin olive oil

1 (4- to 6-oz) piece of salt-cured foie gras, or foie gras torchon, frozen the night before

To serve, divide among 4 salad plates. Top generously with hazelnut crumble and Mimolette, and garnish with fennel pollen, chervil, and a drizzle of oil. Using a microplane and working quickly (as foie gras will melt), finish by grating frozen foie gras over the salads.

NOTE Chinese black vinegar is primarily made from glutinous rice and has a malty, smoky flavor with a hint of sweetness. Look for it at Asian markets like Mekong Supermarket and H Mart.

Banyuls vinegar is a French vinegar made from fortified Banyuls wine, which gives it a sweet-tart flavor with notes of nuts and dried fruit. It can be found at specialty food stores such as Whole Foods. Both vinegars can also be purchased online.

4 (4- to 6-oz) turbot fillets (or halibut, sole, or other flat white fish)

Kosher salt and white pepper, to taste

¼ cup extra-virgin olive oil, divided

1 bunch fresh thyme, divided

6 fresh bay leaves, divided

1–2 Tbsp olive oil

1 large shallot, peeled and shaved thin

Pinch of turmeric

12 small mussels, cleaned

2 cups white wine

1 cup dry vermouth

2 (2-inch-long) orange peels, cut using a vegetable peeler to avoid white pith

1 medium lemon, zested and juiced (juice divided)

1 cup fish fumet (fish stock)

2 Tbsp crème fraîche

8 uni tongues (sea urchin roe)

1¼ cups (2½ sticks) high-quality butter, such as Isigny, Plugrà, or Kerrygold

4–6 oz Dungeness or peekytoe crabmeat

1 Tbsp chopped chives

1–2 oz (30–60 g) caviar

1 oz smoked salmon roe

Chervil sprigs, for garnish

Fruits de Mer with Uni Beurre Blanc, Caviar, and Smoked Salmon Roe

SERVES 4 A celebration of ocean bounty, this luxurious dish features sweet Dungeness crab, mussels, and turbot bathed in a silky sea urchin beurre blanc gilded with caviar and smoked salmon roe. While the specialty ingredients may seem daunting, you can source everything you need at quality fishmongers like Nelson's Meat + Fish (page 166).

Assembly To sous-vide, fill container with water, attach immersion circulator, and heat water to 114°F. Season fish with salt and pepper.

Place each fillet in a vacuum-seal bag with 1 tablespoon of extra-virgin olive oil, a sprig of thyme, and a bay leaf. Submerge bags and sous-vide for 15 minutes. Set aside. (Alternatively, fish can be steamed: Place seasoned fillets in a bowl and add extra-virgin olive oil, thyme, and bay leaves. Toss to coat, then allow to marinate 2–3 hours in the refrigerator. Reserving herbed olive oil, steam fish for 8–10 minutes, or until just cooked through. Set aside.)

Heat 1–2 tablespoons of olive oil in a deep sauté pan over medium heat. Add shallots, 2 sprigs of thyme, 2 bay leaves, and turmeric and sauté for 3–5 minutes, until shallots are translucent. Add mussels and stir to coat. Add wine, vermouth, orange peels, lemon zest, and half of the lemon juice. Cook mussels until opened, stirring occasionally. (Discard any mussels that do not open.) Remove mussels as they open, extract meat, and reserve.

Continue reducing sauce until au sec, or almost dry. Add fish fumet and reduce by half. Stir in crème fraîche and uni. Transfer mixture to a blender (or use an immersion blender) and blend until smooth. Cut butter into tablespoons, and add a piece at a time, blending each addition until smooth and emulsified. Strain sauce through a fine-mesh strainer and season with salt, pepper, and additional lemon juice to taste. Stir in reserved mussels, crabmeat, and chives. Adjust seasoning again and keep warm.

If using sous-vide, remove fish from bags, reserving herbed olive oil for garnish. Briefly grill cooked fillets (or finish under a broiler) until just warmed through. Place a fillet on each serving plate and ladle approximately ¼ cup of seafood sauce over each portion. Top with caviar and smoked salmon roe, and garnish with reserved olive oil and chervil.

ZUZU

Russell LaCasce

When Hotel Valley Ho opened its doors in 1956, it quickly became a favorite of Hollywood royalty—think Bing Crosby crooning by the pool, Zsa Zsa Gabor dahling-ing her way through the lobby, and Humphrey Bogart plotting his next film noir between sips of Scotch. Since then, its mid-century modern color palette, breeze block facades, and lush palm-dotted grounds have continued to blend vintage glamour with a fresh, contemporary vibe.

As the historic resort's executive chef, Russell LaCasce oversees the hotel's culinary offerings, from poolside bites at the OH Pool to the seasonally changing menu at the hotel's signature restaurant, ZuZu. It is named after the beloved matriarch of the family that owns the property, who was known for her open-door hospitality. Zuzu's legacy lives on through the restaurant's warm, welcoming vibe.

Today, LaCasce channels her spirit of generosity with a dash of modern flair. "She came from a place of love and community, and we want to re-create that here so it feels like your home away from home," he explains. "While ZuZu is a fun, hip, casual experience, we operate at a high level with a service team that is polished and knowledgeable and knows how to have fun with their guests."

It's a balance that delivers. "Like ZuZu, who loved to feed everyone, it's important to all of us that we share that same vibe," continues LaCasce. "You're coming into our home as our guests. We want you to feel the hospitality, feel the love in the air, enjoy good food and drink, and take home great memories."

▶ Blistered Romanesco with Whipped Fromage

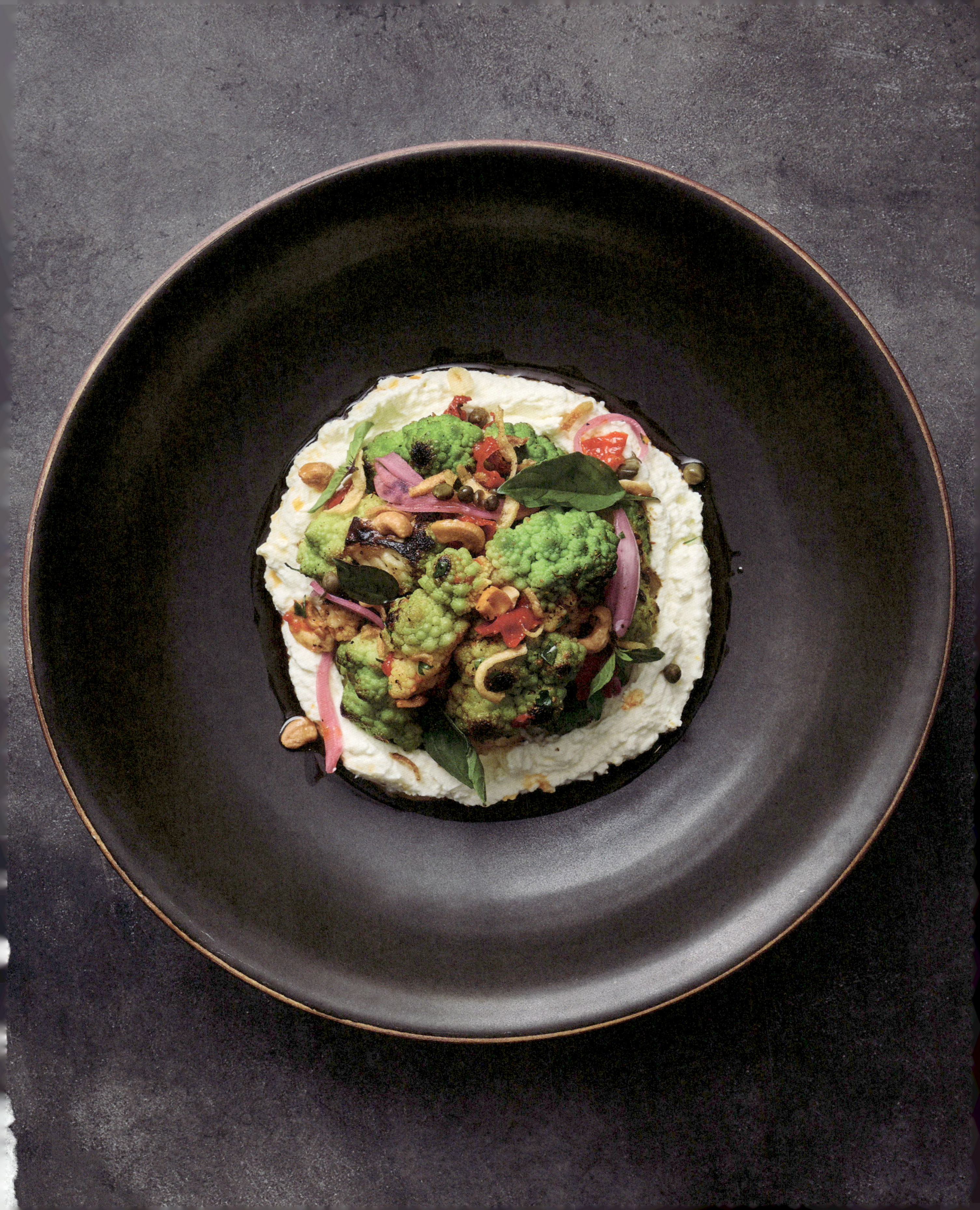

WHIPPED FROMAGE
1 cup (8 oz) fromage blanc
½ lemon, zested
¼ cup heavy cream
1 Tbsp whole milk

PICKLED RED ONIONS
1 large red onion, thinly sliced
1 cup red wine vinegar
1 tsp grenadine
1 Tbsp pickling spice
½ cup granulated sugar
2 Tbsp kosher salt

Blistered Romanesco with Whipped Fromage

SERVES 4 Romanesco cauliflower, also known as romanesco broccoli, is worth seeking out for its vibrant green color and unique fractal design. "I love how versatile cauliflower is," says Russell LaCasce. "Romanesco is an elevated approach and a great vehicle for the big flavors in this dish." Fromage blanc, a fresh spreadable cheese often packaged in tubs, can be found at local specialty grocers.

Whipped Fromage Using a stand mixer fitted with the paddle attachment (or a hand mixer), blend fromage blanc and lemon zest together on medium speed. Gradually add cream and milk and blend until smooth.

Whipped fromage will keep refrigerated for up to 5 days. Use leftover fromage as a spread for toast with figs and prosciutto or jam and on sandwiches and burgers, or in desserts such as tarts and parfaits.

Pickled Red Onions Place onions in a heatproof bowl.

In a medium pot, combine the remaining ingredients over medium heat, stirring until sugar and salt are dissolved. Pour pickling liquid over onions. Use a plate, if necessary, to keep the onions submerged.

Allow to cool to room temperature, then transfer to a container and refrigerate overnight, or up to 2 weeks.

Assembly Preheat oven to 350°F.

In a small saucepan, heat vegetable oil over medium-high heat to 350°F. Add shallots and fry 2–3 minutes, stirring often. Once golden and crispy, immediately remove with a slotted spoon to drain on a paper towel–lined plate. Set aside.

Toss romanesco florets in a bowl with olive oil, salt, pepper, and berbere spice until evenly coated. Arrange in a single layer on a baking sheet and roast for 25–30 minutes, until tender and caramelized.

ASSEMBLY

½ cup vegetable oil, for frying
1 large shallot, sliced
1 large head romanesco, cut into florets
2 Tbsp olive oil
½ tsp kosher salt
¼ tsp black pepper
1 Tbsp berbere spice (see Note)
2 Tbsp roasted cashews
¼ cup Thai basil leaves
¼ cup flat-leaf parsley leaves
¼ cup Pickled Red Onions (see here)
1 Tbsp capers in brine, drained
2 Tbsp chopped Calabrian chiles (see Note)
½ cup Whipped Fromage, or to taste (see here)
Sea salt, to taste
2 Tbsp Calabrian chile oil, or to taste

In a large bowl, toss roasted florets with cashews, basil, parsley, pickled onions, capers, and Calabrian chiles.

To serve, spread whipped fromage across the bottom of a large serving platter or shallow bowl, creating ridges to form pockets for the oil and toppings.

Mound florets over whipped fromage, ensuring all other ingredients in the bowl are evenly distributed over the florets, and sprinkle with sea salt.

Garnish with fried shallots and a drizzle of Calabrian chile oil.

NOTE Berbere is an Ethiopian spice blend featuring chiles, garlic, ginger, and spices like cinnamon and allspice. Look for it at stores such as Baiz Market and New Africa Supermarket, gourmet grocers like Whole Foods, and specialty spice shops.

Calabrian chiles from Italy are moderately spicy peppers commonly sold preserved in olive oil. Look for jarred whole or chopped Calabrian chiles at specialty grocers such as AJ's Fine Foods and Whole Foods and Italian markets. Berbere and Calabrian chiles can also be found online. If unavailable, substitute with your favorite brined or marinated chiles.

DRY RUB

3 Tbsp ground ginger
1 tsp ground cardamom
1 Tbsp Korean chili powder
1 Tbsp togarashi
2 Tbsp black pepper
1 Tbsp white pepper
1 Tbsp Sichuan pepper
1 Tbsp ground pink peppercorn
1 Tbsp ground green peppercorn
1 Tbsp celery salt
2 Tbsp green chile powder
2 Tbsp ground coriander
1 Tbsp dried thyme
1 Tbsp dried rosemary
1 Tbsp granulated onion
1 Tbsp granulated garlic

Sticky Icky Iberico Spareribs with Funky Daikon Salad

SERVES 4 "Everyone loves ribs, but I wanted to add a dynamic punch of flavor with the Asian-esque rub and umami glaze," notes Russell LaCasce, who suggests stocking your pantry with his versatile sixteen-spice blend: "It's good on everything, like pork shoulder, steak, burgers, and barbecue. Try dusting it on a piece of salmon, drizzling with a little honey, and baking—delicious!" Look for Korean chili powder (gochugaru), togarashi (a Japanese spice blend), and Sichuan pepper at Asian markets like Lee Lee International Supermarket and H Mart, or find them online.

Dry Rub Combine all ingredients well. Store in an airtight container for up to 6 months.

Funky Daikon Salad Rinse and drain daikon and place in a large bowl.

Blend garlic, ginger, gochujang paste, and fish sauce in a blender. Add remaining ingredients and blend until smooth. Pour over daikon and mix well.

Store in the refrigerator for up to 10 days. Leftover salad can be served with other grilled meats or fish, used as a topping for burgers, sandwiches, and tacos, tossed with salad greens, or folded into fried rice.

Umami Glaze Heat canola oil in a pot over medium heat. Add garlic and ginger and sauté until fragrant, about 2 minutes. Stir in the remaining ingredients, except cornstarch slurry. Increase heat and bring to a boil. Whisk in slurry and simmer until sauce reaches a glaze-like consistency. Allow to cool.

Glaze will keep 2–3 weeks in the refrigerator. Leftover glaze can be used as a stir-fry sauce, marinade, potsticker dip, or glaze for chicken wings and seafood.

Iberico Spareribs Preheat oven to 300°F.

Place rib rack on a cutting board and slide butter knife under the thin membrane (silver skin) on back of ribs. Peel off and discard.

Cover ribs generously with dry rub on both sides.

FUNKY DAIKON SALAD

1 medium daikon radish, peeled and cut into large dice (see Note)
4 cloves garlic, minced
2 Tbsp peeled and minced ginger
½ cup gochujang paste
2 tsp fish sauce, such as Red Boat
1 tsp togarashi
½ cup chopped pineapple
¼ cup granulated sugar
¼ cup sesame oil
½ cup unseasoned rice wine vinegar
¼ cup soy sauce
¼ cup honey
1 cup water
1 tsp Korean chili powder

UMAMI GLAZE

2 Tbsp canola oil
2 Tbsp minced ginger
2 Tbsp minced garlic
¾ cup mirin
¾ cup unseasoned rice wine vinegar
½ cup soy sauce
½ cup granulated sugar
½ cup gochujang paste
1 tsp togarashi
¼ cup honey
¼ cup sesame oil
2 cups water
Cornstarch slurry (4 Tbsp cornstarch mixed with 2 Tbsp water)

IBERICO SPARERIBS

1 (2-lb) rack of Iberico pork spareribs (see Note)
Dry Rub (see here)

ASSEMBLY

Cooked Iberico Spareribs (see here)
1 cup Umami Glaze, plus more to taste (see here)
Funky Daikon Salad (see here)
Radish sprouts, for garnish

Wrap ribs in aluminum foil and place on a baking sheet. Bake for 1 hour and 20 minutes, or until fork tender but not falling off bone.

Allow ribs to cool while still wrapped in foil. Store in the refrigerator for up to 5 days.

Assembly Preheat grill to medium-high heat.

Cut rib rack into single-bone portions and toss with umami glaze until well coated.

Grill ribs, turning every 30 seconds to avoid glaze burning. After 2 minutes, brush with more glaze and cook for an additional 2–3 minutes, until hot and caramelized.

For each serving, stack 4–5 ribs on a plate and drizzle with umami glaze. Top with daikon salad as a garnish (or serve it on the side) and garnish with radish sprouts.

NOTE Daikon radish is a winter root vegetable popular throughout East Asia. The long, white radish has a slightly sweet, less peppery flavor than more familiar radishes. Find fresh daikon at most supermarkets, including Safeway, Sprouts, and Whole Foods, and Asian markets like H Mart, Asiana Market, and Lee Lee International Supermarket.

Iberico spareribs come from the prized Iberico breed of pigs native to Spain, known for their rich flavor. They can be sourced from specialty butcher shops and gourmet grocery stores, or ordered online from high-quality meat purveyors.

Zuzu / 265

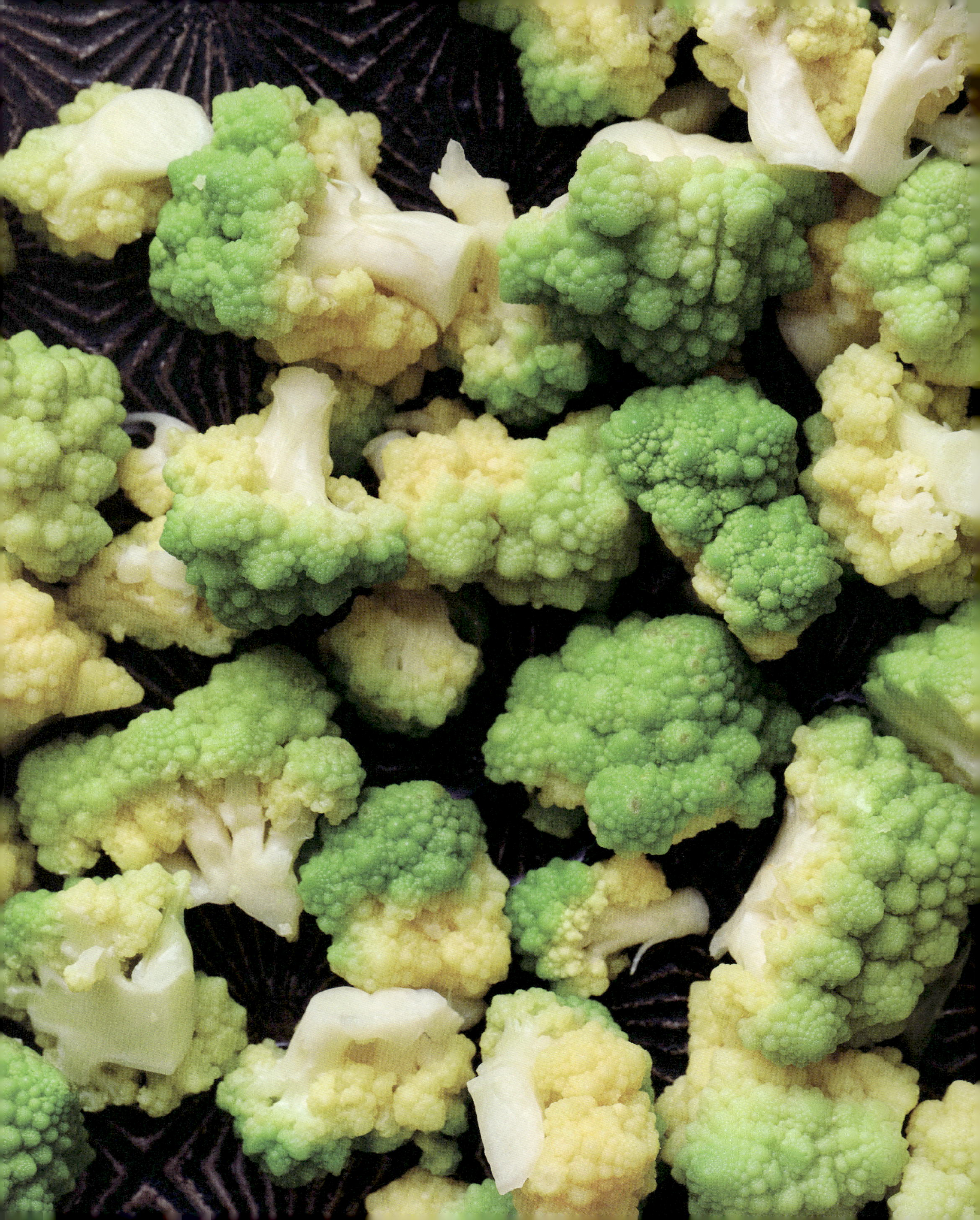

Acknowledgements

First and foremost, thank you to my always-supportive family for their love and encouragement every step of the way.

I'm also grateful to the wonderful team at Figure 1 Publishing for giving me the chance—again!—to shine a light on the amazing talent here in Phoenix. Special thanks to Chris Labonté for believing our city deserved a second book; Lara Smith for her guidance and direction; Tanya Trafford for her keen editorial eye; Pam Robertson for her meticulous copy editing; Breanne MacDonald for her thorough proofreading; Iva Cheung for her precise indexing; and Naomi MacDougall, who brought it all to life with her beautiful book design.

Huge thanks to my immensely talented friend and photographer Joanie Simon and her rockstar team of food stylist Brendan McCaskey and assistant Brittany Ha-Nguyen, who made every shoot so fun and every drink and dish so beautiful.

To Mara Hayes, Kathy Knoop, and Krista Carpenter-Beasley—thank you so much for rolling up your sleeves and helping me test the recipes. I'm so grateful for your time, your thoughtful feedback, and all of your enthusiasm!

And finally, thank you to the chefs, bartenders, and restaurant owners who embraced this project so generously. I'm incredibly grateful you shared your recipes, your stories, and your time with me. This book only exists because of your talent and heart. Phoenix shines because of you, and I hope these pages do justice to you and the pride, creativity, and soul that define our culinary community.

Index

Page numbers in italics refer to photos.

100 Grand, 205

achiote marinade, 212
aioli
    chipotle aioli, 135
    harissa aioli, 94
    malt aioli, 216
    yuzu kosho aioli, 240
albacore tuna tartare toast, *97*, 98
Aleppo chili crisp, 178
almonds
    casarecce trapanese, 119
    saffron couscous, 248
Anaheim chiles
    braised pork shank chili verde, 251
    green chile sauce, 92
ancho chile
    harissa, 94
    salsa roja, 92–93
apple
    albacore tuna tartare toast, *97*, 98
    monkey bread with apples, 64–66
    Verde de la Vida, *97*, 99
apricots, dried, in saffron couscous, 248
arugula
    goat cheese–stuffed lamb burgers, 126–27
    summer peach salad, *17*, 18
avocado
    avocado mousse, 75
    causa rellena de pollo, 132
    Cinco Diablo Burgers, *183*, 184–85
    guasacaca, 213
    ribeye steaks with tepary bean chili, 192–93

bacon
    bacon lardons, 20
    bacon-wrapped dates, 135
    chipotle bacon, 185
    grilled wedge salad, *123*, 124–25
    peppercorn-brandy cream sauce, 70
    tepary bean chili, 192
Baileys butterscotch caramel, 104
balsamic onions, 70
banana Saveiro Madeira, 34
bao buns with hoisin-glazed pork belly and pickled Fresno chiles, *27*, 28–29
barley–macadamia nut breakfast bar, 142
basil oil, 38
beans
    tepary bean chili, 192
    white bean ragu, 82
béchamel, 201, 244
beef
    beef short rib ravioli, 136–37, *138–39*
    birria beef, 154
    bistecca alla Fiorentina, 198, *199*
    Cinco Diablo Burgers, *183*, 184–85
    Copper State beef short ribs, 60–61
    filet au foivre, *69*, 70–71
    Hungarian stuffed cabbage, 163
    The Mile Burger, 164, *165*
    peppercorn steak soup, 101, *102–3*
    quesabirria tacos, 154–55, *155*
    ragu, 200–201
    Sonoran molcajete, *151*, 152–53
    tri-tip kebabs, *225*, 226–27
    Wagyu meatballs, 110
beer-battered poblano chiles, 185
beet-infused Campari, 37
berries, buttermilk pie with, 194–95
birria beef, 154
birria de chivo, 130–31
bistecca alla Fiorentina, 198, *199*

bitters, Heart of Gold, 148
blackberry-infused Rhum J.M 100, 217
blistered romanesco with whipped fromage, *261*, 262–63
blood orange semifreddo, 77, *79*
blue cheese
    bacon-wrapped dates, 135
    blue cheese dressing, 124
    grilled wedge salad, *123*, 124–25
blueberries
    dried, in macadamia nut–barley breakfast bar, 142
    Fresno blueberry margarita, 188, *189*
bordelaise sauce, 160
braised lamb shanks, 247
braised pork shank chili verde, 251
brandy-peppercorn cream sauce, 70
bread
    monkey bread with apples, 64–66
    pistachio pita, 249
breakfast bar, macadamia nut–barley, 142
Breakfast of Champions, 142, *143*
brie, escargot on brioche with, 160–61
brioche
    Cinco Diablo Burgers, *183*, 184–85
    escargot on brioche, 160–61
    foie gras on brioche, 114–15
    goat cheese–stuffed lamb burgers, 126–27
brussels sprouts, charred, 20–21
burgers
    Cinco Diablo Burgers, *183*, 184–85
    goat cheese–stuffed lamb burgers, 126–27
burnt desert blossom honey flan, *231*, 234–35, *235*
butter
    Creole butter, 158

garlic butter, 201
herb butter, 160
buttermilk pie with caramel sauce and fresh berries, *191*, 194–95
butterscotch caramel, Baileys, 104
button mushrooms, in vegan spaghetti bolognese, 220–21

cabbage, Hungarian stuffed, 163
cajeta, 64
cake
   date cakes, 77–78
   elote cheesecake, *45*, 46–47
   gooey butter cake, *103*, 104–5, *105*
Calabrian chiles
   blistered romanesco, 262–63
   lupara, 174, *175*
   shawarma spiced lamb shank, 247–49
calamari, in cioppino, 88, *89*
Campari, beet-infused, 37
candied pecans, 64–65
capers
   blistered romanesco, 262–63
   tapenade, 98
caramel
   Baileys butterscotch caramel, 104
   caramel sauce, 194
   mushroom caramel, 114
carrot shavings, crispy, 137
casarecce trapanese (pasta with Sicilian pesto of Trapani), 119
cascabel chiles, in mafiosa sauce, 152
cashews
   blistered romanesco, 262–63
   vegan ricotta, 220
cauliflower
   blistered romanesco, 262–63
   fried cauliflower, 216
causa rellena de pollo with salsa a la huancaína, *132*, *133*
caviar, fruits de mer with, 258–59

charred brussels sprouts with pickled sultanas, goat cheese, bacon lardons, and mustard vinaigrette, 20–21
charred corn, 46
chayote salad, 233
cheddar, white, in stacked enchiladas, *91*, 92–93
cheesecake, elote, *45*, 46–47
chicken
   causa rellena de pollo, 132
   pollo pibil with guasacaca, 212–13
   Sonoran molcajete, *151*, 152–53
chiles de árbol
   birria de chivo, 130–31
   harissa, 94
   mafiosa sauce, 152
chili, tepary bean, 192
Chil-te-bell, 252, *253*
chiltepin Cointreau, 252
chipotle chile, in pimentón oil, 210–11
chipotle in adobo
   chipotle aioli, 135
   chipotle bacon, 185
   peanut mole, 42
chocolate
   spicy cocoa powder, 24
   vegan chocolate cream, 24
   white, in macadamia nut–barley breakfast bar, 142
chorizo, green, 238
chorizo seasoning blend, 240
chutney, pichuberry, 114
cilantro yogurt, lamb spring rolls with, 228–29
Cinco Diablo Burgers, *183*, 184–85
cinnamon-grapefruit syrup, 33
cioppino, 88, *89*
clams, in cioppino, 88, *89*
cocoa powder, spicy, 24
coffee
   Espiritu de Café, 24, *25*

Silver Fox, 206, *207*
Cointreau, chiltepin, 252
confit duck legs, 51
confit tomatoes, 82
Copper State beef short ribs, 60–61
corn
   corn nage, 82
   corn soubise, 222
   elote cheesecake, *45*, 46–47
   elote moda, 23
   elote rigatoni, 222, *223*
cotija cheese
   elote rigatoni, 222, *223*
   papas verde with green chorizo, *237*, 238–39
couscous, saffron, 248
crab
   fruits de mer with uni beurre blanc, 258–59
   sea bass and crab ceviche, 210–11
cranberries, dried, in saffron couscous, 248
cream cheese
   elote cheesecake, *45*, 46–47
   gooey butter cake, *103*, 104–5, *105*
   honey whipped feta, 108
creamy garlic sauce, 248
crema, jalapeño, 239
cremini mushrooms
   lupara, 174, *175*
   mushroom caramel, 114
   porcini mushroom ragu, 244–45
   vegan spaghetti bolognese, 220–21
Creole butter, 158
crepes, 200
   crepe of Atlantic skate with scallop mousse and lobster sauce, 54–56, *57*
crispy carrot shavings, 137
croquettes, Iberico ham, 94–95

Index / **269**

cucumber
    bao buns with pork belly, 28–29
    cucumber pico de gallo, 75
    sea bass and crab ceviche, 210–11
    Verde de la Vida, 97, 99
curry salt, 229

daikon salad, funky, 265
dates
    bacon-wrapped dates, 135
    date cakes, 77–78
Dead Man's Pocket Watch, 38, 39
desert blossom sticky toffee date
    cake with prickly pear jam, blood
    orange semifreddo, and praline
    pecans, 76–78, 79
dip, smoked salmon, 167
dressing
    blue cheese dressing, 124
    fresh herb ranch dressing, 126
    jalapeño ranch dressing, 184
dry rub
    for hoisin-glazed pork, 28
    for Iberico spareribs, 264
duck three ways, 50–52, 53

eggplant parmigiana panini, 87
eggs
    quail, in causa rellena de pollo, 132
    Sonoran eggs Benedict, 59, 60–63
    stacked enchiladas, 91, 92–93
Elliott's Steakhouse freezer martini,
    69, 73
elote cheesecake, 45, 46–47
elote moda, 23
elote rigatoni, 222, 223
enchiladas, stacked, 91, 92–93
endive salad with foie gras,
    Mimolette cheese, and hazelnut
    mustard vinaigrette, 255,
    256–57
English muffin chips, 60

escargot on brioche with brie and
    bordelaise sauce, 157, 160–61
Espiritu de Café, 24, 25
espresso simple syrup, salted,
    206

Faroe Island salmon tacos with yuzu
    kosho aioli, 240
fennel, in octopus salad, 168–69, 171
feta
    goat cheese–stuffed lamb
        burgers, 126–27
    honey whipped feta, 108
filet au foivre, 69, 70–71
First Street Last Word, 145, 146–47
fish stock, 210
five-spice royal icing, 65
foie gras
    duck three ways, 50–52
    endive salad with foie gras,
        256–57
    filet au foivre, 69, 70–71
    foie gras on brioche, 114–15, 115
Fresno chiles
    Fresno blueberry margarita, 188,
        189
    Fresno chile pesto, 184
    papas verde with green chorizo,
        237, 238–39
    pickled Fresno chiles, 28
    salsa roja, 92–93
    sarsaparilla glaze, 232
    yellowtail crudo, 75
fried cauliflower with pickled onions
    and malt aioli, 215, 216
fried ice cream shake, 181, 182
fromage blanc, whipped, 262
fruits de mer with uni beurre blanc,
    caviar, and smoked salmon roe,
    258–59
funky daikon salad, 265

garlic
    creamy garlic sauce, 248
    garlic butter, 201
ginger simple syrup, 116
glaze
    sarsaparilla glaze, 232
    soy-honey glaze, 42
    umami glaze, 264–65
goat cheese
    charred brussels sprouts with
        goat cheese, 20–21
    goat cheese–stuffed lamb
        burgers, 126–27
goat, in birria de chivo, 130–31
gooey butter cake, 103, 104–5, 105
Gorgonzola cream sauce, 137
grapefruit
    cinnamon-grapefruit syrup, 33
    Faroe Island salmon tacos, 240
    grapefruit-ginger rye sour, 116, 117
green bell peppers, in braised pork
    shank chili verde, 251
green chile sauce, 92
green chorizo, 238
gremolata, 82
grenadine, pomegranate, 141
grilled pineapple–infused tequila,
    205
grilled pork chop with jeow som and
    summer peach salad, 17, 18–19, 19
grilled wedge salad, 123, 124–25
guajillo chiles
    birria de chivo, 130–31
    harissa, 94
    mafiosa sauce, 152
    quesabirria tacos, 154–55, 155
    salsa roja, 92–93
guasacaca, 213
guava, in Tropic Like It's Hot, 33

habanero chiles
    achiote marinade, 212

passion fruit leche de tigre, 210
harissa aioli, 94
hazelnut mustard vinaigrette, endive salad with, 256–57
Heart of Gold old-fashioned, 148–49
herb butter, 160
herb salad, 249
hibiscus, in Heart of Gold bitters, 148
hoisin-glazed pork belly, 28–29
honey
    burnt desert blossom honey, 234
    honey bunch syrup, 148
    honey whipped feta with roasted olives, 108, *109*
    soy-honey glaze, 42
Hungarian stuffed cabbage, 163

Iberico ham croquettes with harissa aioli and Manchego cheese, 94–95
ice cream shake, fried, 181, *182*
icing, five-spice royal, 65
insalata di pomodoro, 198
Italian sausage
    lupara, 174, *175*
    seared polenta with sausage, 177

jalapeños
    cucumber pico de gallo, 75
    jalapeño crema, 239
    jalapeño ranch dressing, 184
    pickled red onions, 193
    pico de gallo, 192–93
    Verde de la Vida, *97*, 99
Jamaican jerk–rubbed salmon with crispy rice and mango salsa, 31
jam, prickly pear, 76
Japanese sweet potatoes with Aleppo chili crisp, 178, *179*
Jennifer's famous birria de chivo, 130–31
jeow som, 18

Kembara's lamb spring rolls with cilantro yogurt, 228–29

lamb
    goat cheese–stuffed lamb burgers, 126–27
    lamb spring rolls, 228–29
    sarsaparilla-glazed lamb ribs, 232–33
    shawarma spiced lamb shank, 247–49
lardons, bacon, 20
Lavender Fairway, 187
leche de tigre, passion fruit, 210
lemon vinaigrette, 168
lettuce
    causa rellena de pollo, 132
    Cinco Diablo Burgers, *183*, 184–85
    grilled wedge salad, *123*, 124–25
    The Mile Burger, 164, *165*
    porcini lasagna, *243*, 244–46
lime leaf mezcal, 141
lobster roe, in scallop mousse, 54
lobster sauce, 55
longaniza sausage, in Sonoran molcajete, *151*, 152–53
lupara, 174, *175*

macadamia nut–barley breakfast bar, 142
Madeira, banana Saveiro, 34
mafiosa sauce, 152
malt aioli, 216
Manchego cheese, Iberico ham croquettes with, 94–95
Mandrake, 37
mango
    mango salsa, 31
    Tropic Like It's Hot, 33
margarita, Fresno blueberry, 188, *189*
marinara, 174

martini, Elliott's Steakhouse freezer, *69*, 73
meatballs, Wagyu, 110
mezcal, lime leaf, 141
The Mile Burger, 164, *165*
Mimolette cheese, endive salad with, 256–57
molcajete, Sonoran, *151*, 152–53
monkey bread with apples, candied pecans, cajeta, and five-spice royal icing, 64–66
Monterey Jack cheese, in quesabirria tacos, 154–55, *155*
morita chiles, in mafiosa sauce, 152
mozzarella
    eggplant parmigiana panini, 87
    porcini lasagna, *243*, 244–46
mulato chiles, in quesabirria tacos, 154–55, *155*
mushroom caramel, 114
mussels
    cioppino, 88, *89*
    fruits de mer with uni beurre blanc, 258–59
mustard
    hazelnut mustard vinaigrette, 256
    mustard vinaigrette, 20

Napa cabbage, in stacked enchiladas, *91*, 92–93
nopal, in Sonoran molcajete, *151*, 152–53

Oaxaca cheese, in stacked enchiladas, *91*, 92–93
octopus salad, 168–69, *171*
oil
    basil oil, 38
    pimentón oil, 210–11
olives
    causa rellena de pollo, 132

Elliott's Steakhouse freezer martini, *69*, 73
  roasted olives, 108
  tapenade, 98
onions, balsamic, 70. *See also* red onions
orange
  blood orange semifreddo, 77, *79*
  Chil-te-bell, 252, *253*
  endive salad with foie gras, 256–57
  Faroe Island salmon tacos, 240
  fruits de mer with uni beurre blanc, 258–59
  guasacaca, 213
  orange whipped cream, 84

pancetta, in ragu, 200–201
panela cheese, in Sonoran molcajete, *151*, 152–53
panini, eggplant parmigiana, 87
papas verde with green chorizo, *237*, 238–39
pappardelle with rabbit ragu, 173
Parmesan/Parmigiano-Reggiano
  casarecce trapanese, 119
  eggplant parmigiana panini, 87
  Fresno chile pesto, 184
  hazelnut crumble, 256
  polenta, 62
  porcini lasagna, *243*, 244–46
  risotto alla Nerano, 120, *121*
  Virtù timballo, 200–202
  Wagyu meatballs with pomodoro sauce, 110–11
  white bean ragu, 82
pasilla chiles
  birria de chivo, 130–31
  mafiosa sauce, 152
passion fruit
  passion fruit leche de tigre, 210
  Tropic Like It's Hot, 33

pasta with Sicilian pesto of Trapani, 119
pastrami, in The Mile Burger, 164, *165*
peach salad, summer, *17*, 18
peanut(s)
  butter, in hoisin glaze, 28
  peanut mole, 42
pecans
  candied pecans, 64–65
  Heart of Gold bitters, 148
  praline pecans, 76–77
Pecorino Romano
  casarecce trapanese, 119
  lupara, 174, *175*
  rabbit ragu, 173
pepitas
  pollo pibil, 212–13
  sea bass and crab ceviche, 210–11
peppercorn
  peppercorn-brandy cream sauce, 70
  peppercorn steak soup, 101, *102–3*
pepper Jack cheese, in The Mile Burger, 164, *165*
pesto
  Fresno chile pesto, 184
  pasta with Sicilian pesto of Trapani, 119
pichuberry chutney, 114
pickled Fresno chiles, 28
pickled (red) onions, 193, 212–13, 216, 226, 239, 248, 262
pickled serranos, 184
pickled sultanas, 20
pico de gallo, 192–93
  cucumber pico de gallo, 75
pie, buttermilk, 194–95
piloncillo syrup, 23
pimentón oil, 210–11
pineapple
  100 Grand, 205
  caramelized pineapple purée, 146

First Street Last Word, *145*, 146–47
  funky daikon salad, 265
  grilled pineapple–infused tequila, 205
  sea bass and crab ceviche, 210–11
  tepache, 146–47
  Tropic Like It's Hot, 33
  Verde de la Vida, *97*, 99
pita, pistachio, 249
plankton powder, 56
Pleasure Island, 141
plums, dried, in macadamia nut–barley breakfast bar, 142
poblano chiles
  beer-battered poblano chiles, 185
  braised pork shank chili verde, 251
  green chorizo, 238
  guasacaca, 213
polenta, 62, 177
pollo pibil with guasacaca and pickled red onions, 212–13
pomegranate grenadine, 141
ponzu, yellowtail crudo with, 75
porcini lasagna, *243*, 244–46
pork. *See also* bacon; prosciutto; sausage
  bao buns with pork belly, 28–29
  braised pork shank chili verde, 251
  green chorizo, 238
  grilled pork chop with jeow som, 18–19
  Iberico spareribs, 265
  ragu, 200–201
  stacked enchiladas, *91*, 92–93
  Wagyu meatballs, 110
potatoes
  causa rellena de pollo, 132
  smashed fingerling potatoes, 238
pots de crème, vanilla, 84–85
praline pecans, 76–77

272 / Phoenix Eats + Drinks

prawns
    cioppino, 88, *89*
    prawns with peanut mole, 42–43
prickly pear jam, 76
prosciutto
    cotto, in Virtù timballo, 200–202
    di Parma, in ragu, 200–201
Provolone del Monaco, in risotto alla Nerano, 120, *121*

quesabirria tacos, 154–55, *155*
queso fresco, in salsa a la huancaína, 132
queso menonita
    papas verde with green chorizo, *237*, 238–39
    quesabirria tacos, 154–55, *155*

rabbit ragu, 173
radicchio, in endive salad with foie gras, 256–57
radishes, in bao buns with pork belly, 28–29
ragu, 200–201
    porcini mushroom ragu, 244–45
    rabbit ragu, 173
    white bean ragu, 82
raisins
    pichuberry chutney, 114
    pickled sultanas, 20
raspberry jacked Hendrick's Gin, 37
ravioli, beef short rib, 136–37, *138–39*
red bell peppers
    cucumber pico de gallo, 75
    Fresno chile pesto, 184
    red bell pepper syrup, 252
    vegan spaghetti bolognese, 220–21
    white bean ragu, 82
red onions
    insalata di pomodoro, 198
    The Mile Burger, 164, *165*

octopus salad, 168–69, *171*
pickled (red) onions, 193, 212–13, 216, 226, 239, 248, 262
sea bass and crab ceviche, 210–11
red wine vinaigrette, 245
reduced duck stock, 50–51
Rhum J.M 100, blackberry-infused, 217
ribeye steaks with tepary bean chili and pico de gallo, 192–93
ribs, sarsaparilla-glazed lamb, 232–33
rice
    Hungarian stuffed cabbage, 163
    Jamaican jerk–rubbed salmon with crispy rice, 31
    risotto alla Nerano, 120, *121*
rich demerara simple syrup, 205
rich simple syrup, 99
ricotta
    porcini lasagna, *243*, 244–46
    vegan ricotta, 220
    Wagyu meatballs, 110
    whipped ricotta, 110
rigatoni
    elote rigatoni, 222, *223*
    lupara, 174, *175*
risotto alla Nerano, 120, *121*
roasted olives, 108
romanesco, blistered, 262–63
rosemary hollandaise, 62
royal icing, five-spice, 65
rye sour, grapefruit-ginger, 116, *117*

saffron couscous, 248
sage-infused green tea, 217
salad
    chayote salad, 233
    endive salad with foie gras, 256–57
    funky daikon salad, 265
    grilled wedge salad, *123*, 124–25
    herb salad, 249

insalata di pomodoro, 198
octopus salad, 168–69, *171*
summer peach salad, *17*, 18
salmon
    Faroe Island salmon tacos, 240
    Jamaican jerk–rubbed salmon, 31
    smoked salmon dip, 167
salmon roe, smoked, fruits de mer with, 258–59
salsa
    chili salsa, 192
    mango salsa, 31
    salsa a la huancaína, 132
    salsa di pomodoro, 87
    salsa roja, 92–93
    tomatillo salsa, 238
salted espresso simple syrup, 206
sarsaparilla-glazed lamb ribs with chayote salad, *231*, 232–33
sausage
    green chorizo, 238
    Italian sausage, in lupara, 174, *175*
    longaniza sausage, in Sonoran molcajete, *151*, 152–53
    seared polenta with tomatoes and sausage, 177
scallops
    cioppino, 88, *89*
    scallop mousse, 54
sea bass and blue crab ceviche with passion fruit leche de tigre, *209*, 210–11
The Sea Queen Punch, *215*, 217
sea urchin roe, fruits de mer with, 258–59
seared polenta with tomatoes and sausage, 177
semifreddo, blood orange, 77, *79*
serrano chiles
    ginger simple syrup, 116
    green chile sauce, 92
    green chorizo, 238

Index / **273**

guasacaca, 213
pickled serranos, 184
tomatillo salsa, 238
tri-tip kebabs, *225*, 226–27
shake, fried ice cream, 181, *182*
shawarma spiced lamb shank, 247–49
shiitake mushroom caramel, 114
short ribs
   beef short rib ravioli, 136–37, *138–39*
   Copper State beef short ribs, 60–61
shrimp
   shrimp tartine with Creole butter sauce, *157*, 158–59
   Sonoran molcajete, *151*, 152–53
Silver Fox, 206, *207*
skate, crepe of, with scallop mousse, 54–56
smashed fingerling potatoes, 238
smoked pork belly, 28–29
smoked salmon dip, 167
smoked salmon roe, fruits de mer with, 258–59
snails on brioche, 160–61
Sonoran eggs Benedict, *59*, 60–63
Sonoran molcajete, *151*, 152–53
soup, peppercorn steak, 101, *102–3*
sour, grapefruit-ginger rye, 116, *117*
Southwest spice, 226
soy-honey glaze, 42
spaghetti bolognese, vegan, 220–21
spicy cocoa powder, 24
spinach, in Gorgonzola cream sauce, 137
Split Decision, 34, *35*
squid ink crepes, 55
stacked enchiladas, *91*, 92–93

steak
   bistecca alla Fiorentina, 198, *199*
   ribeye steaks with bean chili, 192–93
stew, in cioppino, 88, *89*
sticky icky Iberico spareribs with funky daikon salad, 264–65
stock
   fish stock, 210
   reduced duck stock, 50–51
strawberries, in fried ice cream shake, 181, *182*
striped bass with gremolata, white bean ragu, and corn nage, *81*, 82–83
stuffed cabbage, Hungarian, 163
sultanas, pickled, 20
summer peach salad, *17*, 18
sweet potatoes, Japanese, with Aleppo chili crisp, 178, *179*
syrup
   cinnamon-grapefruit syrup, 33
   ginger simple syrup, 116
   honey bunch syrup, 148
   piloncillo syrup, 23
   pomegranate grenadine, 141
   red bell pepper syrup, 252
   rich demerara simple syrup, 205
   rich simple syrup, 99
   salted espresso simple syrup, 206

tacos
   Faroe Island salmon tacos, 240
   quesabirria tacos, 154–55, *155*
tapenade, 98
tea, sage-infused green, 217
tepache, 146–47
tepary bean chili, 192
tequila, grilled pineapple–infused, 205
Thai chile
   cilantro yogurt, 228

   jeow som, 18
   lamb spring rolls, 228–29
Tía Carmen's Southwest tri-tip kebabs, *225*, 226–27
toffee sauce, desert blossom, 78
tofu, in vegan spaghetti bolognese, 220–21
tomatillo salsa, 238
tomatoes
   birria de chivo, 130–31
   casarecce trapanese, 119
   causa rellena de pollo, 132
   chili salsa, 192
   confit tomatoes, 82
   cucumber pico de gallo, 75
   Gorgonzola cream sauce, 137
   grilled wedge salad, *123*, 124–25
   Hungarian sauce, 163
   insalata di pomodoro, 198
   mafiosa sauce, 152
   marinara, 174
   pico de gallo, 192–93
   quesabirria tacos, 154–55, *155*
   rabbit ragu, 173
   ragu, 200–201
   salsa di pomodoro, 87
   salsa roja, 92–93
   seared polenta with tomatoes, 177
   summer peach salad, *17*, 18
   vegan spaghetti bolognese, 220–21
   Wagyu meatballs with pomodoro sauce, 110–11
tortillas
   Faroe Island salmon tacos, 240
   quesabirria tacos, 154–55, *155*
   stacked enchiladas, *91*, 92–93
Tropic Like It's Hot, 33
truffles, in porcini mushroom ragu, 244–45
tuna tartare toast, *97*, 98

turbot, in fruits de mer with uni beurre blanc, 258–59

umami glaze, 265
uni beurre blanc, fruits de mer with, 258–59

vanilla pots de crème, 84–85
vegan chocolate cream, 24
vegan spaghetti bolognese, 220–21
Verde de la Vida, 97, 99
vinaigrette
    hazelnut mustard vinaigrette, 256
    lemon vinaigrette, 168
    mustard vinaigrette, 20
    red wine vinaigrette, 245
Virtù timballo, 200–202

Wagyu meatballs with pomodoro sauce and whipped ricotta, 110–11
walnuts, in prawns with peanut mole, 42–43
watercress, in porcini lasagna, *243*, 244–46
wedge salad, grilled, *123*, 124–25
whipped cream, orange, 84
whipped fromage, 262
whipped ricotta, 110
white American cheese, in Virtù timballo, 200–202
white bean ragu, 82

yellow bell pepper, in white bean ragu, 82
yellowtail crudo with cucumber pico de gallo, avocado mousse, and ponzu, 75
yogurt, cilantro, 228
yuzu kosho aioli, 240

za'atar
    honey whipped feta, 108
    pistachio pita, 249
zucchini
    risotto alla Nerano, 120, *121*
    white bean ragu, 82

ABOUT THE AUTHOR

Christina Barrueta

Christina Barrueta is an award-winning writer who has been inducted into the Arizona Culinary Hall of Fame and received the Arizona Restaurant Association's Foodist Award for Best of the Best Food Writer. She is the author of two books, *Arizona Wine: A History of Perseverance and Passion* and *Phoenix Cooks: Recipes from the City's Finest Chefs*. Her work is widely published in outlets such as *Time Out*, *Men's Health*, *PHOENIX*, *WhereTraveler*, *A Taste of AZ*, and *Phoenix Home & Garden*. Christina is also an Arizona contributing editor for *The Tasting Panel* and for *The Somm Journal*, where she writes her own column, "Sonoran Scoop." Her website, WriteOnRubee.com, has been awarded Best Food Blog by *PHOENIX* magazine and is an eight-time winner of Favorite Local Food Website by *Arizona Foothills*, which also named her 2025's Most Influential in Valley Food. Follow her on social media as @writeonrubee, where her Instagram feed was also named 2025's Favorite Food Feed by *Arizona Foothills*. She lives in Phoenix, Arizona.